STAR WARS

STAR WARS
The Economic Fallout

Council on Economic Priorities

ROSY NIMROODY
Senior Project Director

Foreword by Paul C. Warnke

BALLINGER PUBLISHING COMPANY
Cambridge, Massachusetts
A Subsidiary of Harper & Row, Publishers, Inc.

International Standard Book Number: 0-88730-162-2

Library of Congress Catalog Card Number: 87-22463

Printed in the United States of America

Library of Congress Cataloging-in-Publication Data

Star Wars : the economic fallout/Council on Economic Priorities.
    editor.
    p. cm.
    Rev. and expanded version of: An Economic analysis of the
president's Strategic Defense Initiative. 1984.
    Bibliography: p.
    Includes index.
    ISBN 0-88730-162-2
    1. Strategic Defense Initiative—Economic aspects. I. Council
on Economic Priorities. II. Economic analysis of the president's
Strategic Defense Initiative.
UG743.S735 1987
358'.1754—dc19   87-22463
                                                          CIP

Strategic Defense Initiative Project
Research Group

Senior Project Director	**Rosy Nimroody**
Project Directors	**Stephen Daggett** **Robert W. DeGrasse, Jr.** **William D. Hartung** **Eric Stubbs**
Contributing Author	**Kosta Tsipis**
Editors	**Rosy Nimroody** **Paula Lippin**
Research Staff	**Carey Goldberg** **Martin Ingall** **Scott London**

Strategic Defense Initiative Project
Board of Advisors

The Council on Economic Priorities

THE COUNCIL ON ECONOMIC PRIORITIES is a public service research organization, dedicated to accurate and impartial analysis of some of the most vital issues facing our country today. CEP is nonaligned, independent, and nonprofit.

Founded in 1969, CEP believes that a well-informed community can express its convictions and play a far more effective and influential role in molding public policy when it is acting upon carefully conducted, documented, and factual research.

A clear and primary goal of the council is to enhance corporate performance as it affects society in the critically important areas of energy, the costs and consequences of military spending, political influence, fair employment practices, and environmental impact. CEP acts as a clearinghouse for corporate activities and monitors the role of government as it relates to these social issues.

Credibility is absolutely essential to the work of the council. Our achievements can be measured by the frequency with which congressional committees and administrative agencies invite CEP staff to testify. The national press reports regularly and extensively on the council's work. A broad spectrum of corporations, libraries, and government agencies are institutional subscribers. We receive support from individuals and foundations who share our concerns and beliefs.

The remarkable impact of CEP studies on policymakers, the media, and government is a result of careful and unbiased research. But the council is far more than a research and reporting organization. Once a completed study points to a course of action that we believe to be correct, we are willing to adopt that point of view and press vigorously for its wide acceptance.

Our country is faced with issues of unimaginable magnitude and complexity. The role of the Council on Economic Priorities is to assist in uncovering the facts behind these issues and to bring them to the attention of both the public and the government in such a way that they can be effectively resolved in a logical, humane, and public-spirited manner.

To Herbert Scoville, Jr.,

whose insight, courage, and indefatigable spirit
have inspired us all

CONTENTS

FOREWORD

With this study, the Council on Economic Priorities (CEP) continues its incisive review of the economic implications of the president's Strategic Defense Initiative (SDI) program. In addition to updating the previous analysis of likely costs and cost exchange ratios (*An Economic Analysis of the President's Strategic Defense Initiative: Costs and Cost Exchange Ratios*, October 1984), the Council has added a new section on the steadily proliferating network of contracts and corporate involvement that threatens to precipitate hasty decisions on actual prototype development and testing. The effect of ill-considered choices could be profoundly harmful to future arms control and reduction efforts and to overall U.S. strategic policy.

A threshold difficulty in dealing with the Star Wars questions is the fact that the concept will not hold still. It continues to mean different things to different people. And this lack of clarity contributes to its central and blocking role in arms control negotiations. The explanations are confusing and conflicting, and the Russians, as well as our allies, are both suspicious and concerned. The Star Wars in his eyes blinded President Reagan to the magnificent opportunity offered at Reykjavik.

The president's view of the Strategic Defense Initiative—he does not like the term Star Wars—is an ambitious and attractive one. He foresees a world in which we no longer will need to base security on deterrence—the threat of mutual assured destruction—and instead can devise a magic shield that will render nuclear weapons impotent and obsolete. Speaking to students in the Young Astronauts Program on October 16, 1986, the President said his refusal to compromise on SDI at Reykjavik was necessary, "to develop technology that may someday protect you and your families from nuclear missiles."

It is hard to object to this concept. If a technology existed that could destroy all nuclear weapons on lift-off or during flight, this would be better than any conceivable arms control agreement. But regrettably, nothing under development, nothing under consideration, and nothing yet scientifically conceived can provide us with such a perfect defense. Perhaps this kind of scientific breakthrough will be achieved some day. It is worth, as I see it, continuing with an advanced research program at something like 1985's level of funding. A ban on research would be unverifiable as well as imprudent. Both sides will continue to probe the frontiers of science, if only to make sure that the other side does not come up with a rude surprise in the form of a hitherto unexpected technology.

The president continues to insist on his initial vision of a space shield that will render nuclear missiles impotent and obsolete. But this is not what his SDI office has in mind. It is working on a missile defense designed to enhance deterrence, not replace it. It would deploy a strategic defense using technology currently available. To members of the SDI Organization, the program involves no abandonment of deterrence doctrine, no brave new nuclear-free world. They argue that by protecting our missiles and our command and control we can protect deterrence. Moreover, they assert that our Strategic Defense Initiative program has brought the Russians back to the bargaining table and will persuade them to accept significant reductions in their strategic missiles, particularly their very large land-based intercontinental ballistic missiles (ICBMs).

I am sorry to say that I consider this to be dangerous nonsense. The record at Reykjavik confirms that SDI is powerful incentive for negotiations. But it also shows that the Soviet Union will not bargain away its retaliatory deterrent. Our development and deployment of the kind of defensive systems that are now available (perhaps permanently) prevent control and reduction of Soviet offensive missile systems. As the Council's study demonstrates, the Soviet reaction will inevitably be to match us in a defensive systems race, to deploy more nuclear missiles and nuclear warheads, and to develop decoys, chaff, and other techniques to make sure they can overwhelm any

U.S. defense. Warheads on nonballistic missile delivery systems, such as sea-launched cruise missiles, will increase exponentially. Accordingly, an imperfect defense—the only kind we can put in place—is not an acceptable alternative to arms control. It will drive both sides to seek security in unilateral action, rather than negotiation.

I have no doubt that concern about U.S. plans for strategic defense has helped put the Soviets in a mood to negotiate. I believe we convinced them in the late 1960s and early 1970s that a defensive arms race could only stimulate the further accumulation of offensive systems and leave both countries, and the rest of the world, in a more precarious situation.

Some scientists have said that the SDI project is not yet even in the concept stage. Even SDI supporters disagree as to the program's purpose and the likelihood that any part of a defense system will be ready for deployment within years or even decades. But there is no doubt whatsoever that the cost of any missile defense system will be massive. The amounts necessary to achieve the enormous lift capability and to put in place both the hardware and the software that have yet to be visualized threaten to make Gramm-Rudman a joke and the defense budget a disaster area. Meanwhile, the American taxpayer will be asked to pay, on the average, $5,000 to $12,000.

Today the president's Star Wars proposal is being rapidly converted from stardust and moonbeams to the great pork barrel in the sky. The "race for contracts," as the Council calls it, is becoming an international event. At a Wehrkunde Meeting of defense specialists in Munich in 1984, Secretary of Defense Caspar Weinberger hinted that our NATO allies could share in the benefits of an SDI program. A British participant responded that "our snouts are already twitching to get to the trough." A subsequent article in Britain's *Economist* predicted that West Europeans' receptivity to the Strategic Defense Initiative would depend on how great a share of the action they could receive. Japanese reactions have shown a similar blend of caution and cupidity.

So the stampede is on. It threatens to sweep away the Anti-Ballistic Missile Treaty, the one formally effective treaty that exists to control strategic arms. Moreover, the current commercial degradation of the president's dream can mean the scuttling of that treaty long before evidence exists of any real contribution to our security.

The first study of its kind, the CEP report pulls the Star Wars debate down from the stratosphere of technical terminology and uncovers the economic forces behind the program. Its cogent analysis of the program's impact on the nation's industrial productivity, the SDI industrial complex, the potentially cheaper and more effective Soviet responses to SDI, and CEP's recommendations deserve, indeed demand, a thoughtful reading by those who will make these grave decisions.

Paul C. Warnke

ACKNOWLEDGMENTS

Tackling a subject as complex and important as the impact of SDI on the economy has required the help of many people from diverse backgrounds.

This study was made possible by the generous contributions of The Public Welfare Foundation, The William Bingham Foundation, The W. Alton Jones Foundation, The Ploughshares Foundation, The Norman Foundation, George Wallerstein, Malcolm Wiener, The Joyce Mertz-Gilmore Foundation, Saul and Amy Cohen, Laura Scheuer, Stewart Mott, The Glickenhaus Foundation, William and Helen Mazer Foundation, The Edward H.R. Blitzer Fund, The Bread and Roses Community Fund, The Louise Ottinger Foundation, The Phoebe Haas Charitable Trust, Donald B. Lippincott, Lee B. Thomas, Jr., and anonymous donors and members. All of us on the staff and board of the Council on Economic Priorities are deeply grateful for those donations as well as for the general financial support of the Council's other donors.

Alice Tepper Marlin worked with the authors to structure this four-year study and provided expert editorial oversight of the overall study. Paula Lippin provided stylistic editing for the preliminary stages of the draft. Rosy Nimroody condensed and edited the final manuscript into book form.

Kosta Tsipis traced the evolution of SDI's mission from the original promise of population defense to the current actual goal of missile defense. Stephen Daggett tackled the complicated issues surrounding the cost-effectiveness of SDI and its technical obstacles. Robert W. DeGrasse, Jr., addressed the macroeconomic issues regarding SDI's drain on budgetary resources and technical talent. Rosy Nimroody and William Hartung identified and analyzed the program's contracting network and documented SDI's pork-barrel politics at work. Eric Stubbs provided the incisive analysis concerning Soviet strategic defenses and their likely response to SDI.

Carey Goldberg and Martin Ingall skillfully conducted research and data preparation for analysis of Soviet strategic defense research. Scott London's expert research was invaluable in compiling contract information through freedom of information requests and in creating CEP's database for SDI contracts. This database, which includes over 3,000 SDI contracts, is the first of its kind and has been of service to the media, Congress, and concerned citizens.

Ballinger Publishing Company speedily edited and produced the book with the assistance of Barbara Roth and Carolyn Casagrande. Additional invaluable and knowledgeable editorial help was provided by Henry Epstein and Mary Camper-Titsingh during the hot summer of 1986.

CEP was very fortunate to have the counsel of an active advisory panel whose members carefully reviewed our manuscript at various stages of the project. Their comments enabled us to strengthen both our methods and presentation. The findings and opinions expressed in this book, however, are solely those of the authors and CEP. Although CEP has taken into account the advisory panel comments, the advisors are, of course, not responsible for the final product.

The staff and boards of the Council on Economic Priorities would like to express our deep gratitude to our Board of Advisors and the following individuals for their assistance: P. Amquist, David Blond, Helen Bass, Douglas Braddock, Al Carnesale, Ashton Carter, Peter Clausen, Sidney Drell, Lawrence Forrest, Marshall Goldman, Cindy Gonsalves, Seymour Goodman, Glenn Kent, Ronald Kutscher, David McNicol, Stephen Meyer, Richard Oliver, Judith Reppy, Delores Turner, Jean Vanski, and Peter Worden. CEP is also grateful to Senator William Proxmire and Representative George Brown and staff aides Douglas Waller and Sybil Francis for their active response to CEP's many recommendations.

The Council on Economic Priorities received its funding from a broad spectrum of individuals, foundations, and other institutions. Royalties earned from the book will go toward research and other relevant activities at CEP.

INTRODUCTION

A day of reckoning is at hand. In March 1983, President Reagan challenged the scientific community to develop technologies that would render nuclear weapons "impotent and obsolete." The goal is noble. If truly achievable, it is worth a hefty cost. But since the opening salvo in 1983, the stated mission of the Strategic Defense Initiative (SDI) has experienced rapidly diminishing returns. Instead of providing a leakproof shield to defend the entire U.S. population, SDI's goal now is to enhance deterrence by developing a partial defense system for missile installations. If even a small number of hostile missiles evade a limited defense system, hundreds of millions of people would be killed and America's society decimated as the last frontier—space—becomes our last battlefield.

The U.S. and Soviet space programs have had military applications since their inception. Similar technologies are used both for satellite boosting rockets and for intercontinental ballistic missiles; space satellites are important for military surveillance and for civilian communications; and the space shuttle is used to launch military payloads. The two nations' military surveillance systems have contributed to peace by denying the element of surprise to an attacker and thereby eliminating an advantage of a first strike. Because these space systems provide at least a modicum of time for analysis, confirmation, consultation, and deliberations, they make hair-trigger responses less likely. They have also provided the technical means of verification without which arms control would not be possible.

But the proposed SDI program would change all of that. President Reagan's SDI program has introduced a new element into the military use of space. The program calls for basing large numbers of weapons platforms and components in space, transforming space into a potential theatre of war from which Earth could not escape. Anti-satellite (ASAT) weapons extend this militarization. Because so much of U.S. national security is dependent on the peaceful use of space for communication and surveillance, the argument for accelerated development and eventual deployment of a strategic defense system to protect missiles ring hollow.

THE SDI PORK BARREL

Despite compelling strategic, scientific, and economic arguments against proceeding with the SDI program, the White House has induced Congress to spend over $9 billion for research and development since fiscal year 1984 as a downpayment for what could become the most expensive military venture ever to be undertaken in the history of the world. The nation's defense corporations have become de facto participants in the SDI policymaking process. A politically interdependent relationship exists between the Department of Defense, the key committees and members of Congress, and the private interest of the defense industry that generates momentum for the program. Political scientists describe the use of this interdependency to protect the private interests of all three parties as "pork-barrel politics." Strong ties between the Pentagon and its contractors and their joint ability to lobby Congress successfully have done much to foster the otherwise untenable SDI program. Indeed, the role of pork-barrel politics may be more important than that of national security in keeping arguments for SDI alive. By creating economic constituencies, the administration may be able to "sell" SDI as it has sold other questionable weapons systems, such as the MX missile and the B-1 bomber.

From the point of view of the nuclear arms industry, the timing for launching SDI could not have been better. Although pressures for disarmament had been building since the "ban the bomb" movement of the 1950s, the basing of Pershing and cruise missiles in Europe in 1981 and the president's loose talk of winning a limited nuclear war rudely reawakened the American public to the dangers of the arms race. A campaign for a bilateral U.S.-Soviet freeze on the testing, production, and deployment of the new generation of nuclear weapons systems won broad support in community and state referenda. In June 1982 a million people marched to the United Nations calling for a bilateral freeze and disarmament. National public opinion polls supported it, and the House of Representatives voted for it. Thus the president's Star Wars speech of March 1983 came as citizen pressure to halt the nuclear arms race reached a peak.

By promising yet another technical fix to the arms race, Reagan's Star Wars speech stole the thunder from the freeze campaign. Not only has it diverted public attention from more immediate political solutions to the nuclear arms race, thereby keeping funding for the new generation of nuclear weapons alive, but it has also created a profitable and growing stream of new research and development contracts. Yet while military contractors prosper as a result of SDI, this megaproject will have serious adverse implications for most of the business community and for the economies of both the United States and the Soviet Union.

THE COUNCIL ON ECONOMIC PRIORITIES STUDY

Soon after the president's 1983 speech, the Council on Economic Priorities undertook a study of the economic motivation and the potential economic impact of SDI. While the strategic, military, and technical merits of the program have been analyzed, little had been said about the economic ramifications of pursuing what could become a trillion dollar proposition. It is this economic engine that may drive the program forward, however deeply flawed it may be.

We hope this book will contribute significantly to the ongoing debate on SDI by exploring the economic underpinnings of the program. This debate must continue if decisions on production and deployment are to be based on national security grounds. Major weapons programs, unfortunately, gain a momentum of their own and are difficult to stop once they build constituencies. If the SDI momentum remains unchecked, the "window of opportunity" for arms control will be slammed shut. The nation will be exposed to Star War's economic fallout, and the United States and the Soviet Union will move closer to nuclear disaster.

1

THE REAGAN SDI VISION

Let me share with you a vision of the future which offers hope. . . . What if free people could live secure in the knowledge that their security did not rest upon the threat of instant U.S. retaliation to deter a Soviet attack; that we could intercept and destroy strategic ballistic missiles before they reached our own soil or that of our allies? . . . I call upon the scientific community who gave us nuclear weapons to turn their great talents to the cause of mankind and world peace; to give us the means of making those nuclear weapons impotent and obsolete.

—*Ronald Reagan*
March 23, 1983

The mission of SDI has proved to be a moving target. SDI's first goal, as promised by President Reagan in 1983, was to provide safety and security for all by delivering us from our present status as nuclear hostages in a world dominated by Mutual Assured Destruction (MAD). SDI was envisioned as a program that could restore the United States' control over its own security through a new policy of Mutual Assured Survival (MAS). Instead of deterrence, based on the "immoral threat of nuclear retaliation," we were promised a more "moral" strategic standoff based on defense weapons. When we can "kill weapons instead of people," we will not need to depend on retaliation to deter war.

It is now apparent that his vision contrasts sharply with the technical and strategic objectives that actually guide the SDI program.

1

Despite continued promises of an invulnerable America, which remain the basis of public support for the program, SDI's goals are much more modest in practice. The gap between public rhetoric and actual policy is due largely to the widespread recognition among experts, both inside and outside of government, that the president's vision is unlikely ever to be realized. The promise to defend people in cities has devolved to the reality of defending missiles in silos. How has the debate over SDI's mission evolved, and what motivated the changes in the vision?

THE EVOLUTION OF SDI'S MISSION

In a 1983 speech before the National Space Club, President Reagan explained his SDI mission in unambiguous terms: "We're *not* discussing a concept just to enhance deterrence, not just an addition to our offensive forces, but research to determine the feasibility of a non-nuclear defense system; a shield that could prevent nuclear weapons from reaching their targets."[1] The leakproof system envisioned by the president must be able to intercept all nuclear weapons aimed at the United States. If even a few nuclear weapons leak through the "shield" and reach urban targets, America would suffer hundreds of millions of casualties, witness the decimation of entire cities, and lose the core of its industrial capacity.

Yet the Strategic Defense Initiative Organization (SDIO) established to implement President Reagan's plan aims only at developing systems to counter intercontinental ballistic missiles (ICBMs). No provisions are foreseen for defense against low-flying bombers and cruise missiles that could also deliver nuclear weapons against U.S. targets. Nor did the program purport to safeguard against the clandestine ground or small-aircraft transport of nuclear explosives across American borders.

This gap between rhetoric and policy could have been foreseen. As early on as April 1983 the president's own Commission on Strategic Forces (the Scowcroft Commission) concluded that "*no* antiballistic missile defense technologies appear to combine practicality, survivability, low cost, and technical effectiveness sufficiently to justify proceeding beyond the stage of technology development."[2] And Dr. Richard DeLauer, then undersecretary of defense for research and engineering, struck an even more pessimistic note in July 1983, when he said, "There is no way an enemy can't overwhelm your defenses if he wants to badly enough. It makes a lot of difference in what we do if we have to defend against 1,000 reentry vehicles (i.e., nuclear weapons or decoys that look like them) or 10,000."[3]

In April 1984 two White House panels—a Defense Technologies Study Team headed by NASA chief James Fletcher and a Future Security Strategy Study headed by Fred S. Hoffman—commissioned to study the technical and strategic feasibility of SDI, issued conflicting reports. Whereas the widely publicized Fletcher panel recommended researching a system that could provide a 99.9 percent effective defense, the more pessimistic Hoffman panel recommended beginning with current technology to build defenses to protect military targets in the United States.

Despite the theoretical potential of multilayered defenses, even officials responsible for the SDI do not claim it is possible to build a fully effective defense unless the Soviets reduce their offensive forces. The acting director of the Pentagon's office of strategic defense policy was quite blunt: "No one I know believes we could reach that goal by purely technical means. . . . We do not see . . . a defense system that could defend against every kind of missile threat. There is no such thing as a leakproof defense."[4]

Skepticism among the nation's leading scientists is even stronger. A 1986 poll found that, by a margin of over twenty to one, members of the National Academy of Sciences believed that an SDI system could not be made survivable and cost-effective in the next twenty-five years.[5] This pessimism was reflected in a 1987 report by the American Physical Society, the nation's most prestigious professional society of physicists, which cast severe doubt on the wisdom of proceeding with SDI at any cost. Citing formidable technical obstacles that must be overcome to produce useful weapons, the panel of experts concluded that the survival of any space-based antimissile system against enemy attack was "highly questionable": "The discrepancy between the present state-of-the-art . . . and the ultimate requirements is so large that major gaps in technical understanding must be closed before engineering technology verification could become productive."[6]

With so many administration officials conceding that it is impossible to create a "leakproof" defense for the American population through a technology masterstroke, a new scenario has been enunciated as the path to the president's vision. A partial defense, whose technical prospects are more promising, is now promoted as an interim step to more extensive deployments. This more realistic goal, which directly contradicts President Reagan's call for a perfect defense, has been promoted in White House documents and by Lt. Gen. James Abrahamson, the director of the SDI Organization, to justify continuation of the program. In a speech of October 25, 1984, Abrahamson observed that "from the technical viewpoint, we are pursuing this program to increase deterrence and stability."[7] And in a March 1987 report from Senator William Proxmire's (D-WI) office, the Pentagon's actual plans to deploy a partial defense system by 1994 were unveiled:

> We have been told that SDIO has a "black program" that is developing a reference architecture for a near-term deployment of strategic defenses—that is, a highly classified program which is developing a blueprint for deploying strategic defenses in the near term. . . . In fact, it appears that most members of Congress are being kept in the dark about this secret program.[8]

Thus, despite the administration's campaign to sell SDI to Congress and the American people as an alternative to the "immoral" doctrine of deterrence, SDI has emerged as simply more MAD. And at least two new rationales have been developed to support partial defenses.

RATIONALES FOR PARTIAL DEFENSE

The most frequently cited rationale for a partially effective missile defense is that it would strengthen deterrence by increasing the uncertainties facing the Soviets if they were to contemplate a first strike. This argument raises at least two questions.

Does the United States need to enhance its ability to deter a preemptive Soviet attack? According to the 1983 Scowcroft Commission, although U.S. land-based missiles are theoretically vulnerable to a Soviet ICBM attack, the majority of U.S. strategic warheads are based on submarines and bombers that would escape preemption even in the highly unlikely event that all ICBMs were to be destroyed. Consequently, the United States could deliver a devastating blow even if all of its land-based missiles were destroyed in a Soviet strike. It would simply be unnecessary to deploy partial SDI defenses in order to strengthen the survivability of U.S. land-based missiles.

Even if we assume that a partial defense system could increase Soviet uncertainty of a first strike, would this added uncertainty decrease the likelihood of a Soviet attack? A partial defense system designed to protect retaliatory forces against a first strike can also shield an aggressor against retaliation following an attack on the adversary's nuclear forces. Consequently, in a crisis situation, the incentive of both countries to inflict the first nuclear blow would be greatly increased, thereby aggravating the very problem SDI was intended to solve.

In view of this danger, Paul Nitze, one of President Reagan's top advisors on arms control, articulated two criteria that must be satisfied before any SDI system can sensibly be deployed. In a February 20, 1985, speech before the Philadelphia World Affairs Council, Nitze introduced the notion that the United States and the Soviet Union would increasingly emphasize defenses, while de-emphasizing offensive forces.[9] The development of defenses that were highly effective even against any conceivable Soviet countermeasure, that were cheaper to deploy than were increases in offenses (i.e., that were "cost effective at the margin"), and that could survive direct attack might convince the Soviets that ballistic missiles were no longer worth deploying. In this way the United States could essentially force the Soviets to accept a world without nuclear armed missiles. Nitze acknowledged, however, that it would be "tricky" to ensure that the nuclear balance remained stable as the transition proceeded, and he stressed that negotiated deployments would be preferable.

Nonetheless, Abrahamson and other SDIO officials have been making a case for the "phased deployment" of strategic defenses even without Soviet cooperation. If a system were not highly effective and were vulnerable to countermeasures, Abrahamson implied, the Soviets might still be discouraged from investing in responses by the knowledge that a more effective system, which would defeat their countermoves, would be forthcoming. But even Secretary of Defense Casper Weinberger, in a 1984 report to the president on Soviet violations of arms control agreements, asserted that the possibility of a Soviet missile defense will have a "profound impact on our strategic deterrent forces" and concluded that "a probable territorial defense would require the United States to increase the number of our offensive forces and their ability to penetrate Soviet defenses to assure that our operational plans could be executed."[10] So, well-founded fears of nuclear annihilation will persist as SDI's actual goals are unraveled by either side.

Another rationale for partial defenses was made clear at the Reykjavik Summit. It has been argued that defenses should be developed as an incentive to persuade the Soviets to agree to an arms control accord that eliminates ballistic missiles. At Reykjavik, the president proposed a ten-year program that would reduce all strategic nuclear arms by 50 percent over the first five years and phase out the remaining ballistic missiles over the next five years, as the United States proceeded to develop defensive technologies. Defenses would then be deployed as an insurance policy against minor cheating by either side and would be shared with the Soviets.

Certainly strategic defenses could be built to defend against a small number of Soviet missiles. But why should the promise to deploy such defenses convince the Soviets to reduce their missile deployments rather than increase them sufficiently to overwhelm such defenses? Far from displacing MAD, SDI is destined to lead to an even more dangerous spiral in the arms race, one that couples the old offensive deterrence with defensive deterrence.

However questionable the wisdom of proceeding with SDI, the program is clearly geared for early deployment. Secretary Weinberger continues to proffer population defense as bait to attract support and momentum for the strategic defense build-up, while simultaneously endorsing the early deployment of an initial partial defense against nuclear missiles. As he told one SDI symposium, "The real worry about pursuing anything other than the proper, ultimate, full goal is that it runs the risk of exhausting the momentum that can and should be developed for defense and also would leave us basically with a system that is not as effective as it should be."[11]

Despite the administration's continued attempts to sell SDI as a program for population defense, an increasingly aware Congress and public have begun to impose conditions on their support. A 1986 amendment introduced by Representative Jim Courter (R-NJ) to reorient SDI toward deployment of a "point defense" of missile silos (one type of partial defense system) was defeated by a margin of 2 to 1 (293 to 124). Similarly, 81 percent of the Americans sampled in an April 1987 public opinion poll conducted by Cambridge Reports, Inc. supported a perfect system—one that could successfully defend against all incoming weapons—but just 15 percent supported a system designed to protect only U.S. missiles, key military bases, and Washington, D.C.[12] But, as the next chapter illustrates, it is the political agenda behind SDI's crash research that in the end may drive the program forward.

2

SPACE-BASED MISSILE DEFENSES

Herman Kahn: If we deploy a full-scale antiballistic missile system, we can save 50 million lives.

Bernard Brodie: Herman, in order to save 50 million lives, you've got to have a war.

B uilding defenses against ballistic missiles is not a new idea. Almost from the dawn of the missile age in the late 1950s, the United States has worked on devising defenses. By the late 1960s, both the United States and the Soviet Union had developed land-based, nuclear-tipped anti-missile-missiles designed to destroy nuclear warheads either just above the atmosphere or as they re-entered the atmosphere in the final seconds of flight. But the Anti-Ballistic Missile (ABM) Treaty of May 1972, with a protocol signed in 1974, prohibited implementation of a nationwide missile defense and limited each country to deploying ABMs at a single site with no more than one hundred interceptors.

In the early 1970s, the United States deployed the Safeguard ABM system at Grand Forks Air Force Base in North Dakota. This system used ground-based radars to track incoming nuclear warheads and interceptor missiles to destroy them. Only a few months after Safeguard became operational, however, the government abandoned its ABM effort and dismantled the system as ineffective.[1]

9

Even if some of their problems could be overcome with new technology, the early ABMs were inherently limited in being aimed at offensive weapons only in the last seconds of flight. At best, such systems could provide only a partial defense. They might ensure survival of some U.S. missile silos but could not defend cities.

Technological advances have now made it possible to conceive of a potentially more effective defense, in which missiles and warheads could be attacked in each of the four phases of flight:

1. The boost phase, lasting one to five minutes, in which a missile bearing a payload of warheads takes off from the ground and is accelerated by rocket engines into space.
2. A postboost phase, lasting a few minutes after the rocket motors burn out, in which a maneuvering post-boost vehicle ("bus") pushes off warhead-carrying re-entry vehicles (and possibly decoys) onto separate paths.
3. The midcourse phase, lasting twenty minutes or more, when the warheads continue through space toward their targets.
4. The terminal phase, in which the re-entry vehicles re-enter the atmosphere and streak down toward their targets. If these vehicles are aimed against cities, interception must occur above 10,000 or 20,000 feet. If silos are the target, interception is possible all the way to the ground.

In theory, such a multilayered defense can be highly effective even if each layer is only partially effective. If, for example, each layer of a four-tiered system can destroy 75 percent of its targets, the first layer will allow 25 percent of the warheads to leak through, the second about 6 percent, the third less than 2 percent, and the fourth just 0.4 percent. SDI officials have discussed deploying as many as seven layers of defense.

It is one thing to theorize, however, and quite another to design a practical multitiered system. If each layer of defense is to multiply the effectiveness of the preceding ones, all tiers must be completely independent. Otherwise, if two tiers share any components, a failure in one tier might be replicated in the next. Moreover, success against a large missile attack hinges on accomplishing a myriad of difficult tasks. In every component, the complexity of the problem is daunting and the opportunity for failure great.

THE NATURE OF THE SDI PROGRAM

The complexity of the task immediately poses a key question for policymakers: is the SDI technology development program reasonable at the projected level and pace of funding? The term "technology development" is used advisedly. The SDI program involves much more than "research," strictly defined. Its intent is to allow actual engineering development of a functioning weapon system to begin in the early 1990s. That would require that the design, performance, cost, technical risk, and development schedule of all components be accurately and reliably specified by then. As the Strategic Defense Initiative Organization reported to Congress in 1986, "the majority of effort needed from that point on should be engineering in nature rather than experimental."[2] In short, the program is "schedule driven," in the words of a Senate staff study. Its goal is not just to investigate the feasibility of various approaches to strategic defense but to prepare all the pieces needed to begin building a defensive system in the 1990s.[3]

In part because the SDI research and development (R&D) program is designed to enter full-scale engineering development so soon, its budget is heavily oriented toward construction and demonstration of hardware. Some 49 percent of the requested fiscal year (FY) 1987 SDIO budget was devoted to experiments designed either to demonstrate the capabilities or to prove the feasibility of promising technologies (see Table 2-1). Already some less promising technologies have been eliminated from serious consideration ("down-selected"), to give priority to those more likely to pay off quickly and allow for early deployment of a partial defense (see Table 2-2). Partly so as to display technical progress to the public, Congress, allies, and even the Soviet Union, the SDI R&D program is investing very heavily in elaborate and expensive technology demonstration projects.

Unfortunately, the technology demonstration projects that seem likely to succeed cannot provide a sound basis for an overall defense scheme. It will be a more demanding task of developing key enabling technologies needed for either a highly effective multilayered defense or for a near-term partial defense. The president's original goal is a worthy one, but it does not appear feasible in the near term, while technologies that may be more promising are very far from fruition.

Table 2-1. SDI Budget Request, FY 1986-89 (*million dollars*).

	1986	1987	1988	1989
Surveillance, Acquisition, Tracking, and Kill Assessment (SATKA)				
Radar discrimination and data	21.0	12.7	22.6	34.7
Optical discrimination and data	117.7	90.6	87.9	80.1
Imaging radar technology	30.5	26.2	32.0	38.1
Laser radar technology	75.4	96.4	148.3	177.6
Infra-red sensor technology	82.2	78.7	93.7	98.8
Boost surveillance and tracking	81.1	130.1	256.1	344.7
Space surveillance and tracking	49.0	47.6	191.8	242.2
Airborne optical surveillance	134.9	99.5	104.0	140.7
Terminal imaging radar	31.8	26.3	117.0	136.4
Interactive discrimination	7.6	4.5	32.2	61.7
Signal processing technology	94.7	105.9	134.6	145.1
SATKA integration and support	95.0	149.6	248.0	311.2
Countermeasures	0.7	0.8	0.0	0.0
Innovative science and technology	25.4	42.1	24.5	48.4
Total	847.0	911.0	1,492.7	1,859.7
Directed Energy Weapons (DEW)				
Technology base development	435.5	339.7	340.5	408.6
Acquisition, targeting, and pointing (ATP)				
Technology	51.9	39.8	39.8	51.5
Chemical laser devices	108.6	79.9	80.0	58.0
Excimer lasers	39.1	12.4	12.4	30.0
Free electron laser technology	41.5	23.4	42.0	48.5
Other	93.1	27.0	32.3	28.0
Particle beam technology	34.8	38.5	57.8	46.0
Skylite	46.5	43.0	45.0	20.0
X-ray laser	20.0	8.0	30.0	25.0
Reserve	0.0	67.8	1.3	101.6
Technology Integration Experiment (TIE)	329.4	402.1	587.9	646.1
ATP TIEs	185.9	137.6	147.0	198.5
Free electron laser TIE	84.8	158.0	158.0	201.5
Space-based laser TIE	0.5	2.0	0.0	42.0
Integrated space experiment	58.2	104.5	142.2	204.0
TIE acceleration	0.0	0.0	139.2	0.1
Reserve	0.0	0.0	1.5	0.0
Concept formulation and technical	18.7	26.8	32.3	28.0
Support programs	19.7	62.4	115.0	128.2
Innovative science and technology	0.0	12.7	28.0	35.0
Total	803.3	843.7	1,103.7	1,245.9

Table 2-1. continued

	1986	1987	1988	1989
Kinetic Energy Weapons (KEW)				
Space-based kinetic kill vehicle systems	134.4	126.8	303.5	357.4
SBKKV experiments	117.2	107.0	250.7	305.7
SBKKV technology	17.1	19.8	52.8	51.7
Exoatmospheric KKV systems	61.6	107.6	220.6	307.6
Exoatmospheric KKV experiments	53.7	102.8	186.1	259.4
Exoatmospheric KKV technology	7.9	4.8	34.5	48.2
Endoatmospheric KKV systems	76.7	111.3	237.6	238.8
Endoatmospheric KKV experiments	45.6	100.7	198.7	179.9
Endoatmospheric KKV technology	31.1	10.6	38.9	58.9
Mini projectiles	56.0	74.5	102.9	134.7
Test and evaluation	185.9	252.1	109.3	46.9
Allied/theater defense	69.9	44.3	72.9	79.2
Innovative science and technology	11.4	13.0	28.0	35.0
Total	595.9	729.6	1,074.8	1,199.6
Systems Analysis and Battle Management (SABM)				
SDI strategic architecture	63.5	58.4	91.0	78.0
SDI systems engineering	12.1	20.2	39.0	53.6
Theater architecture	1.7	39.8	38.4	37.9
Battle management and C3 technology	70.9	88.5	121.8	134.1
Battle management and C3 experimental systems	23.4	80.7	172.9	203.5
National test bed	12.0	60.6	119.2	228.4
Countermeasures	5.1	5.0	0.0	0.0
Innovative science and technology	13.4	18.1	28.0	35.0
Civil applications	0.0	2.0	2.0	2.0
Medical free electron laser	9.2	13.5	15.0	15.0
Total	211.3	386.8	627.3	787.5
Survivability, Lethality, and Key Technologies (SLKT)				
Systems survivability	59.4	60.0	94.2	98.3
Lethality and target hardening	78.3	78.0	102.5	98.4
Power and power conditioning	50.0	85.7	158.0	186.9
Space transportation and support	20.7	36.4	433.8	606.2
Materials and structures	0.0	14.2	22.5	40.5
Countermeasures	8.7	26.7	42.8	78.4
Innovative science and technology	0.0	18.2	28.0	35.0
High Energy Laser System Test Facility	0.0	18.8	18.5	18.5
Total	217.1	338.0	900.3	1,162.2

Note: Does not include Department of Energy SDI activities.
Source: "Strategic Defense Initiative 1986–1989 Budget," *Defense News*, March 9, 1987, p. 14.

Table 2-2. Status of SDI SATKA, DEW, and KEW Programs.

	Major Experiments	Down-Selected	Up-Selected	New Mission
Surveillance, Acquisition, Tracking, and Kill Assessment (SATKA)				
Radar discrimination and data				
Optical discrimination and data				
Imaging radar technology		X		
Laser radar technology				
Infrared sensor technology				
Boost surveillance and tracking	X		X	
Space surveillance and tracking	X			X
Airborne optical surveillance	X			
Terminal imaging radar	X	X		
SATKA integration				
Countermeasures				
Innovative science and technology				
Shuttle recovery				
Directed Energy Weapons (DEW)				
Technology Base Development				
Technology Integration Experiments				
ATP experiments	X			
FEL experiments	X		X	
SBL experiments		X		
Integrated space experiment	X			
TIE acceleration				
Reserve				
Concept formulation				
Support programs				
Innovative science and technology				
Kinetic Energy Weapons (KEW)				
SBKKV systems				
SBKKV experiments	X		X	
SBKKV technology			X	
Exoatmospheric KKV systems				
Exo KKV experiments	X		X	
Exo KKV technology			X	
Endoatmospheric KKV systems				
Endo KKV experiments	X		X	
Endo KKV technology			X	

Table 2-2. continued

	Major Experiments	Down- Selected	Up- Selected	New Mission

Mini projectiles
  EML technology
  Low endo
  Laser-guided HV projectiles
  Advanced endo projectiles				

Test and evaluation
  Significant technological
    milestones
  Range instrumentation
  Special instruments
  Targets
  HWIL and simulation
  Special data collection
	X		X	

Allied/theater defense Theater missile defense				
Innovative Science and technology				

Sources: Strategic Defense Initiative Organization, Reports to Congress, June 1986 and June 1987; John Pike, Federation of American Scientists, Washington, D.C.

TECHNOLOGY DEMONSTRATION PROJECTS

A clue to which defensive technologies are most likely to be selected for engineering development lies in the major experiments in which the SDIO is investing. Over the past year, the most promising technologies have been "up-selected" for more rapid exploratory development, while other technologies have been officially "down-selected."

Two technologies are receiving special emphasis for boost-phase defense. In the short term, the principal candidate is space-based rocket interceptors—or space-based kinetic kill vehicles (SBKKV) in the SDI lexicon. A longer-term possibility is ground-based free electron lasers that convert electrical energy into beams that may be able to penetrate the atmosphere efficiently.

Space-based rocket interceptors, using existing technology, could probably be developed within ten to fifteen years. It would take longer, however, to decrease the weight of such systems significantly and thus reduce the cost of lifting them into space.[4] Guidance systems available in the near term would be of limited sophistication, but might provide some capability against Soviet rockets that have not been upgraded to complicate the problem. SDIO officials discuss deploying several hundred satellite carriers, each with just a few interceptor rockets.[5] This is the technology they have in mind when they speak of an interim, less "robust" deployment beginning before the turn of the century.

There are critical problems with rocket interceptors, however, that make any such interim deployment unjustifiable. With any kind of effective guidance system, interceptors would necessarily be quite costly compared with possible cheap boosters that might be deployed in response. The cost of lifting relatively heavy rockets into space would also be extremely high. Additional offensive missiles would almost certainly be less expensive to deploy than additional space-based rocket interceptors. Moreover, kinetic kill vehicles would burn up or be blinded by heat on entering the atmosphere. As a result, any SBKKV deployment could be overcome with "fast-burn" rockets that end their boost phase inside or not far above the atmosphere. Finally, orbiting satellite battle stations would be vulnerable to direct attack. It does not appear reasonable to expect such systems to perform at the level required for effective defense.

In the longer run, one promising technology seems to be ground-based free electron lasers (FEL). FEL beams would be targeted against missiles in the boost phase by sets of mirrors in orbit—relay mirrors in high orbit and targeting mirrors in low orbit passing over potential missile sites. The SDIO proposes to spend roughly a billion dollars to build new high-powered FELs at White Sands Missile Range for tests of power scaling (the ability to "scale up" power output to the necessary intensity) and "up-link" experiments with mirrors in space. The main technical basis for SDIO's optimism is the development of concepts for "atmospheric compensation" (the ability to overcome distortions caused by the atmosphere).

But there are many technical and operational problems to be overcome with FELs. These include adequate scaling to high power levels; deterioration of beam quality caused when the beam itself heats up the atmosphere through which it passes; and the need to develop and protect extremely sophisticated space mirrors. Some research into FELs is certainly warranted, but not at the level now projected (any more than a major government investment in a moon landing scheme would have been justified in 1939). More important, given the uncertainties involved in FEL development, it is wholly inappropriate to count on achieving a breakthrough soon after an early deployment of "less robust" defenses.

An effective defensive system could conceivably be deployed without a boost phase layer, but only with very high levels of performance in the midcourse. According to the Senate staff study referred to earlier, the key consideration for midcourse defense is estimating the size of the threat. It now appears that ten times as many decoys might be used as seemed likely even a year ago, greatly increasing the need for discrimination between warheads and decoys. No credible technologies are likely to be available in the near term for discriminating among so many objects in space. We may eventually develop a discrimination capability (see below), but probably no sooner than FELs, since it would require very new, untested technologies.

One set of technologies may be viable on a predictable time line: land-based rocket interceptors aimed at warheads in the terminal phase or (assuming no proliferation of decoys) at the late midcourse phase. The SDIO is investing heavily in three such systems: the exoatmospheric re-entry vehicle interception system (ERIS), the high endoatmospheric defense interceptor (HEDI), and a possible low endoatmospheric defense interceptor (LEDI), which may evolve out of the recent FLAGE (flexible, lightweight, agile guided experiment).

Development of these systems has progressed further than any other SDI program, with tests of prototypes either under way or expected by the early 1990s. Full-scale engineering development could reasonably begin on the schedule laid out by the SDIO. On such a tight schedule, it seems likely that "direct impact" kill systems could not be developed, and interceptors would rely on nuclear warheads.

Taken together, these technologies could provide a two- or three-layered defense capable of protecting missile fields and perhaps offering some thin defense of populated areas. They would not begin to offer the kind of highly effective defense that the president discussed, however. Indeed, ERIS would probably be rendered wholly ineffective by Soviet deployment of cheap decoys.

Continuation of a rapidly growing development program will create momentum toward deployment of systems like LEDI, HEDI, and ERIS together with space-based rocket interceptors. But such a deployment, though it may be feasible around the turn of the century, would not begin to fulfill the criteria that administration officials themselves acknowledge are important to an effective defense. It is extremely premature to expect future systems, like FELs or midcourse kill systems with effective discrimination devices, to be any more effective. In short, while the up-selected systems may prove to be technically feasible, they will not accomplish SDI's stated objectives.

KEY ENABLING TECHNOLOGIES

The SDI R&D program's investment in the various technologies necessary to construct an entire defense system is based on an assumption that all the building blocks of the system will be successful and available when needed. If some key enabling technologies prove difficult to develop or disappointing in performance, however, the wisdom of heavy early investment in technology projects to meet the schedule-driven and demonstration-oriented pace of the program becomes questionable.

Three technical problems in developing multilayered strategic defenses are considered particularly difficult: developing computer software for battle management, devising a means of discriminating warheads from decoys in the midcourse phase in outer space, and ensuring cheap space lift capability.

The Pentagon group that devised the SDI research program (the Defensive Technologies Study Team, also known as the Fletcher Commission after its chairman, Dr. James Fletcher) estimated that a full-fledged multilayered strategic defense would require a minimum of 10 million lines of computer code and possibly ten times as much. By comparison the space shuttle required some 500,000 lines.[6] No one knows if reliable software of such unprecedented length and complexity can be developed.

The SDIO insists that battle management software can be developed. A group of computer experts brought together by the SDIO concluded that "computing resources and battle management software for a strategic defense system are within the capabilities of the hardware and software technologies that could be developed within the next several years." But the panel also criticized SDI officials for presuming that computing capabilities could be developed to complement whatever strategic defense hardware would eventually be chosen. SDI planners, the study panel complained, "treated battle management as something that is expected to represent less than 5 percent of the total cost of the system, and therefore, could not significantly affect the system architecture. They have developed their proposed architectures around the sensors and weapons and have paid only 'lip service' to the structure of the software that must control and coordinate the entire system."[7]

The comments of these software experts suggest that it may be foolish to go full speed ahead with developing hardware for system designs whose feasibility will depend on the computing capabilities that can be demonstrated and adequately tested in the future. Obviously certain technologies will be necessary whatever computing capabilities and system architectures are selected. But until there is stronger evidence that software limitations will not unduly constrain the effectiveness of the entire system, a large up-front investment seems premature.

In a similar vein, both critics and supporters of SDI acknowledge that discriminating between real warheads and sophisticated light-weight decoys in the vacuum of outer space may be extraordinarily difficult. While SDI officials initially predicted that midcourse discrimination could be handled by infrared, millimeter wavelength, radar, and other familiar tracking devices, they are now pursuing interactive discrimination.[8] This technique involves "nudging," or irradiating, potentially threatening objects with either a laser or a particle beam in order to distinguish between weapons and decoys. Presumably a heavy warhead will react differently from a light decoy when irradiated by a low-power directed energy beam.

While interactive discrimination may hold greater promise than long-wavelength infrared sensors for use in mid-course defense, it is far too soon to tell. As a Senate staff study concluded, interactive discrimination is still "little more than an interesting and promising concept."[9] Proof of its feasibility depends on technology not yet shown to be cost-effective and feasible. Even if a certain degree of interactive discrimination capability can be demonstrated, its effectiveness against a massive increase in decoys is very far from being assured.[10] And until the feasibility of midcourse discrimination is proven out in some way, it is premature to invest in technology demonstrations of programs like the ERIS ground-launched missile system, which aims to intercept warheads in the late midcourse phase.

A third linchpin of strategic defense is the simple matter of space logistics. SDI officials acknowledge that reasonably cost-effective, space-based components of a strategic defense cannot be deployed unless the cost of space lift is cut to no more than 10 percent of current levels.[11] Reducing costs so substantially would require an industrial revolution in the building of space lift systems and would entail an unnecessarily large technical risk. In fact, it remains impossible to determine whether or not space lift costs can be driven down as far as the SDIO requires. Again Congress and the public are being asked to spend billions of dollars on the premise that exceedingly difficult tasks can be accomplished quickly—with no realistic basis for assessing the chances of success.

Beyond that, substantial investments in R&D will be required very soon if we are to develop inexpensive space boosters by the mid-1990s, whether derived from the space shuttle or based on new technologies. Huge up-front expenditures may make sense if strategic defenses with space-based systems are certain to be deployed. But without such certainty, an immense early expenditure is probably not justified.

In short, the prospects for strategic defense depend on reliable battle management software, effective midcourse discrimination, and cheap space logistics. If any of these enabling technologies turns out to be infeasible or prohibitively expensive, the entire SDI research effort will prove abortive. None is close to being demonstrated.

All these difficulties are dwarfed, however, by the operational problems of a multilayered defensive system. Such a system can never be tested or exercised under realistic conditions, nor can these conditions be fully simulated. The tens of millions of lines of computer code that must support the operations of the system's massive computational network can never be confidently debugged. The codes can never be tested against the possibility of failure under unforeseen circumstances.[12] The possibility that some computers of the defensive system will grind to a halt will always exist. Faced with the unexpected, therefore, the system as a whole will probably degrade ungracefully.

Furthermore, the Soviet Union could disrupt the myriad of command, control, and communications (C3) links (several orders of magnitude more extensive and more complex than the C3 of our current offensive weapons) in a number of ways before or during a nuclear attack. While the defense has only half an hour to perform its function perfectly, with little or no prior knowledge of the exact configuration of the threat, the offense can prepare for years, devise secret countermeasures, and choose the moment and the form of attack.

In sum, a highly effective strategic defense is, at present, so far from fruition that the odds do not justify a crash program to demonstrate defensive technologies by the early 1990s.

PROBLEMS WITH A PARTIAL DEFENSE SYSTEM

Since the only technologies likely to prove feasible in the foreseeable future could at best provide only a partial defense of selected targets, the real question of concern involves the strategic value of limited defense, rather than the distant prospect of a highly effective defense against all ballistic missiles.

Partial defenses can be designed to protect missile silos and other strategic targets and perhaps to provide some defense of urban areas against small attacks. The rationale for defense of strategic military targets is quite straightforward. Protection of silos could safeguard U.S. retaliatory forces and thus help preserve the U.S. deterrent. The technology is at hand.

The case against such partial defense systems is equally clear and more compelling, however. First, there is no reason to believe that U.S. retaliatory forces are currently vulnerable enough to encourage a Soviet strike even in a military confrontation. As the Scowcroft Commission noted, the Soviets might be able to destroy either U.S. land-based missiles or bombers on the ground but not both simultaneously. Bombers or land-based missiles together with invulnerable U.S. submarine-based missiles ensure a robust, survivable retaliatory force. The Scowcroft Commission officially and firmly closed the so-called window of vulnerability.

In addition, planned U.S. weapons, including the Trident II missile and the Midgetman small ICBM, will further increase the share of invulnerable weapons able to carry out any required retaliatory strike against the USSR. More fundamentally, it is not clear that this problem must be solved through technology. Arms control agreements that reduce the number of large Soviet land-based missiles could diminish the threat against theoretically vulnerable U.S. retaliatory forces. This seems a far better route than to go ahead with a strategic defense of retaliatory forces that seem fated only to ensure a Soviet response in kind and escalate the arms race.

Still more questionable would be a strategy of enhancing defenses that goes beyond silo protection, including partial city defenses, but does not render missiles obsolete. Well-known strategic experts such as Keith Payne and Colin Gray seem to endorse as extensive a defense as can be developed under almost any circumstances.[13] Occasionally, official documents repeat the kinds of arguments made by these nongovernmental experts. A January 1985 White House description of the SDI, for example, argued:

> To achieve the benefits which advanced defensive technologies could offer, they must, at a minimum, be able to destroy a sufficient portion of an aggressor's attacking forces to deny him confidence in the outcome of an attack or deny an aggressor the ability to destroy a militarily significant portion of the target base he wishes to attack.[14]

In this view, deterrence is enhanced to the extent that defenses make a prospective enemy uncertain about the outcome of an attack.

The case for using extensive strategic defense to deny the Soviets confidence in achieving military goals has a number of problems, however. First, the theory depends on Soviet goals. The USSR may believe it can win a nuclear war by targeting U.S. strategic forces while either limiting the damage from a retaliatory strike (through defenses of its own and/or through civil defense) or deterring the U.S. response. If so, there is some logic to the case for strategic defense, although it would make more sense for the U.S. simply to strengthen its retaliatory forces. On the other hand, the Soviets may regard their nuclear weapons simply as a way of deterring American use of nuclear weapons in a deteriorating situation in which the USSR is prevailing with nonnuclear forces.[15] Whatever Soviet goals may be at present, defenses may simply force the Soviets to adopt an old-fashioned assured destruction doctrine.

Second, if the United States deploys strategic defenses, the Soviets will certainly respond in kind. Paradoxically, partial defense might do more damage to the United States' ability to accomplish its military goals than to the Soviet Union's. It is generally assumed that the USSR plans for a rather massive initial strike if conflict reaches the nuclear level. A massive first strike would certainly accomplish something even given a partial defense. In contrast, the United States plans more limited initial uses of nuclear weapons. Partial defense would be less effective in the face of a massive Soviet attack than against a limited American one.

Third, coupled with offensive forces, partial defense presents the threatening prospect of a first strike with defense against a degraded retaliation. In his speech of March 23, 1983, President Reagan explicitly acknowledged this problem. "I clearly recognize that defensive systems have limitations and raise certain problems and ambiguities," he said. "If paired with offensive systems, they can be viewed as fostering an aggressive policy, and no one wants that." At the very least such a posture would accelerate the arms race and, in a crisis, could invite a pre-emptive strike by the other side.

Finally, the demands on technology and costs will be equally formidable whether the goal is a partial defense or the more ambitious multilayered defense of the population. If, for example, components of the defense could not survive attack, they invite pre-emptive attack and may be destabilizing. Costly defenses also encourage offensive countermeasures. Even partial defense, therefore, needs to meet the same standards as more effective defense.

The argument that defenses need not be perfect, or even close to perfect, in order to be useful, therefore, should not be allowed to justify deployment of technologies that merely invite countermeasures. The worst situation would be for the United States to deploy systems that the Soviets can attack directly or that they can overcome merely by proliferating offensive weapons. Such a U.S. deployment would be extremely destabilizing. In a crisis, vulnerable defenses would encourage a direct attack on space systems. Indeed, the Soviets may wisely feel that destroying space defenses during a crisis would discourage rather than encourage retaliation. And any defense that is more expensive than offensive countermeasures will undermine the prospects for arms control and drive the arms race forward.

CONCLUSION

SDI today represents a tangle of proposals and shifting research projects covered by confusing, even contradictory, statements about the true aims of this effort. From the outset the claims of SDI supporters have been contradictory (in terms of population defense versus "hard point" site or missile defense) and, in many cases, exaggerated. As a result, the shift from promising an end to deterrence to assuring enhanced deterrence borders on deliberate obfuscation. So imperfectly does SDI match its stated objectives that any thoughtful observer must worry what the real intentions and effects of the system are.

The political benefits that emerge from such confusion are significant. To garner public support, a system to "harden our missiles from space" and thus to enhance deterrence is being developed under the name of population defense. In fact, a very large fraction of monies appropriated by Congress for SDI is being spent on research for systems suitable only for defending "hard targets" like missile sites and totally inadequate for defense of cities. Meanwhile expensive technology demonstrations are being prematurely funded even before key enabling technologies prove feasible. The danger is that our heavy investment will create an irreversible momentum to deploy less than fully effective defenses—a choice we would not make if we considered the question carefully from the start. President Reagan's original vision of a future without nuclear weapons has immense popular appeal. That appeal should not be allowed to obscure debate about the logic of the more limited defenses that may alone prove feasible.

WHAT PRICE STRATEGIC DEFENSE?

The military establishment, not productive in itself, necessarily must feed on the energy, productivity and brain-power of the country, and if it takes too much, our total strength declines.

—Dwight D. Eisenhower
May 18, 1953

The SDI program should be judged not only by its strategic merit and its technical feasibility, but also by its impact on the economy. In a time of peace, the costs to the economy must be weighed against the benefits, if any, of proceeding with such a rapidly paced, high-risk research program.

Much controversy surrounds the potential costs of an SDI system. With burgeoning federal deficits and a widely acknowledged need to restrain expenditures, the decision to launch the SDI program is increasingly critical to both national and economic security. This chapter therefore first discusses the long-term costs of deploying an SDI system. It then examines the nature of SDI research and its short-term funding. Other research and development projects related to defensive technologies are also discussed. Finally, the impact of SDI programs is assessed by comparing them with aggregate measures of similar activities. Marginal changes that occur as a result of the new emphasis on strategic defense are of greatest concern. If SDI requires too large a share of new research and development resources, it cannot help but crowd out other projects in both defense and civilian areas.

PRODUCTION COSTS FOR STRATEGIC DEFENSE

SDI is not just another expensive weapons program. Some official sources, including Lt. Gen. James Abrahamson, project its ultimate cost at $500 billion.[1] Independent estimates made by former secretaries of defense James Schlesinger and Harold Brown put the final price tag closer to $1 trillion.[2] Yet Abrahamson and other administration representatives argue that since planners have not even begun to define the technologies and the final architecture of a strategic defense system, no valid cost estimates are possible.

Although the full price of SDI cannot yet be predicted accurately, a preliminary estimate can be obtained by projecting production costs from initial research and development funding. In many weapons projects, such as those for the B-1 bomber, Trident II, and MX missiles, production and deployment costs have been generally between two to five times the research and development costs.[3] An independent 1979 study by the Boston Study Group estimated that the total cost of producing and deploying a typical weapon system is about six times R&D costs.[4] If these cost ratios hold, a completed strategic defense system might cost roughly $400 billion to $1 trillion.[5] The lower range of this estimate assumes the initial five-year program will lead immediately to full-scale development (FSD). Given the high uncertainty surrounding the technologies, however, pre-FSD spending could continue beyond the next five years, driving ultimate FSD costs still higher.

This range in SDI costs is similar to estimates made by Barry Blechman and Victor Utgoff of the Foreign Policy Institute of John Hopkins University.[6] Their cost estimates include full-scale development (using existing off-the-shelf technology), production, and deployment as well as the cost of ten years of maintenance for four different kinds of defense systems, ranging from one limited to defending missile silos to one intended to protect the population. The four systems are:

Alpha. A system using two types of ground-based interceptors deployed at sites of offensive forces, an early warning aircraft armed with air-to-air missiles, and shorter-range interceptors for air defense. This system, designed to defend only U.S. nuclear retaliatory capabilities, would cost $160 billion.

Beta. A system supplementing Alpha defenses with additional ground-based, long-range interceptors within areas of relatively high population density. This system would defend the forty-seven most densely populated metropolitan areas of the United States and Canada at a cost of $170 billion.

Gamma. A system composed of ground-based Beta interceptors and space-based rockets deployed on satellites in low earth orbits and directed by battle management satellites in 5,000 km orbits. This system is designed to offer comprehensive protection for the entire population of the United States and Canada from Soviet ballistic missiles and aircraft at a cost of $770 billion.

Delta. A system combining ground-based Beta interceptors with chemical lasers in low earth orbit, controlled by battle management satellites in 5,000 km orbits, to destroy Soviet offensive missiles in boost phase. This system is also designed to offer comprehensive protection for the entire population of the United States and Canada from Soviet ballistic missiles and aircraft, for $670 billion.

In estimating these costs, the authors made a series of optimistic assumptions about the sizes of the defensive force and characteristics of the technologies to be employed, how well these approaches might work, and the counterresponse the Soviet Union might take in deploying offensive forces. For example, the authors assumed that the cost of producing components would decrease by 10 percent with each doubling in the number of items produced. Such systematic cost declines, reflecting the so-called "production learning curve," have occurred only rarely in recent weapons programs.

Never before has the nation allocated such large sums to any single program, military or civilian. In today's prices, building an interstate highway system would cost $250 billion. The entire cost of the Vietnam War, from 1965 to 1972, was about $300 billion at 1987 prices. And total U.S. defense spending during the three years of the Korean War came to about $650 billion. Whatever the final costs of an SDI system, it will clearly cost each American household a total of $5,000 to $12,000, spread over eight to twenty years. For the average family earning between $30,000 and $50,000 a year, SDI could increase the annual tax bill by about $570.[7]

Table 3-1. Strategic Defense Initiative Budget Authority (*million dollars*).

	Actual				Total 1984–87
	1984	*1985*	*1986*	*1987*	
Surveillance, acquisition, and tracking	$ 367	$ 546	$ 847	$ 911	$2,671
Directed energy	323	377	803	844	2,347
Kinetic energy	196	256	596	729	1,777
Systems analysis and battle management	83	100	211	387	781
Support	23	118	230	358	729
DOD Total	992	1,397	2,687	3,229	8,305
DOE Total	118	224	285	514	1,141
SDI Total	$1,110	$1,621	$2,972	$3,743	$9,446

Sources: RDT&E Programs (R-1), Department of Defense Budget for Fiscal Year 1988 and 1989, January 5, 1987. Data for FY 1989-92 from SDIO budget breakdown released February 25, 1987, and Congressional Budget office, "Selected Weapons Costs From the President's 1988/1989 Program," April 2, 1987.

RESEARCH COSTS

Although no system has yet been scheduled for production and deployment, the SDI research program is well into its fourth year. The SDI Organization has spent $9.4 billion since FY 1984 and plans to spend an additional $39.2 billion through FY 1992 on research and development of strategic defense systems (see Table 3-1). That figure not only dwarfs the costs of previous major military research programs like the Manhattan Project (about $10 billion in 1986 dollars), but surpasses both the research and production costs of major strategic weapons programs like the MX missile and B-1 bomber. Expenditures for SDI research over the next five years are projected to be more than double those of any other major procurement program in the Defense Department's five-year budget request (see Table 3-2). The two next biggest requests in the Pentagon's five-year plan are for the F-16 fighter ($20.1 billion) and the F/A-18 fighter ($16.8 billion).

Table 3-1. continued

Requested					Total
1988	1989	1990	1991	1992	1988-92
$1,493	$1,859	—	—	—	
1,104	1,246	—	—	—	
1,075	1,200	—	—	—	
627	787	—	—	—	
922	1,190	—	—	—	
5,221	6,282	7,400	8,400	9,800	37,103
569	390	390	390	390	2,129
$5,790	$6,672	$7,790	$8,790	$10,190	$39,232

Strategic defense funding is carried out under the management of the Department of Defense (DOD) through the SDI Organization. Effective SDIO management of the research and technology program requires careful coordination with various armed service agencies such as the Army Strategic Defense Command, the headquarters of the Air Force, and the Defense Nuclear Agency as well as various national laboratories of the Department of Energy (DOE) including Lawrence Livermore National Laboratory, Los Alamos National Laboratory, and Sandia National Laboratory. As a result, the SDI program is funded from both the DOD and the DOE budgets.

The SDI is only a part of the total strategic defense R&D program. Secretary of Defense Weinberger stated on March 27, 1984, that the goal of the SDI was to create a "thoroughly reliably and effective defense against both ballistic missiles and cruise missiles."[8] Current SDI funding, however, includes only research and development on ballistic missile defense (BMD). The Defense Department's SDI budget does not include many projects that would eventually be part of a comprehensive defense against nuclear weapon delivery systems. Nor does the DOE SDI budget cover spending for nuclear defense programs. Among the related programs not included in the SDI are

Table 3-2. Procurement Program Budget Authority (*million dollars*).

	1987	1988	1989	1990	1991	Total 1987–91
Army						
M-1 Abrams MBT	2,125	2,191	1,886	105	73	6,380
Navy						
F-14A/D	696	963	1,248	1,354	1,768	6,029
F/A-18	3,407	3,598	3,232	3,535	3,075	16,847
Trident II submarine	1,515	1,557	1,605	1,661	1,716	8,054
SSN-688 submarine	2,419	2,174	2,361	3,041	997	10,992
SSN-21 submarine	455	163	1,579	608	2,595	5,400
DDG-51 destroyer	2,539	2,385	2,554	2,490	4,105	14,073
Trident D-5 missile	1,426	2,316	2,359	2,331	2,047	10,479
Air Force						
F-15	2,027	2,101	2,176	1,993	1,989	10,286
F-16	3,843	3,877	4,154	4,120	4,140	20,134
C-17A	217	1,363	1,274	1,971	2,788	7,613
Midgetman ICBM (RDT&E)	1,376	2,495	2,737	2,130	1,473	10,211

Source: Congressional Budget Office, *Selected Weapons Costs from the President's 1987 Program* (Washington, D.C.: CBO, April 9, 1986).

those exploring particle beam weapons, laser weapons, and missile surveillance.[9] The Federation of American Scientists (FAS) has identified an additional $8 billion in research related to directed energy weapons to be carried out between 1985 and 1989. These projects include ballistic missile defense, air defense against bombers, and antisatellite weaponry.

Through SDIO the Defense Department is funding projects in five technical areas (Figure 3-1) for the purpose of "conduct[ing] research on those technologies which might enable the development of defensive systems capable of intercepting ballistic missiles after they have been launched and preventing them from hitting their targets."[10] Directed energy research sponsored by the Department of Energy also falls under the SDI budget. These programs are described briefly below.

Surveillance, acquisition, tracking, and kill assessment (SATKA) projects are to develop the capability to detect, identify, locate, and track ballistic missiles and re-entry vehicles. Various sensors support the decision to initiate a defensive engagement, manage the battle, and assess the status of forces during the attack. SATKA will receive the bulk of SDI funding over the next three years (FY 1987-89), a total of $4.3 billion.

Directed energy weapons (DEW) projects explore and test various types of laser devices and particle beam weapons to be based on land or in space for use in destroying ICBMs in boost and post-boost phases of flight. In addition to developing the means of driving these speed-of-light weapons, means of controlling the beams and focusing them on targets will also be funded. Directed energy weapons will receive funding of $3.2 billion over the next three years.

Kinetic energy weapons (KEW) projects focus on the development of conventional rockets and small hypervelocity projectiles for use in attacking ICBMs in any phase of their flight path. The three-year budget for this program element is $3.0 billion.

Systems analysis and battle management is divided into two projects. The first aims at developing technologies necessary for a "highly responsive, ultra-reliable, survivable, endurable, and cost effective" battle management system. The second uses modeling and simulation techniques to assess the technological risks and

Figure 3-1. Growth in SDI Funding, FY 1984-88 (*million dollars*).

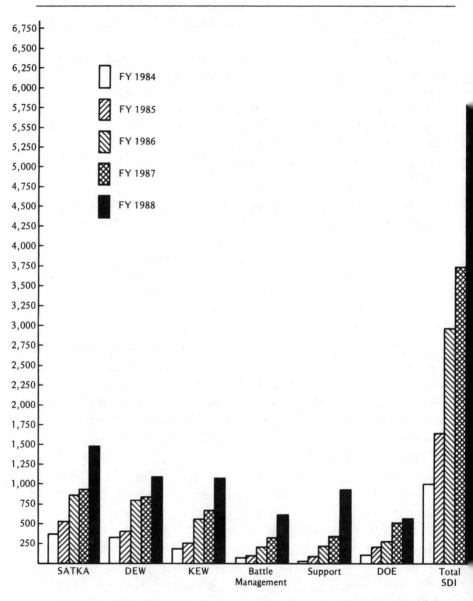

costs of developing such a complex system. Projected funding in this area is $1.8 billion over three years.

Support programs include testing the lethality of different weapons concepts against Soviet ICBMs and re-entry vehicles, developing means for defending the strategic defense system against attack, and exploring new means for launching large payloads into space and providing long-term power for platforms in space. These programs will receive $2.5 billion over three years.

Funding for strategic defense had been growing even before the president's 1983 speech. Budget authority for SDI-related program elements grew by 81 percent in constant dollars between 1980 and 1983.[11] More dramatic increases came in 1985 and 1986. Appropriations increased by 41 percent in 1985 alone, and during 1986 budget authority almost doubled in real terms.

Since some growth was already planned, new funding resulting from the president's initiative did not become a large part of the budget until 1986. Indeed, as a result of congressional budget actions, SDI funding for 1985 was $130 million *lower* than previously planned (Table 3–3). But in 1986, new funds accounted for 32 percent of the total.

Without access to long-range budget plans (these are classified), it is difficult to determine precisely the overall increase in strategic defense funding resulting from the president's initiative. Moreover, ongoing and previously planned projects exploring defensive technologies have been resurrected and reorganized under the central SDIO office. In many cases the reorganization included only part of some "program elements" (the building blocks of the Pentagon's budget). Because the Defense Department's selection of activities to include in the SDI is somewhat arbitrary, it is difficult to trace the increases resulting from the initiative. According to the Congressional Budget Office:

> Even by the narrower definition of SDI that limits it to ballistic missile defense, a number of projects closely related to SDI could have been included in the funding estimates. The summaries that accompany the 27 program elements [now merged into 5 program elements] from which SDI funds are drawn describe projects that relate to SDI but are not included in SDI funding. The basis upon which portions of these program elements are included or excluded is not readily apparent, particularly since the funds transferred to SDI are rarely associated with a particular project or projects.[12]

Table 3-3. New Budget Authority for SDI (*million dollars*).

	1984	1985	1986	Total 1984-86
Current Dollars				
Funding from existing program elements	941	1,527	1,809	4,277
New funds	51	-130	866	787
Total	$992	$1,397	$2,675	$5,064
Constant 1987 Dollars				
Funding from existing program elements	1,047	1,641	1,879	4,567
New funds	57	-140	899	816
Total	$1,104	$1,501	$2,778	$5,383

Source: Congressional Budget Office, *Analysis of the Costs of the Administration's Strategic Defense Initiative, 1985-1989* (Washington, D.C.: CBO, May 1984), p. 5. Updated using data from RDT&E Programs (R-1), Department of Defense Budget for Fiscal Year 1987, February 4, 1986.

Two estimates, however, have been offered. Lt. Gen. James Abrahamson has suggested that DOD plans formulated before the SDI called for spending roughly $12 billion on strategic defense research between 1984 and 1989 (see Table 3-4). Thus SDI would add over $7.6 billion to research on defensive systems.[13] After adjusting for inflation, the increase would be about $7.4 billion (in 1987 dollars).

An independent assessment of strategic defense funding performed by John Pike of the Federation of American Scientists (FAS) found that additional funding attributable to SDI amounts to over $12.6 billion between 1984 and 1989, or about $12.3 billion after adjusting for inflation (Table 3-5). According to FAS, estimates from SDIO are based on assumptions that are no longer pertinent because predecessor programs changed significantly even before the initiation of SDI. For example, SDIO has not taken into account the fact that the administration had cancelled deployment of the low-altitude defense system (LOADS) and deferred the advanced warning system (AWS) and the space-based surveillance technology (SBSS) deployments before the advent of SDI.[14] Consequently, SDIO showed bigger pre-SDI budgets than did FAS.

A $39 billion five-year program is not likely to bankrupt an economy producing more than $4 trillion worth of goods and services

Table 3-4. New Budget Authority for SDI, FY 1984-89 (*SDIO View*) (*million dollars*).[a]

	1984	1985	1986	1987	1988	1989	Total
SDI Funds							
Current dollars	992	1,397	2,687	3,229	5,221	6,282	19,808
Constant 1987 dollars	1,104	1,501	2,790	3,229	5,042	5,885	19,551
Pre-SDI Funds							
Current dollars[b]	985	1,527	1,802	2,181	2,699	2,982	12,176
Constant 1987 dollars	1,096	1,641	1,871	2,181	2,606	2,794	12,189
Increase/Savings							
Current dollars	7	-130	885	1,048	2,522	3,300	7,632
Constant 1987 dollars	8	-140	919	1,048	2,436	3,091	7,362

a. Data are for DOD budget only.

b. Figures from SDI Organization, "SDI: Progress and Challenges," staff report submitted to senators William Proxmire, J. Bennett Johnston, and Lawton Chiles, March 17, 1986. Data are for DOD SDI budget only.

Table 3-5. New Budget Authority for SDI, FY 1984-89 (*FAS View*) (*million dollars*).[a]

	1984	1985	1986	1987	1988	1989	Total
SDI Funds							
Current dollars	992	1,397	2,687	3,229	5,221	6,282	19,808
Constant 1987 dollars	1,104	1,501	2,790	3,229	5,042	5,885	19,551
Pre-SDI Funds							
Current dollars[b]	970	1,030	1,128	1,236	1,319	1,441	7,124
Constant 1987 dollars	1,079	1,107	1,171	1,236	1,274	1,350	7,217
Increase/Savings							
Current dollars	22	367	1,559	1,993	3,902	4,841	12,684
Constant 1987 dollars	25	394	1,619	1,993	3,768	4,535	12,334

a. Data are for DOD budget only.

b. Figures provided by John Pike, "The Strategic Defense Initiative Budget and Program" (Washington, D.C.: Federation of American Scientists, February 10, 1985).

Table 3-6. SDI and DOD RDT&E Budget Authority (*million dollars*).

	Actual					Tota
	1983	*1984*	*1985*	*1986*	*1987*	*1984–*
Strategic Defense Initiative						
Department of Defense	912	992	1,397	2,687	3,229	8,3(
Department of Energy	54	118	224	285	514	1,1⁴
Total SDI	966	1,110	1,621	2,972	3,743	9,4⁴
DOD RDT&E	22,798	26,867	31,327	33,609	36,724	128,5:
DOD SDI as a percentage of DOD RDT&E	4.0%	3.7%	4.5%	8.0%	8.8%	6.:
National research						
Basic research	10,935	12,105	13,300	14,655	16,206	56,2(
Applied research	20,245	21,190	22,925	24,374	26,008	94,4:
Total national research	31,180	33,295	36,225	39,029	42,214	150,7(
SDI as a percentage of national research	3.1%	3.3%	4.5%	7.6%	8.9%	6.:

Table 3-7. SDI and DOD RDT&E Budget Authority (*million constant 1987 dollars*).

	Actual					Tota
	1983	*1984*	*1985*	*1986*	*1987*	*1984–*
Strategic Defense Initiative						
Department of Defense	1,051	1,104	1,501	2,790	3,229	8,6
Department of Energy	62	131	241	296	514	1,1:
Total SDI	1,113	1,235	1,742	3,086	3,743	9,8(
SDI growth	—	122	507	1,344	657	2,6.
	—	10.9%	41.0%	77.2%	21.3%	37.(
DOD RDT&E	26,271	29,889	33,660	34,900	36,724	135,1
DOD RDT&E growth	—	3,618	3,771	1,240	1,824	10,4
DOD SDI growth as a percentage of DOD RDT&E growth	—	1.5%	10.5%	104.0%	24.1%	20.:
National research	35,930	37,040	38,922	40,529	42,214	158,7(
National research growth	—	1,110	1,883	1,606	1,685	6,2:
SDI growth as a percentage of national research growth	—	11.0%	26.9%	83.7%	39.0%	41.:

e 3-6. continued

	Requested					Total
	1988	1989	1990	1991	1992	1988-92
tegic Defense Initiative						
partment of Defense	5,221	6,282	7,400	8,400	9,800	37,103
partment of Energy	569	390	390	390	390	2,129
l SDI	5,790	6,672	7,790	8,790	10,190	39,232
) RDT&E	43,719	44,203	39,586	39,652	42,278	209,438
) SDI as a percentage						
DOD RDT&E	11.9%	14.2%	18.7%	21.2%	23.2%	17.7%
onal research						
sic research	17,871	19,618	21,438	23,363	25,627	107,917
plied research	27,673	29,311	30,906	32,499	34,396	154,785
l national research	45,544	48,929	52,344	55,862	60,023	262,702
as a percentage						
national research	12.7%	13.6%	14.9%	15.7%	17.0%	14.9%

e 3-7. continued

	Requested					Total
	1988	1989	1990	1991	1992	1988-92
egic Defense Initiative						
partment of Defense	5,042	5,885	6,756	7,494	8,488	33,666
partment of Energy	550	365	356	348	338	1,957
l SDI	5,592	6,251	7,112	7,842	8,826	35,623
growth	1,849	659	861	730	984	5,083
	49.4%	11.8%	13.8%	10.3%	12.6%	19.6%
) RDT&E	42,220	41,412	36,142	35,375	36,619	191,768
) RDT&E growth	5,496	-808	-5,270	-767	1,244	-105
) SDI growth as a						
centage of DOD	33.0%	-104.4%	-16.5%	-96.3%	79.9%	-5003.2%
T&E growth						
onal research	43,983	45,839	47,789	49,837	51,989	239,437
onal research growth	1,769	1,856	1,950	2,048	2,152	9,775
growth as a percentage						
national research growth	104.5%	35.5%	44.2%	35.6%	45.7%	52.0%

each year. Nonetheless, this kind of investment entails a significant opportunity cost: it consumes money that could be spent in many other areas. The economic impact of SDI depends on both the level of funding and the marginal spending increase involved in the project. The total spending level equals the amount of resources, both human and capital, involved in the project. The marginal increase measures the new demand for resources the program will make on the economy.

CROWDING OUT R&D RESOURCES

How great a shift of resources will be required to carry out strategic defense funding? SDI increases could consume hefty shares of the total growth in military and civilian R&D. SDI spending is projected to grow from 11.9 to 23.2 percent of the Defense Department's total research, development, testing, and evaluation (RDT&E) budget between 1988 and 1992 (Table 3-6). SDI's share of the yearly increases in research funds is even greater. In the last four years, SDI accounted for 20.8 percent of the $10.5 billion growth in the Defense Department's budget for RDT&E (see Table 3-7). By 1992, it will claim a staggering 5003 percent of the anticipated increase in the Pentagon's entire RDT&E account. (The RDT&E budget actually decreases during 1989, 1990, and 1991 while SDI research increases.) As Chuck Spinney, a budget analyst for the DOD, has testified, the Defense Department often underestimates total defense RDT&E in order to obtain increased funds for new weapons projects.[15] This practice, often referred to as getting the camel's nose under the tent, helps to spur initial financial momentum for the program.

Furthermore, the need to reduce the federal deficit may have prompted the Defense Department to reduce requested funds for other RDT&E requirements. Consequently, SDI, as proposed, will consume an even greater share of research funds at the expense of other defense projects that may be more beneficial to our national security. This impending drain on other defense projects has elicited protests from the various armed services.[16]

More importantly, SDI growth consumed almost 84 percent of the 1986 increase in national research funds, both basic and applied, for public and private sector technology. By 1988, SDI's share could peak at 105 as a result of the expected decline in national research funds. Since national research is key to any progress in the development of civilian technology, these cuts may hurt the economy. Chapter 8 will discuss this issue in greater detail.

So long as SDI dodges the Gramm-Rudman cuts and President Reagan opposes tax increases, SDI spending is likely to lead to further shrinking of civilian research programs. Research on toxic-waste cleanup, biomedical research on cancer, AIDS research, fuel-efficient cars, renewable energy, and other important endeavors will end up on the back burner.

CONCLUSION

By any standards, the SDI program represents a substantial demand for new R&D resources. Rapid growth in the early years of the program could crowd out other federal R&D efforts with less political clout. Moreover, expenditures of such large sums are certain to have an impact on the civilian economy. Thus consideration of the economic impact of SDI is crucial to decisions on the defense budget, particularly in peacetime. A severe adverse economic impact should be weighed as a factor in determining whether to continue accelerated development of strategic defense systems. But as the next chapter illustrates, the pattern of SDI contracting has left it up to the contractors themselves to make many of the decisions regarding which technologies are developed and on what timetable.

4

THE RACE FOR CONTRACTS

Will you find a place in this state-of-the-art cornucopia expected to be a greater undertaking than the Apollo program?

—American Society of Mechanical Engineers
November 16, 1984

While the scientific and arms control communities remain deeply divided about the feasibility of SDI, discussion and competition are proceeding on another less visible but equally important front: the struggle to determine which corporations will define, build, and profit from a strategic defense system. It is that competition that may settle the question of which system will be built, one intended to protect missiles or one intended to protect people. The analysis of feasibility may be not whether SDI is feasible but who does the feasibility studies and which companies can sell the Pentagon on their designs. SDI contractors are already building a momentum that may carry the program through the tangles of the political process.

As the largest and fastest-growing military venture ever proposed, SDI could soon become the leading area of growth for the nation's major military contractors. And now that SDI spending has exceeded $9 billion—with billions more to come—many scientists find the pork too luscious to refuse. In fact, an important political constituencey for the Strategic Defense Initiative program has emerged, based on its current and future economic benefits to key contractors, communities, and research institutions.

The nation's largest defense contractors will supply the core of this support. Politicians have long understood that contractors whose economic survival depends on defense spending can generate a strong political constituency for questionable weapons programs. The Reagan administration has successfully used such pork-barrel politics to garner support for SDI from the earliest research stage. Today a serious danger exists that the program may develop an unstoppable economic momentum. The program offers tremendous benefits to contractors who have powerful lobbying mechanisms at their disposal.

Major military corporations, historically dependent on Department of Defense prime contract awards for a substantial share of business, can hardly afford not to become involved in SDI research. As one company executive said in an interview with the *Christian Science Monitor,* "All of the major aerospace industries are deeply and heavily into this now, and all of them view this as an opportunity that they can't pass up. Twenty-five billion dollars is an awful lot of money. That's a strong incentive for any company to pursue it, even if Congress cuts it in half and we only get 10 percent."[1]

SDI R&D contracts are not an end in themselves but a key step toward the potentially much more lucrative production contracts that could follow. Not surprisingly, many of the corporations with strong positions in the strategic defense market—Lockheed, TRW, Rockwell International, Boeing, and Martin Marietta—have also been involved in developing the United States' offensive nuclear arsenal. A move toward deployment of a full strategic defense system could play the same sustaining role for these firms in the 1990s that production of a new generation of offensive nuclear weapons is playing in the 1980s. Indeed, a failure to shift to defensive strategic weapons could be economic suicide for these companies as the budget shrinks for offensive weapons and swells for defensive ones. SDI research not only staves off pressure for an immediate halt to the production of nuclear weapons in the 1980s, but will provide the seed money for the next wave of contracts as production of some major weapons like the MX, cruise, and Pershing missiles and the B-1 bomber winds down over the next five years. As one Pentagon expert on SDI has noted, "This isn't just a new area of opportunity for the major contractors; they've adopted the attitude that this is their future. That it's life or death."[2]

Consequently, it is by no means premature to raise questions about the economic and bureaucratic underpinnings of the SDI program now, before strategic defense systems go into production. What is the nature of the SDI contracting procedure? How will the contractors affect future directions and preferred technologies of the program?

THE CONTRACTING PROCESS

Much of the early competition among contractors has been spurred by the Pentagon's SDI Organization and Lieutenant General Abrahamson, a former manager of the expensive and controversial F-16 fighter and space shuttle programs. Abrahamson was asked to head up SDI because of his demonstrated ability to steer projects through the congressional budget process and promote them to the public.[3]

Much of Abrahamson's work to date has involved closed-door conferences with defense industry representatives to discuss SDI strategies and technologies in detail. These efforts are primarily directed at convincing defense contractors that SDI is here to stay, so that it is worth their while to bid for contracts and assign the best scientific and engineering talent available to the effort. In August 1984, defense contractors were invited to a three-day secret strategy session with DOD officials of the American Institute of Aeronautics and Astronautics. In addition to giving industry representatives an overview of SDI spending priorities, the symposium's objective was to help "foster development of a national commitment to the Strategic Defense Initiative." But perhaps the hardest sell of all was made by the American Society of Mechanical Engineers in a conference entitled "Find Your Role in SDI Battle Management/C^3." An overview of contracting and career options in the "state of the art cornucopia for high technology" was presented. In these and other industrial conferences on strategic defense, Abrahamson and other SDIO officials gave briefings.[4]

Bidding for strategic defense contracts is already intense. Over 240 contractors bid on the initial ten $1 million contracts to begin defining the systems architecture, or engineering model, of a strategic defense system. These contracts are designed to "provide an initial definition and assessment of several alternative constructs of systems . . . that can detect, identify, discriminate, intercept, and negate ballistic missiles in their boost, post-boost, mid-course and/or terminal phase."[5] In addition, the contractors are "to provide a set of requirements . . . that can make the individual architecture a viable and cost-effective strategic defense system." Abrahamson described this contracting process as a "horse race" approach. SDIO rewards the firms that respond "first with the best" ideas with follow-on contracts.

In December 1984, the Pentagon chose 10 of the 240 companies to undertake the first round of SDI concept designs. The first-phase study teams were led by General Research Corporation, Hughes Aircraft, Lockheed, Martin Marietta, McDonnell Douglas, Rockwell International, Science Applications International Corp., Sparta Inc., Teledyne Brown Engineering, and TRW. In a second phase, $5 million follow-on contracts for more detailed system architecture studies were awarded in the summer of 1985 to five of the original study teams, headed by Rockwell, Martin Marietta, TRW, Sparta, and Science Applications. Major hardware contractors including General Electric, General Dynamics, Boeing, Westinghouse, and LTV were selected as members of the second-round study teams.[6]

Firms involved in architecture studies can both determine the type of strategic defense system that may ultimately be deployed and receive future contracts for the components of such a system. There is a clear danger in this approach. First, firms hired to determine the feasibility of developing effective defenses against ballistic missiles are also the most likely beneficiaries of weapons production. Their own interests are best served by recommending full speed ahead on strategic defense whether or not a total workable system for population defense is possible. As Senator William Proxmire told the *New York Times*, "It's an enormous potential conflict of interest. There is no way these contractors can raise a skeptical eye. They look at SDI as an insurance policy that will maintain their prosperity for the next two decades."[7]

Second, many of these contractors have been involved in development of ballistic missile defense technologies since the 1970s and have the technology needed to begin production. Thus they may tend to push for what would best serve their short-term interests: a partial defense system. As one contractor representative told the *Washington Post*, "Everyone knows that you don't make money on technology research programs. We've got to have deployment."[8]

The contractors' tendency to push for early deployment is aided by the administration's increasing support for a partial defense system. Limited defense for U.S. ICBM silos can be achieved with extensions of the technology developed over the past ten years under the Army's ballistic missile defense programs. In fact, despite the administration's original stress on "novel concepts" and new technologies, most of the contracts awarded to date involve pre-existing programs. These programs are more applicable to terminal and midcourse defense than to the much more problematic task of postboost defense—the critical phase essential to population defense—and would allow for early deployment.

Of the $3,818 million in large, long-term contracts awarded since the beginning of FY 1983, 46 percent involve research for midcourse and terminal defense, 34 percent for boost-phase defense, and 20 percent for supportive technologies for all phases. The Army is administering about $1.4 billion in projects aimed at developing techniques for destroying ICBM re-entry vehicles late in their flight path, either just before or after return to the atmosphere en route to targets in the continental United States. Another $370 million in SDI research contracts administered by the Air Force has been allocated for midcourse and terminal defense systems. Many of these contracts are continuations of pre-existing programs (see Table 4–1).

Contractor pressure for deployment of a strategic defense system has already begun, even before the initial conceptual and feasibility studies have been completed. Lockheed asserted it had the technology to build a midcourse defense system soon after the success of its homing overlay experiment (HOE) in June 1984, which relied on infrared sensors and an unfolding umbrellalike projectile to destroy a dummy missile warhead. According to David Montague, a Lockheed vice president, "We have clearly demonstrated . . . a non-nuclear defense system that can unequivocally destroy ballistic missile warheads and could be used for defense of U.S. missile sites."[9] He vowed that such a partial defense system could be built for $30 billion and would destroy 85 percent of the delivery vehicles in an ICBM attack on the United States. The system is also expected to protect cities from "light" attack by accidental enemy launches or blackmail threats.

But Montague's Star Wars timetable is far more optimistic than Pentagon plans, which call for much more research before any decision is made on building the system. While the success of the HOE experiment demonstrated that one can "hit a bullet with another bullet," much more will be needed for a complete strategic defense

Table 4-1. SDI Contracts over $30 Million (*million dollars*).

Company	$ Value	Description of Work	Armed Service Agency
Ball Corp.	32	Space pointing and tracking experiment (SPATE)	Air Force Systems Command
Boeing	209	Airborne optical system (AOS)	Army Strategic Defense Command
	58	QUEEN MATCH-restructure DOT (designating optical tracker)	Army Strategic Defense Command
EG&G	243	Excalibur x-ray laser-cables and other test support	Department of Energy
	105	Excalibur x-ray laser-diagnostic equipment	Department of Energy
Gencorp Inc.	49	High endoatmospheric defense interceptor (HEDI) kill vehicle	Army Strategic Defense Command
	34	Infrared sensor for AOS	Army Strategic Defense Command
General Electric	200	SP-100 space nuclear reactor	Department of Energy
General Motors	167	Exoatmospheric re-entry interceptor system (ERIS) subsystems	Army Strategic Defense Command
	120	HEDI terminal stage kill vehicle	Army Strategic Defense Command
	111	Infrared sensor for AOS	Army Strategic Defense Command
Lawrence Livermore National Laboratory	278	Nuclear directed energy concepts	Department of Energy
	86	Induction free electron laser technology	Army Strategic Defense Command
Lockheed	301	ERIS-functional technology validation demonstration program	Army Strategic Defense Command
	64	SPATE	Air Force Space Division
	174	Integration of the TALON GOLD instrument with the space shuttle	Air Force Ballistic Missile Office
Los Alamos National Laboratory	236	Nuclear-driven directed energy concepts	Department of Energy

Company		Description	Agency
LTV Corp.	76	Small radar homing intercept technology (SRHIT)	Army Strategic Defense Command
McDonnell Douglas	163	HEDI development and test	Army Strategic Defense Command
	71	Terminal defense program radar	Army Strategic Defense Command
MIT Lincoln Lab	36	OAMP sensor system/data reduction-Optical data analysis and discrimination	Air Force Electronic Systems Division
	34	Imaging laser technology	Air Force Electronic Systems Division
	241	Anticipated SATKA work	Air Force Electronic Systems Division
Rockwell International	31	GaAs low-power rad-hard complex LSI fabrication pilot-line	Air Force Systems Command
Sandia National Laboratory	188	Nuclear directed energy concepts (and other support)	Department of Energy
SDI Institute	125	SDI support and analysis	Strategic Defense Initiative Organization
Systems Planning Corp.	39	SDI technical counters and Soviet response	Defense Supply Service/SDIO/DARPA
Teledyne Inc.	112	Systems engineering and technical assistance contract (SETAC)	Army Strategic Defense Command
Textron	63	Excimer moderate-power raman-shifted laser device (EMRLD) program	Air Force Kirtland Contracting Center R&D
TRW	141	ALPHA I laser-fabrication, testing, and evaluation	Air Force Kirtland Contracting Center R&D
Westinghouse Electric	31	Thunderbolt ground-based electromagnetic launcher facility	Defense Nuclear Agency
Total	$3,818		

Source: Council on Economic Priorities SDI database.

system. Even if Montague's optimistic assessment is accurate, the proposed system would not prevent the destruction of the United States by the 15 percent of missiles not intercepted. Despite these limits, Lockheed's homing overlay technology has been touted by Max Kampelman, the administration's chief arms negotiator, and by Robert Jastrow and Zbigniew Brzezinski as a key element in a partial strategic defense system they proposed for deployment in the early 1990s.[10]

The bias of defense contractors in determining the architecture of SDI affected even the initial decision to proceed with SDI research. The Defensive Technologies Study Team, or Fletcher Commission—a presidentially appointed commission charged with assessing the technical feasibility of the program in order to determine whether there should be a major financial commitment to SDI research—was heavily influenced by major defense contractors. More than a third of its members were employees or board members of military corporations that have since received $2.8 billion in contract awards for SDI research.[11] Similarly, of the fifty-seven non-Defense Department members of the Future Security Strategy Study Group, or Hoffman Panel, appointed to address the policy implications of SDI, at least forty-nine worked for organizations that have received SDI contracts. Fred Hoffman, who headed the panel, also worked for Pan Heuristics, a division of R&D Associates—in turn a subsidiary of a major SDI contractor, Logicon. Logicon received almost $22 million in SDI contracts between FY 1983 and FY 1986.

Furthermore, of the forty-eight members of the Defense Science Board, which deals with a variety of defense policy issues including SDI, thirty-one represented organizations with SDI contracts. The chairman of the board, Charles Fowler, is also senior vice president of the Mitre Corporation, which has about $1.5 million in SDI contracts. Finally, of the six non-Defense Department members of the eight-member Eastport Study group, four worked for organizations with SDI contracts.[12] While major weapons projects cannot be planned without the expertise of military contractors, it is dangerous to rely so heavily on their judgments, given SDI's far-reaching implications for the future of arms control and nuclear strategy.

The Pentagon has long relied on the companies that will profit from building a weapons system as the main source of information on its cost and technical feasibility. As Merton Peck and Frederic Scherer of the Harvard Business School noted in a landmark 1962 study of weapons acquisition:

Although weapons program decisions are made at high levels, they are based upon information collected largely at lower levels. The most important sources of information are the service operating agencies and commands, which in turn obtain much of their data from the contractors. Thus defense firms are not only major sources of new weapons program ideas, but they also provide information on the technological feasibility of new concepts and on estimated development costs and schedules,[13]

While Peck and Scherer acknowledge the value of "contractor-furnished information" to the program decision-making process, they add that "the information may be colored by the fact that it is provided in hopes of starting a program in which the contractor will participate."[14]

Objective technical assessment alone, however, is obviously not enough to produce sound decisions on weapons programs, as evidenced in the development of the ICBM in the 1950s. Study contracts for the ICBM contained a clause excluding the firms studying the feasibility and design concepts from bidding on hardware contracts.[15] The key motivating factor that propelled the program forward was the imaginary "missile gap" later used by the Kennedy administration to justify a 1,000-strong force. In the case of SDI, however, technical considerations will have a great influence on whether Reagan's original promise to protect the U.S. population has any hope of realization. Thus, technical and cost assessments by experts not employed by military contractors may be even more important than they were for the ICBM.

Congressman Thomas Foglietta (D-PA) and Senator William Proxmire (D-WI) have introduced amendments for a congressionally appointed review panel to provide this vital independent assessment.[16] Instead, in response to congressional pressure, SDIO Director James Abrahamson recommended the establishment of the SDI Research Institute in 1986. This federally funded "technical organization" is charged with providing impartial advice on SDI's feasibility. The institute's unofficial estimated cost is between $20 million and $30 million, and its staff size is estimated at between 100 and 200 scientists invited by the SDI Organization to participate.[17] It excludes experts from military industry involved in SDI work. At first glance, this appears to be a substantive step in the right direction. As we shall see, however, the issue of potential conflict of interest remains unresolved.

Most federally funded research centers are largely free of control by the agencies to which they report. But according to Senator Carl Levin (D-MI), the Pentagon is creating "enormous potential for abuse" in the SDI Institute, for at least three reasons.[18] First, Secretary of Defense Caspar Weinberger "has invited certain prominent individuals in the science fields" to form the organization. Not only are the identities of these scientists kept confidential, but they have been "extended the privilege of dealing with the federal government on a sole-source basis concerning a long-term contract." No one else will be invited to bid. Second, SDI Director James Abrahamson will be choosing the center's top staff members, resulting in an "unprecedented" level of control. Finally, the administration has refused to enact "revolving door" prohibitions against scientists moving from the institute to private companies whose performance the institute will evaluate. According to Senator Levin, employees could recommend a contract award and "six weeks later accept a job with the firm that submitted the winning proposal." Under the 1986 Defense Authorization Act, former DOD personnel who go to work for defense contractors must file a report for at least two years, disclosing their past and present employment activities.

Another study concludes that the institute could end up shaping the research done on the system.[19] As long as the three problems mentioned above are not resolved the institute will perpetuate the very conflict of interest it was initially conceived to eradicate. As Senator Paul Simon (D-IL) stated, "If there is one thing the Pentagon does not need, it is a taxpayer-funded lobby" for Star Wars.[20]

Early response to SDI from the defense industry indicates that institutional momentum for pursuing strategic defense is already gathering. Without an objective assessment of SDI, contractors will have a free rein in pushing for the program regardless of its technical and strategic wisdom. As key military firms become more involved in SDI research, the emphasis may be on *what type* of strategic defense system to build rather than whether to build one at all. For many military contractors, SDI has already become a significant base for business.

THE MILITARY SPACE BUSINESS

Contractors are already benefiting from Star Wars-related spending. The Council on Economic Priorities has identified almost $6.8 billion in prime contracts awarded in the last four years, $619 million awarded during FY 1983, $1,479 million in FY 1984, $2,446 million in FY 1985, and $2,215 million in FY 1986. An additional $561 million in contract options for FY 1987 was also identified.[21]

Table 4-2. The Top Twenty SDI Contractors, FY 1983-86.

Company	Value of Contracts (thousand dollars)	Share of Total SDI Contracts (percent)
Lockheed[a]	720,961	9.8
General Motors	612,698	8.4
Boeing	373,697	5.1
TRW	373,117	5.1
DOE Lawrence Livermore National Laboratory[a]	366,685	5.0
EG&G[a]	360,300	4.9
McDonnell Douglas	338,224	4.6
MIT Lincoln Lab	327,542	4.5
DOE Los Alamos National Laboratory[a]	285,588	3.9
General Electric	260,797	3.6
DOE Sandia National Laboratory[a]	226,530	3.1
Rockwell International	197,405	2.7
Teledyne Inc.	181,145	2.5
Gencorp Inc.	175,455	2.4
SDI Institute	125,000	1.7
Textron	120,331	1.6
LTV Corp.	105,657	1.4
Flow General	90,226	1.2
Raytheon Co.	81,819	1.1
Martin Marietta	77,781	1.1
Total	$5,400,958	73.8%

Note: Data are from FY 1983 to December 1986. Total contract values for this period equal $7,321 million. Since only three months of 1987 are included in the estimates, final figures may differ from those listed here.

a. Figures include $492 million in FY 1987 priced contract options that have yet to be exercised. Of this, Lockheed is to receive $34 million, Lawrence Livermore $83 million, EG&G $154 million, Los Alamos $123 million, and Sandia $99 million.

The distribution of these SDI contracts—74 percent went to just twenty private contractors and national laboratories—has set the program's economic landscape for the future (Table 4-2). An analysis of space weapons contracts awarded so far reveals three significant qualities.

First, SDI research and development contracts are highly concentrated. Of the total awards identified to date, 60 percent, or $4.4 billion, went to twenty military corporations (Table 4-3). Thirteen

Table 4–3. Top Twenty Corporate Military SDI Contractors, FY 1983–86 (*thousand dollars*).

Company	FY 1983	FY 1984	FY 1985	FY 1986	Total 1983–86	Total Share of Contracts, 1983–86 (percent)
Lockheed[a]	80,225	173,304	78,383	355,949	720,961[b]	9.8
General Motors[c]	10,304	148,083	128,223	326,088	612,698	8.4
Boeing	48,430	237,088	79,290	8,889	373,697	5.1
TRW[d]	61,878	153,713	142,939	14,587	373,117	5.1
EG&G	17,000	20,600	68,400	100,600	360,300[e]	4.9
McDonnell Douglas	38,932	91,846	17,951	189,495	338,224	4.6
General Electric[f]	3,077	11,177	37,889	208,654	260,797	3.6
Rockwell International[d]	18,521	59,423	104,324	15,137	197,405	2.7
Teledyne	15,201	97,039	41,229	27,676	181,145	2.5
Gencorp[g]	1,148	44,800	72,023	57,483	175,455	2.4
Textron[h]	12,877	3,978	65,005	38,472	120,332	1.6
LTV	77,871	4,632	19,934	3,220	105,657	1.4
Flow General	2,781	12,539	50,736	24,170	90,226	1.2
Raytheon	13,180	33,224	11,363	24,052	81,819	1.1
Martin Marietta[d]	15,270	14,754	43,784	3,973	77,781	1.1
Honeywell	10,007	26,941	32,841	351	70,140	1.0
Science Applications[d]	9,461	16,231	31,485	10,196	67,373	0.9
Westinghouse	295	878	17,935	43,481	62,589	0.9
Nichols Research	8,887	9,219	33,986	6,206	58,298	0.8
Litton	6,710	29,958	10,253	4,832	51,753	0.7
Total	$452,055	$1,189,427	$1,087,973	$1,462,611	$4,379,767	59.8%

a. Lockheed merged with Sanders Associates Inc. in July, 1986. Sanders received $1,640,991 in 1985, while Lockheed received $76,742,127. Sanders received no SDI contracts in 1983–84.

b. Total includes $34,000 in FY 1987 priced contract options.

c. General Motors merged with Hughes Aircraft on Dec. 31, 1985. Hughes received $124,294,969 in 1985 and $125,552,246 in 1984, while GM received $3,927,937 in 1985, $22,531,052 in 1984. GM received no SDI contracts in 1983.

d. Companies that won the second phase of "systems architecture" contracts to assess the feasibility of space defense. The fifth contract was awarded to Sparta.

e. Total includes $153,000,000 in FY 1987 priced contract options.

f. General Electric merged with RCA in Feb. 1986. RCA received $9,331,387 in 1985, while General Electric received $28,557,662. RCA received no SDI contracts in 1983–84.

g. In 1984 Gencorp replaced General Tire and Rubber Co. as the parent company. Total also includes SDI contracts to the company's Aerojet General division.

h. Textron acquired AVCO in Feb. 1985. AVCO received $3,259,783 in SDI contracts in 1984, and $7,745,321 in 1983, while Textron received $717,722 in 1984 and $5,131,40 in 1983.

Table 4-4. DOD Contracts for Top Twenty SDI Contractors, FY 1985 (*thousand dollars*).

Contractor	Prime DOD Contracts		DOD Awards as Percent of Sales	Prime DOD RDT&E Contracts		SDI Contracts	
	Dollar Value	Rank		Dollar Value	Rank	Dollar Obligations	Percent of RDT&E
Lockheed[a]	5,550	5	53	1,710	1	54	3
General Motors[b]	5,076	7	5	507	9	84	17
Boeing	5,458	6	40	1,070	3	118	11
TRW	1,079	25	18	457	12	93	20
EG&G[c]	NA	NA	NA	9	156	68	NA
McDonnell Douglas	8,857	1	77	692	5	19	3
General Electric[d]	7,205	3	19	1,167	2	10	1
Rockwell International	6,264	4	55	625	6	50	8
Gencorp	566	38	19	131	28	31	24
Teledyne	694	33	21	104	34	48	47
Textron[e]	1,920	13	47	244	22	37	15
LTV	1,585	17	19	171	26	27	16
Flow General[f]	NA	NA	NA	21	85	15	71
Raytheon	2,999	9	47	365	14	16	4
Martin Marietta	2,717	11	62	911	4	20	2
Honeywell	1,908	14	29	246	21	16	6

Science Applications[g]	235	70	NA	100	37	26	26
Westinghouse	1,941	12	18	519	8	8	2
Nichols Research[g]	NA	NA	NA	13	122	12	90
Litton	1,528	18	33	98	38	9	10
Total	$55,582		23%	$9,160		$761	9%

a. Total for Lockheed includes contract awards to Sanders Associates Inc., which merged with Lockheed in July 1986.
b. Total for GM includes contract awards to Hughes Aircraft Corporation, which merged with GM on December 31, 1985.
c. All of EG&G's SDI contracts were awarded by the Department of Energy; therefore, they are not included in DOD RDT&E figures.
d. Total for GE includes contract awards to RCA, which merged with GE in February 1986.
e. Total for Textron includes contract awards to AVCO, which merged with Textron in February 1985.
f. Flow General and Nichols Research do not rank among the top 100 contractors. Value of prime contracts is therefore not available.
g. Science Applications and Nichols Research as privately held companies and do not make public their sales figures.

of these leading space weapons research contractors were among the Department of Defense's top twenty contractors in FY 1985, the most recent year for which these rankings are available.[22] These firms with the most valuable contracts for developing defenses against nuclear missiles are also the key contractors for the new generation of nuclear weapons: the MX missile (Rockwell, TRW, AVCO, Martin Marietta), the B-1 bomber (Rockwell, AVCO, Boeing, LTV), the Pershing missile (Martin Marietta), the Trident missile (Lockheed), and cruise missiles (Boeing, Litton). AVCO, Boeing, and LTV also received a total of $432 million in antisatellite contracts between 1983 and 1985.[23] While SDI research awards will not make or break these military giants today, the corporations' continued profitability may well depend on their receiving new large awards upon completion of their current nuclear weapons programs.

As financial analyst Alan Benasuli of Drexel Burnham stated, "SDI will probably take up the slack of regular military spending, which is scheduled to start leveling off in 1988."[24] Already, DOD awards accounted for 5 percent to 77 percent of sales for leading SDI contractors in FY 1985, while over 9 percent of their RDT&E awards were related to space weapons (Table 4–4).

Second, with a potential to generate a whole new network of military subindustries in the 1990s, Star Wars could also underwrite the financial standing of a wide range of corporations seeking to reap profits from the next arms build-up. A number of smaller computer and electronics companies are hoping to collect their share of what one investors' newsletter called "money from Heaven" (Table 4–5). Of the $18,874 million in DOD RDT&E awards distributed to over 500 defense contractors in FY 1985, a full 8 percent was spent on SDI.[25]

One such company is Kaman Corporation, one of the few Vietnam-era contractors to apply military technology (in helicopter production) to a peaceful use (making guitars). It has been awarded almost $31 million to study how well weapons and communications facilities could survive a nuclear attack. One of the least likely SDI contractors is Corning Glass Works. Best known for its housewares, Corning has become a major supplier for Defense Advanced Research Projects Agency (DARPA's) large optics demonstration experiment, which aims to produce the mirrors needed to redirect laser beams in space. A number of such smaller companies will do quite nicely with the crumbs from the Star Wars pie.

Table 4-5. Smaller SDI Contractors, FY 1983-86 (*thousand dollars*).

Company	1983	1984	1985	1986	Total
System Planning Corp.	1,526	1,827	2,902	6,092	45,847[a]
Ball Corp.	0	0	1,624	17,288	33,512[b]
Kaman Sciences	3,921	10,865	15,404	400	30,590
W. J. Schafer	4,569	4,073	9,841	10,928	29,411
Sparta Inc.	4,247	7,457	12,423	4,881	29,008
Western Research	1,810	9,103	9,576	8,011	28,500
SRS Technologies	3,220	6,044	2,663	10,146	22,073
Dynetics Inc.	826	1,481	18,465	0	20,772
Atlantic Research Corp.	162	59	12,525	6,832	19,578
SRI International	1,946	2,476	11,849	781	17,052
Mission Research	1,165	2,457	8,942	3,641	16,205
Rutherford Appleton Lab.	0	0	0	15,000	15,000
Riverside Research	2,055	1,771	5,659	4,917	14,402
Maxwell Laboratories	1,375	3,806	8,502	650	14,333
Physical Research	1,314	3,016	8,112	907	13,349
Arthur D. Little	2,614	1,570	7,295	250	11,729
New Technology Inc.	4,246	3,445	3,681	0	11,372
Perkin Elmer	643	1,569	8,609	317	11,138
Acurex Corp.	4,927	356	5,446	0	10,729
Verac Inc.	0	2,238	488	7,997	10,723

Note: Companies are not listed among top 100 Department of Defense Prime Contractors in FY 1985.
a. System Planning Corp. total includes $33,500,000 in 1987 priced contract options.
b. Ball Corp. total includes $14,600,000 in 1987 priced contract options.

Third, the nation's federally funded research and development centers and armed service facilities also have much at stake in the SDI program. As Table 4-6 indicates, over $1.5 billion in SDI contracts has been distributed to twenty laboratories or defense facilities since FY 1983. With $367 million in contracts for laser research, the Department of Energy's Lawrence Livermore Laboratory is the leading SDI national laboratory. M.I.T. Lincoln Laboratories, with $328 million, is also a leader in SDI research, specializing in surveillance research.

The SDI Organization depends on these contractors for its core of support. While technical and strategic criticisms of the program cast doubt on its viability as an arms control solution, the distribution of

Table 4-6. Value of SDI Controls: Top Twenty Federally Funded Research and Development Centers or Armed Service Divisions SDI Contractors, FY 1983-86 (thousand dollars).

	1983	1984	1985	1986	Total
DOE Lawrence Livermore National Laboratory	20,000	40,000	83,105	140,900	366,685 [a]
MIT Lincoln Laboratories	0	0	303,797	23,745	327,542
DOE Los Alamos National Laboratory	15,000	20,000	65,301	62,487	285,588 [b]
DOE Sandia National Laboratory		18,000	37,830	71,800	226,530 [c]
SDI Institute			0	125,000	125,000
DOE Hanford National Laboratory			0	27,100	27,100
AF Weapons Laboratory			22,877	1,100	23,977
AF Geophysics Laboratory			13,190	5,470	18,660
DOE Brookhaven Laboratory			5,843	11,600	17,443
Army Corps of Engineers			3,698	12,537	16,235
NASA, Lewis Research Center [d]			11,130	1,770	12,900
AF Space Command (BMD)			9,800	1,775	11,575
Army BMD Advanced Technology Center			9,201	1,500	10,701
Naval Research Laboratory			9,874	550	10,424
Army Missile Command			5,561	3,401	8,962
Army White Sands Missile Reserve			4,540	554	5,094
Naval Surface Weapons Center			3,533	1,300	4,833
Naval Sea Systems Command			4,687	50	4,737
DOE Argonne National Laboratory			0	4,000	4,000
AF Space Division			3,261	483	3,744
Total	$35,000	$78,000	$597,228	$497,122	$1,511,730

a. Total for DOE Lawrence Livermore National Lavoratory includes $82,680,000 in FY 1987 contract options.
b. Total for DOE Los Alamos National Laboratory includes $122,800,000 in FY 1987 priced contract options.
c. Total for DOE Sandia National Laboratory includes $98,900,000 in FY 1987 priced contract options.
d. Total includes awards to NASA received by the Goddard Space Flight Center ($2,445,000), the Ames Research Center ($1,236,000), the Jet Propulsion Laboratory ($225,000), the Marshall Space Flight Center ($166,000)...

research and development contracts will strengthen SDI's base of political support. Many of these companies, national laboratories, and defense facilities have made major structural changes to accommodate the rapid pace of SDI research. The next chapter focuses on the technology being researched by the top ten SDI military corporations. Most of these companies are involved in producing prototypes for experiments in technologies intended for early deployment.

5

THE TOP TEN SDI CONTRACTORS

The defense budget will grow only marginally for the rest of the decade. By the 1990s, some of the industry's biggest players will be scrambling for growth. . . . One bright hope for new growth is Reagan's Strategic Defense Initiative.

—Fortune Magazine
August 5, 1985

The SDI program followed the longest and largest military buildup in U.S. peacetime history. Appropriations for defense doubled from $144 billion in 1980 to $293 billion in 1987. This steady growth in weapons outlays has made the military giants increasingly dependent on the Pentagon budget. In fiscal 1984, twenty-three of the Department's top hundred contractors received more than 25 percent of their yearly revenues for Pentagon awards.[1] Since SDI is expected to take 80 percent of new funds for DOD R&D by FY 1992, the top DOD firms are likely to become increasingly dependent on SDI research money.[2] For many, SDI is already a key source of income.

The following profiles of the top ten SDI companies outline their financial involvement, major projects, and wherever possible their view of the role of SDI in their future. How important are SDI R&D contracts for their present projected business base? What role will each key contractor play in SDI? And how have they reorganized

61

their companies to deal with the initiative? To answer these questions, SDI obligations—the actual amount of SDI contract money spent—are compared to total defense research funds for each company in FY 1985. The fiscal 1985 budget marked the sixth consecutive year of substantial real increases in military spending, with weapons research and development accounting for the largest share. Companies are listed in order of their total SDI awards since 1983.

1. LOCKHEED MISSILES AND SPACE

SDI obligations (FY 1985): $54.5 million
   Share of DOD RDT&E awards: 3 percent
DOD awards (FY 1985): $5,550 million
   Share of sales: 53 percent

Lockheed ranked number one among all strategic defense contractors, with $721 million received since FY 1983.[3] This position reflects the company's traditional strength in the defense industry. In FY 1985, Lockheed was among the top ten prime DOD and RDT&E contractors, largely because of its work on the Trident II fleet ballistic missiles.

Lockheed has already taken a leap into this new defense market, with 3 percent of its FY 1985 DOD RDT&E awards (some $54 million) involved in strategic defense. The corporation is pursuing the same line of technology today as it did before Reagan's March 1983 speech: DARPA's laser program and the Army's ballistic missile defense (BMD) drive. In the laser program, the company is currently the prime contractor for two parts of DARPA's three-pronged Triad laser experiment: Talon Gold, which is the laser pointing and tracking experiment, and the large optics demonstration experiment (LODE).

Under a $139 million increase on its contract for Talon Gold, Lockheed originally scheduled to test the system—essentially a telescope that would enable lasers to spot and fire at missiles as they are launched—aboard the space shuttle in 1984. Given the technical complexity of the task, the test date slipped back to 1989. Recently, Talon Gold's mission has shifted from space testing to a modest series of ground-based experiments in pointing and tracking. Testing in space, however, is viewed as essential to evaluating the system's workability in strategic defense. Therefore, an advanced version has been scheduled for space testing in the early 1990s. In the meantime, this multiyear contract, awarded in early 1984, will spur Lockheed's interest in pursuing the project at a more energetic pace and sustain its enthusiasm for the president's national security directive. Lockheed will also direct LODE, the effort to create a hinged mirror to point the laser beam to its target. A total of $24 million has been awarded to the company over the past two fiscal years.

The Army's $300 million homing overlay experiment (HOE), one part of its BMD, is the most advanced project in kinetic energy weapons development. HOE, terminated after its 1984 test, has already been succeeded by the exoatmospheric re-entry vehicle interceptor subsystem (ERIS) and the high endoatmospheric system (HEDS) programs. Lockheed is doing concept definition work to enable the demonstration of this nonnuclear ground-based ballistic missile defense.

Lockheed has also won concept definition contracts for the booster surveillance and tracking system and is doing additional work on infrared sensors.

2. GENERAL MOTORS/HUGHES AEROSPACE

SDI obligations (FY 1985):	$84.4 million
Share of DOD RDT&E awards:	17 percent
DOD awards (FY 1985):	$5,076 million
Share of sales:	5 percent

General Motors' second-place position is due primarily to its acquisition of Hughes Aircraft Company on December 31, 1985.[4] Hughes had received over $260 million in SDI awards before the merger, and this total jumped to $612 million in 1986. Hughes's extensive involvement in SDI accounted for 17 percent of the two companies' combined DOD RDT&E awards for 1985. The company's contribution to SDI consists mainly of work on kinetic energy weapons (KEW), surveillance, acquisition, tracking, and kill assessment (SATKA), and directed energy weapons (DEW) technologies.

Hughes is one of the leading contractors in the high-endoatmospheric defense interceptor (HEDI) project to develop nonnuclear rocket-launched projectiles to intercept missiles in the terminal phase of their flight. This $120 million award to GM Hughes Electronics Corporation is a subcontract from McDonnell Douglas. The company also won a $167 million subcontract from Lockheed in January 1986, to develop subsystems for ERIS.

In surveillance technologies, Hughes was involved in component building for the space surveillance technology system (SSTS). The Hughes Electro-Optical and Data Systems Group also took a 30 percent share ($111 million) of Boeing's airborne optical system contract to develop infrared sensors. The company has already reported the flight test success of the sensor it subcontracted for the Army's designating optical tracker (DOT) program. The retrievable infrared sensor was used in the tracker/telescope to be rocketed into space and relay what it "sees" to a ground station.

Hughes is also working on laser and particle beam weapons under triservice programs. The company's pre-1983 work on the Sealite beam director included a $66 million contract, which was subsequently supplemented by $25 million to transport the beam director from El Segundo, California, to the White Sands Missile Range in New Mexico and to continue its operation. Further funding can be expected as Sealite is integrated with TRW's mid-infrared chemical laser (MIRACL). Hughes has also contributed to numerous other DEW projects, including concept definition for ground-based lasers that can intercept missiles in their boost phase.

Finally, Hughes's prowess in sensor technology has also gained it an important role in battle management activities of SDI. It won an award in February 1986 for concept definition for the battle management/command, control, and communication project. The company is already developing the infrared sensors for the antisatellite miniature vehicle. Its number two position is due principally to its ability to act as "the eyes and ears" of space defense, based on the maturity of its sensor technology.

The acquisition of Hughes marks a giant leap into aerospace and strategic defense industries for GM. In FY 1985, GM's work in military vehicles and aircraft engines ranked the company seventeenth among DOD prime contractors and seventy-fifth among DOD prime contractors for RDT&E. Ranking eighth and tenth in the same categories and highly experienced in electro-optics and electronics, Hughes promises to make GM a major contender among SDI contractors.

3. BOEING

SDI obligations (FY 1985):	$118 million
Share of DOD RDT&E awards:	11 percent
DOD awards (FY 1985):	$5,458 million
Share of sales:	40 percent

Boeing, the third-ranked SDI contractor for the period FY 1983–86, received $373.7 million in awards. The company has long been involved in offensive nuclear weapons programs, including the air-launched cruise missile, the B-52 and B-1 bombers, research on the Midgetman small ICBM, and research on MX basing modes. Under the present policy of strategic defense R&D coupled with continued deployment of new offensive nuclear weapons systems, Boeing should remain a top DOD contractor.

Boeing's role in SDI is based on its experience during the antiballistic missile (ABM) efforts of the 1960s and early 1970s. Marshall Gehring, the company's manager for SDI battle management/C³ I, explained:

> We concluded that we could not build a cost effective BMD system then because the probability of it doing the job was low. Now, given the technology we have in 1984, it is still beyond our capability to do the full [leakproof] job. Even the largest computer, the Cray computer at Boeing, can't field the job of space-based lasers and other twenty-first-century deals in my lifetime. On the other hand, terminal phase hard-point defense is the genesis and mainstay of ballistic missile defense.[5]

A review of the contracts awarded to the company's Seattle division, the home of the current strategic defense effort, reveals that Boeing's main contribution will be in surveillance, acquisition, tracking, and kill assessment. A $376 million five-year contract was awarded to the company in July 1984 for the airborne optical adjunct. Boeing will spend $209 million of the total, subcontracting $111 million to Hughes, $34 million to Gencorp, and $22 million to Honeywell. The project's goal is to develop airborne infrared sensors that can be sent aloft aboard modified 767 aircraft to aid in the discrimination of warheads from decoys in the terminal phase of the ICBM flight path.

Boeing is also the lead contractor for another tracking program, the Army's designating optical tracker. Its purpose is to demonstrate the capability of long-wave infrared (LWIR) sensors to direct interception of re-entry vehicles above the atmosphere. Between 1983 and 1986 Boeing received $55 million to restructure the DOT program and accommodate two flights from the Army's new rocket launch facility at Shemya Air Force Base, Alaska. The flight tests will carry the DOT telescope, fully equipped with its LWIR sensor package, aboard a rocket to an altitude of over 100 miles. Boeing has also won concept definition awards for the high endoatmospheric defense system and the exoatmospheric re-entry vehicle interception system.

Boeing's role thus far in the kinetic and directed energy weapons programs includes evaluating the integrated on-orbit demonstration of DARPA's Triad space-based laser experiments and designing a concept for the Have Sting program, an effort to examine potential uses of kinetic energy devices. In addition, the company is completing a new test facility for the radio frequency free electron laser (FEL). Another $33.2 million was received for various kinetic energy weapon contracts, including a $20.1 million contract for the Sagittar project. Boeing is also a major contractor in the SDI related anti-satellite (ASAT) program, having completed work on a $46 million contract already, and for the National Aeronautics and Space Administration's orbital transfer vehicle. The NASA vehicle would play a key role in servicing a functioning space-based missile defense system.

Boeing's substantial share of the early SDI contracting effort insures its continued support for the president's program. As Gehring put it, "There is an awful lot of money here and this is the type of activity Boeing is interested in. If we can do something for the government that is within our resources and make money, we will. We are not philanthropic."[6]

4. TRW

SDI obligations (FY 1985):	$93.3 million
Share of DOD RDT&E awards:	20 percent
DOD awards (FY 1985):	$1,079 million
Share of sales:	18 percent

A total of $373 million in SDI contracts over the last four years has made TRW a leading beneficiary of the program. It ranked twelfth and twenty-fifth respectively among the RDT&E and DOD prime contractors of FY 1985. Twenty percent of the company's total DOD RDT&E awards in FY 1985 were from SDI, up from 8 percent in 1983.

TRW's interest in ballistic missile defense dates back to the ABM program of the 1950s. It helped engineer techniques for systems management and coordinated the efforts of thousands of contractors and subcontractors on matters ranging from propulsion, guidance, and re-entry to data processing and site construction. Between 1978 and 1983, at least $60 million in awards assured TRW's continued work on this effort.

Under the new initiative, this technology program is still funded, but TRW's major focus has shifted to directed energy weapons. The company has two contracts totaling $167 million to develop the Alpha chemical laser, one leg of the DARPA Triad experiment. As a leading competitor in high-energy laser technology, the company also completed a $28 million contract in 1982 for the Navy's mid-infrared chemical laser, an effort originally aimed at protecting ships from Soviet cruise missiles but revised under SDI for missile defense. It has received an additional $12.7 million contract in conjunction with the lethality and vulnerability tests against target arrays that took place in the fall of 1985 at the White Sands Missile Range in New Mexico. It has also won contracts for work on the oxygen-iodine chemical laser and excimer laser under Air Force guidance as well as $12 million in contracts for electron laser experiments.

TRW is also advancing its work in space surveillance technology and space survivability. Its principal contract has been a $20 million concept definition (Phase II) award for the boost surveillance and tracking system. The company also received a $10.4 million contract for the space surveillance and tracking system project. In survivability technology, TRW was one of three companies chosen to develop the satellite defense system.

The company's fourth area of research is the orbiting maneuvering vehicle. Under a $1.6 million contract recently awarded, it has already begun design and development of this space transportation system. Because this program will be important in establishing a system in space, TRW can expect much larger revenues in the future.

TRW's commitment to space defense is underscored by the recent creation of a vice presidency to develop the company's SDI business strategy. Traditionally TRW's government sales have stemmed mostly from the aerospace and communications business, primarily through its defense and space systems group. A major restructuring in 1985 promises to focus even more of the company's resources on space defense and related technologies. In that year, the Electronics and Space Systems Division accounted for 57 percent of TRW's sales and 50 percent of its operating profits, in large part because of its work on the MX.[7] This trend helps explain why almost one-quarter of DOD RDT&E came from SDI in 1985 and why this number may grow in the future. Moreover, by awarding TRW a Phase II systems architecture award, the Pentagon has extended its recognition of the company as a key player in the industrial base for Star Wars.

5. EG&G

SDI obligations (FY 1985):	$68.4 million
Share of DOD RDT&E awards:	not available
DOD awards (FY 1985):	not available
Share of sales:	not available

EG&G ranked fifth among the leading SDI contractors, with $360 million awarded since FY 1983. While the company is not currently a significant DOD contractor, it is among the leading recipients of defense contracts from the Department of Energy. It has designed and produced diagnostic and test support equipment along with other services for the nuclear weapons testing program without interruption since 1947. This expertise in developing new nuclear weapons has put EG&G in a strong position to aid in the development of the nuclear-pumped x-ray laser, termed the "third generation" nuclear weapon.

Although President Reagan originally introduced the Strategic Defense Initiative as a nonnuclear defense against nuclear missiles, this new weapon is powered by an atomic explosion that emits powerful x-rays that can be focused and directed. Many scientists claim the laser is impractical because it cannot shoot through the atmosphere to intercept missiles in the boost phase. Many are also uncomfortable with the notion of detonating one atomic bomb to stop another, even if the explosion occurs in space. Nonetheless, the x-ray laser has strong supporters in the administration.

EG&G is the only one of the top ten companies to participate in just a single SDI program. If the projected funding level of $222 million for the x-ray laser from FY 1986–91 is maintained, EG&G will be well placed to receive a large share, increasing an already appreciable source of income. While SDI contracts amounted to only 6 percent of the company's sales in 1985, the $68 million received from the DOE for the x-ray laser already dwarfs the $8.7 million received in RDT&E from the DOD for that same year. Moreover, the company's experience with nuclear power generation, electro-optics, and high-energy pulsed lasers makes it a potential candidate for contracts in other SDI programs.

6. McDONNELL DOUGLAS

SDI obligations (FY 1985):	$18.6 million
Share of DOD RDT&E awards:	3 percent
DOD awards (FY 1985):	$8,857 million
Share of sales:	77 percent

McDonnell Douglas ranks sixth in SDI awards received since 1983, with a total of $338 million, and first in overall DOD prime contract awards for FY 1985. The company has created a new vice presidency at its Huntington Beach, California, plant to deal strictly with SDI-related programs in an effort to stay on top of the program as it unfolds. A leader in earlier ABM efforts, it sends representatives to conferences cosponsored by the SDI Organization to speak on such topics as high endoatmospheric discrimination and battle management.[8]

Having come up with the winning concept for the high endoatmospheric defense system, McDonnell Douglas received $163 million in 1986 to develop and test the HED interceptor. Although the low-altitude defense system (LOADS) program has been cancelled, McDonnell Douglas has had little trouble maintaining its share of SDI spending, receiving over $189 million in 1986 alone.

In keeping with its historical role in ABM systems development, McDonnell Douglas's contracts have focused on terminal defense since the beginning of FY 1983. The company received a $71 million two-year award to develop subsystems for terminal defense in October 1983. In the same year it received $18 million for research on LOADS. McDonnell Douglas has also contributed to the survivability, lethality, and key technologies (SLKT) program, receiving approximately $20 million to develop and test technologies to protect key components from attack and radiation.

7. GENERAL ELECTRIC/RCA

SDI obligations (FY 1985):	$9.6 million
Share of DOD RDT&E awards:	1 percent
DOD awards (FY 1985):	$7,205 million
Share of sales:	19 percent

With $286 million share in space defense contracts since FY 1983, General Electric ranks seventh among the leading SDI contractors.[9] The company is making its principal contributions to strategic defense in the areas of space-based nuclear power generation, kinetic energy weapons, and radar technologies. In February 1986, GE acquired the RCA Corporation, adding significantly to its existing strengths in the aerospace and defense industries. The figures shown above include RCA's SDI contracts, which amount to 3.6 percent of GE's total awards.

To date, GE has received $202 million in awards (77 percent of its total SDI awards) for the SP-100 space-based nuclear reactor program. Because of the huge power requirements of a space-based defensive system, high priority has been given to the development of a 100-300 kilowatt-plus nuclear reactor that can be put into orbit. NASA and the Department of Energy administer this project jointly with SDIO, suggesting its potential for wide-ranging military and nonmilitary applications. Already well entrenched in the development of space power technology, GE is likely to continue its participation in this aspect of strategic defense.

GE also plays an important role in the kinetic energy weapons program, with $26.6 million in awards. These contracts involve design and development of electromagnetic launchers to direct projectiles at missiles during all phases of their flight. Other GE contributions to the KEW program include guidance and fire control, boost surveillance and tracking, sensors, and radar. Within other SDI programs, GE is working on the large-aperture radar sensor technology for which it has received a concept definition contract. This is one of the more mature programs within SDI and is likely to be a key element if early deployment is carried out.

Before its acquisition by GE, RCA had won a number of strategic defense contracts through its proficiency in signal-processing technologies. Its three major contracts have all been with the SATKA program, led by an $8.2 million award for developing radiation-hardened very large-scale integrated (VLSI) circuits component technology.

The GE-RCA team will be a stronger competitor for SDI contracts than either company alone. RCA is a top manufacturer of communications and meteorological satellites, while GE has expertise with defense satellites. GE has already been awarded $8.4 million in SDI radar contracts. RCA will bring to GE its experience with phased-array defense systems for the Navy. RCA is also strong in electro-optics and signal processing. Nineteen percent of GE's sales already comes from DOD awards, and the acquisition of RCA should help the company draw further on this profitable source of contracts. If SDI's momentum continues, the new GE will look forward to prosperous defense contracts for a long time to come.

8. ROCKWELL INTERNATIONAL

SDI obligations (FY 1985):	$49.8 million
Share of DOD RDT&E awards:	8 percent
DOD awards (FY 1985):	$6.264 million
Share of sales:	55 percent

With $197 million in strategic defense awards since FY 1983, Rockwell International is the eighth-ranked contractor for the program. Before the president's speech Rockwell's contribution to strategic defense was predominantly the development of optical sensors. Since then, however, the company has diversified into advanced military space surveillance and KEW technology as well as DEW technology and battle management.

A competitive award of $20 million for the development of an oxygen-iodine chemical laser in September 1982 has established Rockwell as a prime contractor for the Alpha prototype space-based laser. It has won an additional award for laser vulnerability tests at Kirtland Air Force Base.

Rockwell is the major contractor for the DARPA/Air Force Teal Ruby sensor experiment, designed to test infrared mosaic sensor technology in space. In previous efforts, including $21 million awarded before the advent of SDI, the company headed a team that developed the Air Force space-based surveillance system program and improved the technology of infrared sensors for the advanced warning system. In September 1985, the company received a $26 million contract for the development of the mosaic optical sensor technology testbed. It was also one of two companies recently to win a $2.7 million contract for the preliminary design of the SDIO's national testbed.

The company is also a prime contractor for the DARPA/Air Force railgun effort and in September 1984 received a contract to develop a 40 megawatt prime power supply under a $10 million contract. The propulsion system for the interceptor in the homing overlay experiment was also built by Rockwell under a subcontract for Lockheed. An additional $39 million has been awarded to the company for kinetic energy technologies.

In October 1981 Rockwell International published a booklet entitled *Space: America's Frontier for Growth, Leadership and Freedom* with the help of Morgan W. Sanborn, a retired U.S. Air Force colonel. The booklet discusses various unfavorable trends that will lead the United States "to find itself in an increasingly precarious position, beset with problems both at home and abroad." These trends, according to Rockwell, include a decline in economic growth, growing dependence on imported fossil fuels, loss of military advantage, and decline in national morale. Space technology, argues the booklet, can make a major, perhaps decisive contribution to the reversal of these trends.

Against this background, the company proposes its own strategic defense program under a three-stage plan over the next thirty years. In the first stage, the 1980s, efforts to improve reconnaissance, navigation, and other satellites would be a priority for the nation. Progress on space systems will be such as to offer "decisive support" for its military force in the 1990s. By the year 2010, Rockwell hopes to achieve absolute space superiority by orbiting a laser-protected geostationary space base functioning as an all-seeing watchtower that permits "direct, rapid and reliable command and control of all military forces."[11]

Having won a $5 million Phase II systems architecture award in September 1985, Rockwell has solidified its role in defining what SDI will eventually entail. This well-established position in what promises to be the largest military program ever will certainly affect the company's role in the defense industry. SDI is likely to increase its share of the company's DOD RDT&E from 8 percent in FY 1985. And Rockwell will remain one of the largest prime DOD and RDT&E contractors—it was in the top six in FY 1985—not only because of its full-scale engineering development and production of the B-1 bomber and MX missile but, increasingly, because of its share in the strategic defense market.

9. GENCORP

SDI obligations (FY 1985): $31.1 million
    Share of DOD RDT&E awards: 24 percent
DOD awards (FY 1985): $566 million
    Share of sales: 19 percent

GenCorp was ninth among the leading SDI contractors, having received $175.5 million since FY 1983. Its contribution to the program is based largely on its experience with rocket propulsion and optical sensing. In FY 1985, 24 percent of the company's DOD RDT&E came from the SDI program.

Since a major restructuring took place in 1984, changing the parent company's name from General Tire to GenCorp, special efforts have been devoted to technologies relevant to President Reagan's defense build-up. With DOD awards accounting for 19 percent of total sales, these efforts seem to be paying off. Since 1984, Aerojet General, Gencorp's aerospace and defense subsidiary, has made a major role in SDI a top priority.

GenCorp's receipt of $88.7 million for work in the kinetic energy weapons program marks it as a major contributor to propulsion technologies for strategic defense. Of this amount, $49.3 million has been awarded for the high endoatmospheric defense interceptor. The rest has gone to develop rocket propellant for small space-based boosters, cooling technologies, engine components, and optical seekers.

Another $78.5 million has been awarded for participation in the surveillance, acquisition, tracking, and kill assessment program. Of this, $34 million was awarded as a subcontract from Boeing to develop an infrared sensor for the airborne optical system. Additional SATKA contracts include $16.7 million for the precursor above the horizon sensor (PATHS) for space-based surveillance and $15.3 million for designing the warning satellite sensor for the defense support program.

The establishment of the Propulsion Research Institute, where new ideas in lasers, electromagnetism, and antimatter will be explored, further underscores the company's intention to derive a large share of its business from aerospace and defense contracts.

Under the Reagan administration's "peace through strength" strategy, which simultaneously pursues the development of the MX missile and a strategic "Astrodome," GenCorp is likely to emerge as a major beneficiary and benefactor of Star Wars. With an increasing share in SDI research, coupled with hoped-for MX and Midgetman contracts, the company may move up from its current standing as the thirty-eighth largest DOD contractor.

10. TELEDYNE BROWN ENGINEERING INC.

SDI obligations (FY 1985):	$48.3 million
Share of DOD RDT&E awards:	47 percent
DOD awards (FY 1985):	$694 million
Share of sales:	21 percent

Teledyne Brown has had $48.3 million in SDI awards over four years. The company's input to SDI is predominantly in the area of battle management and is based on its expertise in computer technology. The fact that 47 percent of Teledyne Brown's total RDT&E resources were used for SDI-related research in FY 1985 underscores the importance of SDI for the continuation of the company's computer research.

Since 1971, Teledyne has assumed the role of systems engineering technical assistance contractor (SETAC). As such it develops and integrates new technologies into complete defense system concepts for the Ballistic Missile Defense Systems Command in nearby Huntsville, Alabama. SDI has made this a more important role and brought over $147 million in contract awards for systems engineering and technical support for Army testing of ballistic missile defenses.

In the systems analysis/battle management program, Teledyne received a $13 million award for the tactical warning/attack assessment project conducted jointly with the Army Ballistic Missile Defense Command and North American Air Defense (NORAD). In the KEW program, Teledyne has contributed to both the endoatmospheric and exoatmospheric nonnuclear kill projects. It received $4 million in 1985 to develop window cooling technology for the former project.

Teledyne's prowess in radar technologies helped it to obtain a $7.5 million contract for work on optical sensors for the imaging radar project, part of the surveillance, acquisition, tracking and kill assessment program. In another SATKA program, the company has been asked to develop battle management software and surveillance computers such as those used for the designating optical tracker. Since the success of a space-based defense system hinges on critical computer-made decisions during the half-hour flight of an enemy ICBM from launch to re-entry, the accuracy of this technology is of crucial importance, helping to assure Teledyne's continuing involvement in strategic defense.

6

TARGETING ACADEMIA

What I find particularly troublesome about the SDI funding is the effort to short-circuit debate and use MIT and other universities as political instruments in an attempt to obtain implicit institutional endorsement. This university will not be used.

—*Paul Gray*
President, Massachusetts Institute of Technology, 1985

Universities have been a major source of unbiased basic scientific research, driven by neither military requirements nor the imperatives of commercial product development. They have a strong record in extending the boundaries of scientific knowledge through the conduct of applied and basic research. In recent history, universities have benefited from a diversified base of federal support—civilian and military—and an open environment in which research results may be disseminated freely among scientific colleagues. University participation in SDI, however, poses a serious threat to these traditional strengths.

In the fall of 1984 the Strategic Defense Initiative Organization set up an office of Innovative Science and Technology (IST). Its mission, according to program director James A. Ionson, is to "pursue . . . highly innovative, high-risk concepts that could have a revolutionary impact on the Strategic Defense Initiative."[1] Although the office will not limit its awards to university-based scientists and engineers,

Ionson hopes to "tap the reservoir of brilliant minds in the academic community and promote university involvement in the SDI program."[2] Its objective is to convince them that their future, like that of military corporations, depends on participating in Star Wars research.

The rush to involve prominent universities in SDI raises serious questions about the future conduct of scientific research in the United States. Will Pentagon research funding, led by SDI, crowd out federal support for civilian research programs? Will current university involvement in SDI be used to legitimize the program independently of future research findings? How will SDI security restrictions affect the free flow of information that has long been a major strength of U.S. research universities?

THE REAGAN BUILD-UP: DISTORTING
THE RESEARCH PROCESS

The push to involve university researchers in SDI is only the latest and most dramatic example of a growing Pentagon presence at the nation's universities. Today, DOD accounts for 17 percent of all federal spending for university research, up from 12 percent in 1980. American universities are now as strongly dependent on the Defense Department for research funding as they were in 1968, at the height of the Vietnam War. Since 1980 DOD funding for university research has increased by 115 percent, rising from $495 million to $1,065 million (see Figure 6-1).

The next fastest growing sources of federal support for university research have been the National Aeronautics and Space Administration (NASA) and the National Science Foundation (NSF). NASA's funding of campus-based research grew by 97 percent, NSF's by 56 percent over the same period. If DOD funding to off-campus affiliates like M.I.T.'s Lincoln Laboratories is taken into account, the Pentagon is now outspending the NSF and NASA on university research. In addition, the Pentagon is not the only sponsor of military research conducted at universities. Both the Department of Energy and NASA sponsor military projects, including DOE's new SDI innovative concepts program, which awards $3 to $5 million a year. In fact, under the Reagan administration, atomic energy defense activities have increased from $2,991 million in FY 1980 (30% of the DOE budget) to $7,478 million in FY 1987 (78% of the DOE bud-

Figure 6-1. Shifts in Federal Funding for University Research, FY 1980-86.

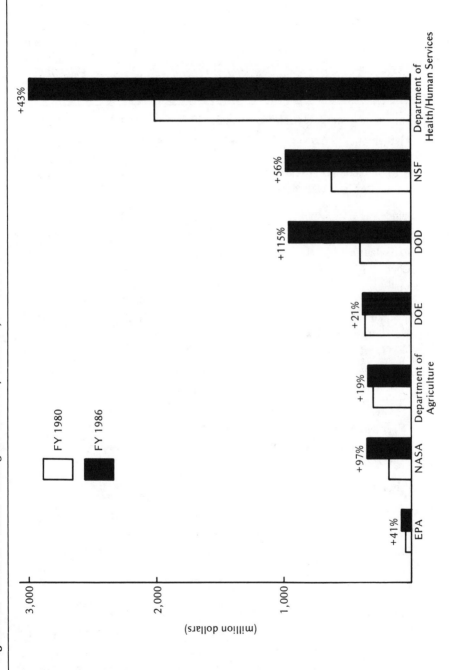

Table 6-1. Pentagon Share of Federal Funding for University Research by Field, FY 1986 (*thousand dollars*).

Field	Total Federal Funding	DOD Funding	DOD Share of Total Federal Funding (percent)
Mathematics/Computer Science	288,285	169,421	58.8
Mathematics	100,953	35,607	35.3
Computer science	113,866	61,398	53.9
Math and computer sciences not elsewhere classified	73,466	72,416	98.6
Engineering	566,801	219,328	38.7
Aeronautical	55,338	29,723	53.7
Astronautical	12,172	8,072	66.3
Chemical	53,083	1,786	3.4
Civil	48,220	4,482	9.3
Electrical	143,974	86,071	59.8
Mechanical	74,638	35,945	48.2
Metallurgy and materials	105,848	51,221	48.4
Other	73,528	2,028	2.8
Environmental Sciences	364,395	94,652	26.0
Atmospheric	114,625	19,417	16.9
Geological	104,600	16,134	15.4
Oceanographic	137,194	58,367	42.5
Environmental sciences not elsewhere classified	7,976	734	9.2
Psychology	127,994	23,790	18.6
Physical Sciences	829,174	112,216	13.5
Astronomy	99,839	6,024	6.0
Chemistry	276,041	41,462	15.0
Physics	433,527	60,786	14.0
Other	19,767	3,944	20.0
Life Sciences	3,055,622	61,990	2.0
Social Sciences	114,191	53	0.05

Source: National Science Foundation, *Federal Obligations for Research to Universities and Colleges by Agency and Detailed Field of Science, Fiscal Years 1973-1986.*

get). In contrast, campus funding from other major federal agencies—including the departments of agriculture and health and human services—has grown *less than half* as fast as DOD support since 1980.

The universities' growing dependence on Pentagon research support is particularly extreme in certain fields. The Pentagon provides a large share of the available federal funding for research in fields like computer science, electrical engineering, and metallurgy (see Table 6-1). Moreover, the growth of military funding under the Reagan administration has shifted the balance away from basic research toward weapons projects. This trend appears to be worsening: in the proposed FY 1987 budget, DOD research and development is scheduled to increase by 24 percent, while basic research will grow by only 7.5 percent. Within the basic research budget, Pentagon-sponsored projects are proposed for a 5 percent increase. Outside the physical sciences, basic research funding will increase by a mere 1.7 percent in FY 1987.[3]

This increased dependence on the Department of Defense has had harmful effects, as will be detailed in Chapter 8. The DOD's increased share of federal funding to universities has siphoned off funds that might otherwise have gone to civilian research projects. The scientific fields that are most dependent on the DOD as a source of money are also key to the future development of U.S. high technology. When support for weapons research comes at the expense of basic research funds, the entire direction of U.S. high technology research will be distorted.

SDI PRESENCE GROWING ON CAMPUS

The SDI Organization's new innovative science and technology program is sure to heighten university dependence on military contracts. The FY 1987 allocation for SDI innovative programs was over $104 million, up sharply from $28 million in FY 1985.[4] Much of this new money went to university researchers.

Since the Innovative Science and Technology Program is slated to receive 3 percent of all SDI funding in each of the next two years, it could be a $500 million program by 1989. Robert L. Park, executive director of the Washington office of the American Physical Society, told the *Chronicle of Higher Education* that researchers in some fields, like plasma physics, may see SDI funding as the only way to keep their research projects alive. "Obviously there are some scientists who are going to apply," says Park. "This is a tight time for a lot of fields."[5] James Duderstadt, dean of the College of Engineering at the University of Michigan, expressed a similar view after attending a Pentagon briefing on SDI. "I was very impressed," he said. "This will be one of the few sources of new money for basic research in the physical sciences in coming years."[6]

The SDIO would like university researchers to investigate a variety of topics. Major areas of interest include ultra-high-speed computing, new space-based power sources, novel laser concepts, new types of optic sensors, microelectronic devices that can operate "in the hostile space environment for extended periods of time," and various studies of "how the natural atmospheric environment might affect the performance of strategic defense surveillance sensors and directed energy weapons." Researchers whose projects do not fit into any of these areas are encouraged by SDI to apply to the individual research grant division of the IST office. This division is "mandated to provide fast reaction funding for . . . research programs that represent totally new or revolutionary ideas that don't easily conform to existing consortia or concepts programs."[7]

The combination of a rapidly growing budget and technical challenges spanning a number of disciplines has already sparked considerable interest in the innovative science program. David Parnas, a computer software expert from the University of Victoria, British Columbia, who resigned from SDI's expert panel on Computing in Support of Battle Management in June 1985, argues that many scientists who do not believe an effective strategic defense system is technically feasible are applying for funding anyway. "During the first sitting of our panel, I could see the dollar figures dazzling everyone involved. Almost everyone that I know within the military industrial complex sees SDI as a new 'pot of gold' just waiting to be tapped," argues Parnas. "For others, the project offers an unending set of technological puzzles that are fun to work on. Several of the speakers at the first meeting of our panel could not hide their delight at the unbounded set of technical challenges implicit in the unattainable goals of the project."[8]

"INNOVATIVE" CONTRACTING TECHNIQUES

The SDIO's aggressive effort to involve universities in Star Wars work officially began with the first annual SDIO/IST Technical Review for

Universities held on March 29, 1985, on the outskirts of Washington, D.C. The meeting, which attracted more than 240 scientists and engineers from 124 colleges and universities, was designed to familiarize university research personnel with the major Star Wars technology needs. Participants were duly impressed by the innovative science program's research shopping list. "SDI seems to want just about everything under the sun," said Richard G. Griskey, dean of engineering at the University of Alabama at Huntsville.[9]

While SDIO's determined pursuit of academic researchers has yielded results, it has also sparked criticism. Some university officials have begun to wonder about the IST's political agenda. Asked why the office was soliciting proposals for FY 1986 funding so far in advance of congressional budgetary decisions, IST director Ionson told *Science* magazine, "It's probably something that's never been done, but this office is trying to sell something to Congress. If we can say that this fellow at M.I.T. will get money to do such and such research, it's something real to sell. That in itself is innovative."[10]

Ionson has streamlined the contracting process to encourage researchers to apply for SDI funding. Each participant at the March briefing was urged to submit a so-called white paper—an informal preproposal "not to exceed ten pages of technical content." SDIO justifies this procedure as a labor-saving device: "Researchers are initially spared the laborious task of preparing a formal proposal requiring corporate or university approval since no budgetary details, lengthy resumes, or grandiose program definition needs to be included."[11] Whatever its rationale, this new method has succeeded in attracting proposals. Less than six months after the March meeting, SDI spokesperson Lt. Colonel Lee DeLorme told the *New York Times,* "We are presently considering over 2600 applications from individuals and universities."[12]

SDI's plan for letting university contracts calls for completing the whole application cycle, from white paper to contract award, in just nine months. University researchers were informed by the innovative science program office that "most of the contracts" for FY 1986 "are anticipated to be let by January 1, 1986." By soliciting proposals before Congress had appropriated FY 1986 funds and by aiming to spend all of its allocations within the first three months of the fiscal year, the office sent out a strong signal to university researchers: the SDI innovative science program can produce funds quickly, but only if they apply *now*. While it is not unusual for the Defense Department to involve universities in new weapons research, SDI university contracts are being funded at a rate that would make any significant peer review impossible. In fact, the IST office has already committed $62 million in long-term contracts to support six research consortia involving twenty-nine universities in sixteen states. These academic-industrial teams have been set up under the IST's Research Thrust Division to "address specific science and technology areas that are known to be of critical importance to the success of SDI." [13] The consortia named to date will investigate the following areas: [14]

Nonnuclear space power: a $19 million four-year program involving Auburn, the State University of New York at Buffalo, Polytechnic Institute of New York, Texas Tech, and the University of Texas at Arlington.

Optical computing: a $9 million three-year consortium consisting of Carnegie-Mellon, Caltech, Georgia Tech, Stanford University, M.I.T.'s Lincoln Laboratories, Battelle Columbus Laboratories, the University of Alabama at Huntsville, and the U.S. Naval Oceans Systems Center.

Electronic circuits for computing, sensing, power generation, and directed-energy beams: a $4 million three-year program involving the University of California at Berkeley, Stanford, Purdue, the University of Florida at Gainesville, and the University of Southern California.

High-speed electronic systems, new dielectric materials for storing power for directed energy and kinetic energy systems, and advance power sources for lasers and particle beams: a $2.5 million three-year program undertaken by SUNY Buffalo, the Naval Research Laboratory, and General Electric.

Composite materials development: a $15 million three-year program involving researchers at M.I.T., Pennsylvania State, Colorado School of Mines, Johns Hopkins, Texas A&M, Brown, Rensselaer Polytechnic Institute, Drexel, SRI International, and the Naval Research Laboratory. They are to team up with such firms as United Technologies, Martin Marietta, Fiber Materials, Aeronautical Research Corp. of Princeton, and Ultrasystems, Inc.

Chemical-laser exhaust problems, spacecraft radiation, electromagnetic waves, and particle beams: a $12.5 million three-year program involving investigators at Johns Hopkins's Applied Research Laboratory, the universities of Arizona, Maryland, Michigan, Iowa, Kansas, and California at Berkeley, Utah State, U.C.L.A., M.I.T., Stanford, N.Y.U., the Naval Research Laboratory, and the Air Force Geophysics Laboratory.

Other long-term consortia to investigate nuclear space power, propellants, and ultra-short-wave lasers are expected to be announced shortly. Some universities that warmed up to SDI as a source of badly needed research funds have already found the partnership enriching. As Table 6-2 demonstrates, the top twenty universities received over $180 million of the total $205 million in SDI contracts awarded between 1983 and 1986 by the IST office and other divisions. In 1985, SDI contracts made up 4.2 percent of these universities' total RDT&E awards from the Pentagon (see Table 6-3). Four of these universities already have become highly dependent on SDI dollars. These awards represent 100 percent of DOD research funds at Texas Technical University, 64 percent at the State University of New York, 49 percent at Auburn University, and 44 percent at Utah Higher Education System. As funding for university contracts increases over the next few years, so will the reliance of these universities on SDI.

A THREAT TO ACADEMIC FREEDOM

Although SDI funds have poured into university research departments, the methods used by the SDIO and the goals of the Star Wars program have stirred campus controversy of an intensity not seen since the anti-Vietnam war protests. Most major U.S. research universities have maintained policies from the Vietnam war era prohibiting classified research on campuses. Many academics are wondering whether the political vulnerability (to say nothing of the military sensitivity) of a program such as SDI will lead to classifying research again on the campus. Many university scientists and administrators are concerned that the introduction of SDI contracts on campuses will interfere with academic freedom to publish and disseminate research findings and with the conduct of basic research, and will be used by SDI officials to legitimize a questionable weapons program.

Publicly, IST director Ionson has stated that "any work for SDI performed on a university campus will not be classified and therefore

Table 6-2. SDI Contracts to Universities, FY 1983-86 *(thousand dollars).*

	1983	1984	1985	1986	Total
Utah Higher Education System[a]	24,808	0	11,524	0	36,332
University of Texas	5,644	950	26,140	499	33,233
Georgia Institute of Technology	2,043	925	23,861	1,344	28,173
Stanford University	0	0	12,411	11,023	23,434
University of California	310	780	5,787	133	7,010
University of Dayton	0	0	5,372	235	5,607
Carnegie-Mellon University	166	772	3,650	796	5,384
Johns Hopkins University	0	0	5,292	0	5,292
State University of New York[b]	0	0	4,976	0	4,976
Auburn University	352	293	3,900	21	4,566
Polytechnic Institute of New York	170	190	3,935	0	4,295
Texas Technical University	0	0	3,965	0	3,965
Pennsylvania State University	0	540	1,460	1,806	3,806
M.I.T.[c]	0	578	2,539	0	3,117
University of Arizona	353	270	2,054	134	2,811
California Institute of Technology	0	0	1,300	664	1,964
University of Alabama	72	281	1,589	0	1,942
Florida State University System[d]	108	100	1,534	89	1,831
Northwestern University	0	0	1,349	0	1,349
University of Massachusetts	0	0	539	701	1,240
Total	$34,026	$5,679	$123,177	$17,445	$180,327

a. Figures for Utah Higher Education System include Utah State University and the University of Utah.
b. Figures for State University of New York include campuses at Albany, Buffalo, and Stony Brook.
c. Figures for M.I.T. do not include Lincoln Laboratory.
d. Figures for Florida State University System include the University of Florida and the University of Southern Florida.

Table 6-3. SDI and RDT&E Awards for Top Twenty University Contractors, FY 1985 (*thousand dollars*).

University	Prime DOD RDT&E Contracts	SDI Contracts (Obligations)	SDI Share of RDT&E (percent)
Utah Higher Education System[a]	18,575	8,113	43.7
University of Texas	39,871	5,983	15.0
Georgia Institute of Technology	40,040	5,200	13.0
Stanford University	32,716	3,303	10.1
University of California	57,558	2,182	3.8
University of Dayton	18,743	1,017	5.4
Carnegie-Mellon University	29,511	910	3.1
Johns Hopkins	304,310	4,842	1.6
State University of New York[b]	1,241	792	63.8
Auburn University	1,972	973	49.3
Polytechnic Institute of New York	2,413	620	25.7
Texas Technical University	572	572	100.0
Pennsylvania State University	24,848	1,164	4.7
M.I.T.[c]	360,104	1,851	0.5
University of Arizona	3,811	633	16.6
California Institute of Technology	5,951	550	9.2
University of Alabama	1,715	373	21.7
Florida State University System[d]	5,979	660	11.0
Northwestern University	2,268	500	22.0
University of Massachusetts	6,141	164	2.7
Total	$958,339	$40,402	4.2%

a. Figures for Utah Higher Education System include Utah State University and the University of Utah.

b. Figures for State University of New York include campuses at Albany, Buffalo, and Stony Brook.

c. Figures for M.I.T. do not include Lincoln Laboratory.

d. Figures for Florida State University System include the University of Florida and the University of Southern Florida.

will not be subject to any control or restrictive clauses or security classifications. . . . You do not stimulate innovation behind closed doors."[15] But in an official memo related to Star Wars publications, Ionson qualified his earlier remarks. Although SDI research on university campuses is funded from the budget for advanced development (with disclosure restrictions), it will be treated as "fundamental basic research" (with no disclosure restrictions). "However," the memo goes on to stipulate, "when there is a likelihood of disclosing operational capabilities and performance characteristics of planned or developing military systems, or technologies unique and critical to defense programs, the responsibility for the release of information resulting from IST research belongs to the sponsoring office." [16]

On the surface, this clause appears to leave open the option for universities to get involved in classified research. But it also gives the Office of IST the right to classify research once findings are deemed applicable to developing strategic defense systems. Since the innovative science program is essentially a "mission-oriented basic research" program, it is only a matter of time before unclassified research at universities becomes "critical" for the SDI program. As one congressional aide told *Defense Week*, "Many Pentagon [research and development] programs begin this way with unclassified efforts. It's an effort to get their nose under the tent." [17]

Controversy over the long-term status of SDI research on campus is prompting some universities to reconsider their long-standing policy banning classified research. While some universities facing potentially serious academic disapproval will ban SDI research before it becomes classified, others may revise policy guidelines to allow badly needed research money from SDI on campus. Researchers at universities where classified research is prohibited may have to choose between giving up their research and staying on campus or moving out of academia and into industry before the research is classified. University administrators are already confronting serious public relations problems as well as internal conflict over accepting SDI research contracts.

The universities that have received the largest SDI awards so far have also been the most vocal in criticizing the Pentagon's promotion of the program. At M.I.T.'s 1985 graduation exercises, President Paul E. Gray criticized Ionson's claim that academic participation in SDI would add "prestige and credibility" and "influence the Congress to be more generous in funding the program." Gray objected to this apparent attempt to use universities as "political instruments" to gain legitimacy for the program. [18]

Yet in justifying the SDI contracts already let to some M.I.T. professors, Provost Francis E. Low stated, "The same tradition of academic freedom that permits professors to take public positions on public issues permits them to work on research projects of their choice, provided that the projects . . . are appropriate projects for the university. . . . Our acceptance of research under the SDI program in no way constitutes an institutional position on the SDI program."[19]

At the California Institute of Technology, President Marvin Goldberger accused SDIO officials of making "manifestly false" statements about the university's participation in SDI's consortia in an effort to build public support for the program. Although one Caltech electrical engineering professor received a $50,000 subcontract for research on optical computing from Dayton Research Institute, Goldberger insisted the university institution itself had not signed an agreement with any SDI consortium.[20]

Whether SDI research is conducted on campus by individual professors or through formal institutional consortium arrangements, universities will not find it easy to distance themselves from the research being done. Universities and academic research personnel will have to decide soon where they stand on the goals and the methods of the SDI IST Program. With constraints on other funding sources, many campus-based scientists will be tempted to apply for SDI funding regardless of their views of its goals. Others will participate on the grounds that SDI is strictly a research program that can advance scientific knowledge even if its overall goals are never achieved. This would be tantamount to conceding control of our nation's advanced scientific research effort to the Department of Defense. Furthermore, given the strong promotional atmosphere in which SDI contracts are being awarded, the Pentagon is likely to claim that academic researchers' participation in the program represents an endorsement of the technical feasibility of a strategic defense system.

Any SDI on-campus research could spark new confrontations between students and faculty members involved in the project and those opposed to such work. Despite Ionson's claims that "virtually everyone on every campus" wants to become involved in SDI, a campaign to boycott Star Wars research is fast gaining ground in university science and engineering departments.[21] The movement began spontaneously in mid-1985, when the physics departments of the University of Illinois and Cornell University took the unprecedented step of drawing up a petition calling the SDI program "deeply misguided and dangerous" and pledging "not to solicit nor accept SDI funds, and to encourage others to join in this refusal."[22]

At the University of Illinois, organizers drew up the anti-SDI petition on May 16, 1985, and more than half of the science and engineering faculty had signed by May 20. Michael Weissman of the physics department asserts that the effects of SDI funding on the university research process were a secondary consideration in his decision to help organize the petition drive: "I really see Star Wars as a life and death issue. Star Wars is a big step towards nuclear war, and everything else pales in comparison with that."[23]

Physicist David Wright of the University of Pennsylvania, who helped organize the early anti-SDI petition at Cornell, stresses that the pledge targets individuals rather than institutional policies against accepting SDI funds to avoid violating the academic freedom of those researchers choosing to do Star Wars work. Wright asserts that many signatories at Cornell were convinced that "the political reality is that by sending in a proposal you will be giving legitimacy to this program."[24]

With the help of the Washington-based United Campuses to Prevent Nuclear War (UCAM), the petition to boycott Star Wars on campus is now being circulated at 110 research universities in forty-one states.[25] Never has there been such a level of dissent aimed at specific weapons programs. Unlike other recent university-based campaigns led by undergraduates, this movement is spearheaded by faculty members and graduate researchers who are potential recipients of SDI research grants. Its more than 3,900 faculty signatories include former Manhattan project scientists Hans Bethe of Cornell and Philip Morrison of M.I.T. Organizers of the petition estimate that more than half of the faculty members at 120 university science and engineering departments in the country have now pledged not to accept SDI funds.

These issues are of special concern at M.I.T. With $360 million, or 28 percent of all DOD research funds let to universities in FY 1985, M.I.T. is the university most sought after by administration promoters of SDI. Its off-campus Lincoln Laboratories alone was awarded $304 million in SDI funds in 1985. In all, M.I.T. and its off-campus affiliate received over $306 million in SDI awards in that year.[26] A nine-member committee has been appointed to review potentially adverse consequences of SDI research for M.I.T.'s academic autonomy and freedom. Other universities are currently reviewing these issues as well.

The phenomenal growth of DOD university funding in general, and the SDI innovative science program in particular, threatens the diversity of funding sources and the open research process. Howard Ris, executive director of the Union of Concerned Scientists, sees a danger in university researchers' rush to obtain SDI funding: "You can basically see the universities becoming another congressional district . . . when scientists discover that SDI is not such a good idea, it will be difficult to turn off the faucet."[27]

7

THE PORK BARREL
Who Pays?

Perhaps the most effective support for Star Wars is being generated not by ideology but good, free-enterprise greed. Firms in the hypertrophic defense industry, along with their thousands of technicians, are manifesting a deep patriotic enthusiasm for Star Wars. Since they are experienced in lobbying and wield heavy influence with members of Congress who have defense plants in their constituencies, they are creating a formidable momentum for the project. Whether or not it would contribute to the security of the nation, it offers them security.

> —*George Ball*
> *Former Under Secretary of State*
> *April 11, 1985*

S DI contractors have used powerful lobbying mechanisms to influence Congress and sway critical votes in favor of the program. Historically, members of Congress from military dependent areas have banded together to vote for programs that will benefit their states.[1] In the case of SDI, members whose home districts have a large financial stake in the program will have a special incentive to vote for funding increases for it. As the size of SDI contracts grows, so will contractor pressure on legislators to authorize still higher funding levels, on the grounds that it will create jobs and income.

SDI contracts are highly concentrated in traditional strongholds of military industries. Almost 85 percent of prime contract awards for SDI research between FY 1983 and FY 1986 were awarded to only five states: California (45 percent), New Mexico (17 percent), Massachusetts (10 percent), Alabama (7 percent), and Washington (6 percent). As SDI moves toward development and production, the distribution of DOD funds could be skewed even further toward the current winners in the competition for contracts (see Table 7-1 and Figure 7-1).

SDI contractors are also well positioned to gain the support of the members of Congress who have the most to say about future spending. Representatives from regions dependent on defense spending have a keen interest in serving on the House and Senate Armed Services Committees and Defense Appropriations Subcommittees, where they can most influence budget decisions on defense spending. To be sure, some states with a significant share of the defense business have tended to resist such pressure. The Massachusetts congressional delegation, for example, voted against funding for the MX missile despite large contracts in that state. But they are the exceptions. In the case of SDI, this pattern is repeated.

About 87 percent of prime contracts in space defense work awarded in FY 1983 and FY 1984 went to states represented by Senate members of the Armed Services Committee and Defense Appropriations Subcommittee. In FY 1985 and FY 1986, the share of SDI contracts awarded to states represented on these two committees increased to 92 percent (see Table 7-2). These states received an average of 50.7 million in SDI contracts, or almost twelve times the average amount received by other states in FY 1983 and FY 1984. In the FY 1985-FY 1986 election cycle, SDI contracts to states represented on these committees increased to $119.8 million, or twenty-two times the average amount received by other states. Tying SDI to regional economies dependent on defense spending will exert considerable pressure on representatives of those regions to support the program.

SDI PACMEN: TARGETING INFLUENCE

Contractors have other ways to exercise influence besides the promise of SDI money and jobs. Like trade unions, professional associations, and special interest groups, corporations often use contributions from Political Action Committees (PACs) to influence the electoral process and congressional decision making. In an effort to identify key congressional figures who might be influenced by PAC con-

Table 7-1. Top Twenty SDI States (*thousand dollars*).

State	SDI Contracts FY 1983–86	Share of Total Awarded SDI Contracts (percent)	SDI Contracts, FY 1985	DOD RDT&E, FY 1985	SDI Share of DOD RDT&E, FY 1985 (percent)
California	3,255,277	44.5	595,646	7,704,324	7.7
New Mexico	1,230,096	16.8	229,574	1,319,770	17.4
Massachusetts	718,347	9.8	178,402	2,483,940	7.2
Alabama	534,790	7.3	135,884	547,403	24.8
Washington	402,739	5.5	120,437	577,475	20.9
Virginia	257,999	3.5	26,368	1,988,375	1.3
Texas	178,900	2.4	44,721	1,049,928	4.3
Colorado	124,348	1.7	26,098	234,389	11.1
New York	110,115	1.5	21,414	1,958,080	1.1
Florida	75,529	1.0	14,086	717,112	2.0
Maryland	62,153	0.8	22,576	2,481,465	0.9
Utah	46,752	0.6	8,241	166,532	4.9
Pennsylvania	41,116	0.6	9,453	669,609	1.4
Ohio	35,359	0.5	17,686	1,029,503	1.7
Connecticut	35,316	0.5	7,050	471,939	1.5
Minnesota	35,218	0.5	8,462	525,642	1.6
Georgia	28,172	0.4	5,200	128,191	4.1
New Jersey	27,368	0.4	7,335	1,446,759	0.5
District of Columbia	26,278	0.4	19,081	1,392,646	1.4
Missouri	18,396	0.3	4,746	555,300	0.9
Total	$7,244,268	99.0%	$1,502,460	$27,448,382	5.5%

Source: Council on Economic Priorities SDI database. Data are from FY 1983 to December 1986.

Figure 7-1. Distribution of SDI Contracts, FY 1983-86.

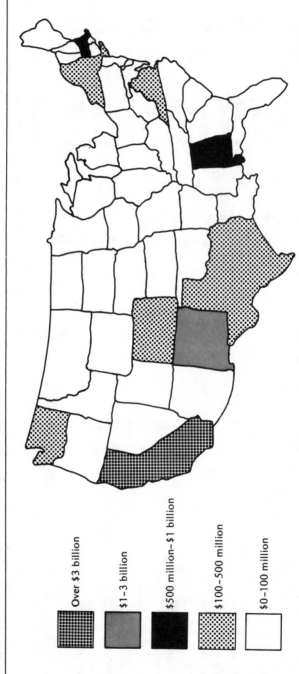

Over $3 billion

$1–3 billion

$500 million–$1 billion

$100–500 million

$0–100 million

Source: Council on Economic Priorities SDI database. Data are from FY 1983 to December 1986.

Table 7-2. SDI Contracts Awarded to States Represented by Senators on
Key Committees, FY 1983-86 (*million dollars*).

	FY 1983-84	FY 1985-86
Senate Armed Services Committee		
California (Pete Wilson)	$1,069	$2,069
New Mexico (Jeff Bingaman)	104	729
Massachusetts (Edward Kennedy)	125	593
Alabama (Jeremiah Denton)	—	310
Virginia (John Warner)	25	200
Colorado (Gary Hart)	31	79
Texas (John Tower, Phil Gramm)	101	78
Georgia (Sam Nunn)	3.0	25
Illinois (Alan Dixon)	—	10
Arizona (Barry Goldwater)	3.4	9.1
Indiana (Dan Quayle)	—	2.9
Maine (William Cohen)	1.0	2.6
New Hampshire (Gordon Humphrey)	0.5	2.4
Michigan (Carl Levin)	—	2.1
North Carolina (John East)	—	0.3
Washington (Henry Jackson)	286	—
Total	$1,748	$4,113
Share of total SDI contracts	83%	88%
Senate Appropriations Subcommittee on Defense		
New York (Alphonse D'Amato)	21	$90
Florida (Lawton Chiles)	28	47
Connecticut (Lowell Weicker)	3.0	32
Utah (Jake Garn)	25	22
Tennessee (Jim Sasser)	—	4.5
New Hampshire (Warren Rudman)	0.5	2.4
Wisconsin (Bob Kasten, William Proxmire)	—	1.0
Hawaii (Daniel Inouye)	—	0.2
Missouri (Thomas Eagleton)	0.8	—
Louisiana (J. Bennett Johnston)	0.4	—
Total	$78	$199
Share of total SDI contracts	4%	4%

Source: Council on Economic Priorities SDI database.

tributions and lobbying, for example, Martin Marietta published a booklet entitled "Strategic Defense: A Martin Marietta Commitment."[2] Appended to this booklet is a list of Congressmen worth "concentrating upon" as well as a list of "swing votes" likely to affect the future of Star Wars.

PAC money resembles an investment more than a contribution or gift. By financing politicians, lobbies are buying insurance for their own legislative interests. The net result is a parochial financing structure that exerts economic pressure on political decisions. And as SDI funding requests increase, so will PAC money. Is SDI PAC money talking on Capitol Hill? What congressional votes have been influenced by PAC contributions? Which members of Congress has this new breed of Star Warriors most effectively lobbied?

The Council on Economic Priorities' analysis of Federal Election Commission data indicates that sixteen of the twenty leading SDI contractors contributed almost $6 million through their PACs to candidates running for federal office from 1983 through the spring of 1986 (see Table 7–3). Such contractors use two interrelated criteria to determine the focus of their contributions and ensure the greatest impact from their PAC dollars. They target candidates who hold positions of influence on key committees and those whose constituencies live in or near military plant areas, where the promise of new jobs can be an extremely compelling lobbyist's argument.

The distribution of PAC money reveals a strong link to influential members of Congress on key committees. In 1983–84 over $946,000 of the $3.2 million in contributions by sixteen leading SDI contractors went to only twenty-four candidates in the House and Senate (see Table 7–4). Nineteen of these candidates were members of their house's Armed Services Committee or Appropriations Subcommittee on Defense, with SDI contracts in their states. Moreover, many of the recipients also chaired military-related committees or subcommittees.

This pattern of contributions reflects astute political maneuvering by SDI contractors. They are well aware that, together, the Appropriations Subcommittees on Defense and the Armed Services Committees in the House and Senate wield the greatest influence over decisions about the future of SDI: its budget, its prospects for proceeding beyond the research stage, and its presentation for a full vote of each chamber. The fifty-seven representatives who make up the two House committees—only 13 percent of the House member-

	1983-84			1985-86		
Company	Contributions	Rank	Distribution (%) Rep/Dem	Contributions	Rank	Distribution (%) Rep/Dem
1. Boeing	$175,162	11	57/43	$199,850	4	58/42
2. EG&G	28,450	19	62/38	2,000	19	88/12
3. Gencorp	29,400	18	79/21	26,400	16	67/33
Aerojet General	38,880	17	54/46	26,280	17	51/49
4. General Electric	198,515	5	43/57	147,135	7	41/59
5. General Motors	223,017	4	77/23	145,265	8	76/24
Hughes	175,645	10	55/45	181,305	5	57/43
6. Honeywell	58,230	16	78/22	22,000	18	85/15
7. Litton	224,750	3	79/21	138,834	9	81/19
8. Lockheed	415,441	1	56/44	299,015	1	58/42
9. LTV	141,503	14	38/62	94,725	12	37/63
10. Martin Marietta	175,950	9	56/44	83,325	13	56/44
11. McDonnell Douglas	169,050	12	43/57	164,775	6	49/51
12. Raytheon	138,125	15	50/50	80,073	14	48/52
13. Rockwell International	324,590	2	67/33	279,975	2	68/32
14. Textron	156,549	13	56/44	264,100	3	51/49
AVCO	194,650	6	37/63	40,150	15	59/41
15. TRW	181,325	8	57/43	114,520	11	52/48
16. Westinghouse	188,285	7	41/56	114,610	10	40/60
Total	$3,237,517		56/44%	$2,424,337		57/43%

Source: Federal Election Commission, *Index of Candidates Supported/Opposed*; data are for 1983 through June 1986 for sixteen of the twenty leading SDI military corporations (Teledyne Inc., Flow General, Science Applications, and Nichols Research do not have PACS). Although some of the sixteen corporations have merged, their PAC contributions are listed separately.

Table 7-4. Leading PAC Beneficiaries, 1983–84.

	Contribution	Committees
Senate		
John Warner (R-VA)	$69,050	Chairman, Armed Services Subcommittee on Strategic and Theater Nuclear Forces; member of Committee on Energy and Natural Resources
Roger Jepsen (R-IA)	60,100	Chairman, Armed Services Subcommittee on Manpower and Personnel; member, Subcommittee on Preparedness, and Subcommittee on Tactical Warfare
Ted Stevens (R-AK)	57,800	Chairman, Appropriations Subcommittee on Defense; member, Committee on Commerce, Science and Transportation, Subcommittee on Aviation
Gordon J. Humphrey (R-NH)	51,350	Chairman, Armed Services Subcommittee on Preparedness
Thad Cochran (R-MS)	50,100	Member, Appropriations Subcommittee on Defense
Pete V. Domenici (R-NM)	45,500	Chairman, Budget Committee; member, Appropriations Committee, Energy and Natural Resources Committee
Strom Thurmond (R-SC)	43,000	Chairman, Armed Services Subcommittee on Military Construction; member, Subcommittee on Strategic and Theater Nuclear Forces
William S. Cohen (R-ME)	41,650	Member, Armed Services Subcommittee on Strategic and Theater Nuclear Forces, Government Affairs Subcommittee on Energy, Nuclear Proliferation, and Government Processes
Charles H. Percy (R-IL)	41,600	Chairman, Committee on Foreign Relations and ex facto member of all Subcommittees; chairman, Government Affairs Subcommittee on Energy, Nuclear Proliferation, and Government Processes
J. Bennett Johnston (D-LA)	40,700	Member, Appropriations Subcommittee on Defense, Budget Committee, Energy and Natural Resources Committee
Walter Huddleston (D-KY)	38,650	Member, Appropriations Subcommittee on Defense, Small Business Subcommittee on Export and Promotion and Market Development, vice-chairman of Intelligence Subcommittee on Collection and Foreign Intelligence Subcom-mittee on Collection and Foreign Operations

Sen... (D-CA,)

... Member, Armed Services Subcommittee on Manpower and Personnel, Subcommittee on Seapower and Force Projection, and Subcommittee on Strategic and Theater Nuclear Forces

| | Total | $577,499 | |

House

Joseph Addabbo (D-NY)	$52,653	Chairman, Appropriations Subcommittee on Defense
William Dickinson (R-AL)	47,500	Ranking minority member, Armed Services Subcommittee on Research and Development
William V. Chappell Jr. (D-FL)	45,750	Member, Appropriations Subcommittee on Defense
Charles Wilson (D-TX)	40,250	Member, Appropriations Subcommittee on Defense
W. G. (Bill) Hefner (D-NC)	32,500	Chairman, Subcommittee on Military Construction; member, Appropriations Subcommittee on Defense, Budget Committee
John P. Murtha (D-PA)	24,200	Member, Appropriations Subcommittee on Defense
James Jones (D-OK)	22,650	Chairman, Ways and Means Subcommittee on Social Security; member, Subcommittee on Health
Norman Dicks (D-WA)	22,562	Member, Appropriations Subcommittee on Defense
Don Fuqua (D-FL)	21,650	Chairman, Science and Technology Committee
Bob Michel (R-IL)	20,750	Ex officio member, Permanent Select Committee on Intelligence; House Republican minority leader
Joseph D. McDade (R-PA)	20,250	Member, Appropriations Subcommittee on Defense
Richard B. Ray (D-GA)	18,550	Member, Armed Services Subcommittee on Military Installations and Facilities, Subcommittee on Procurement and Military Nuclear Systems, Subcommittee on Readiness, and Defense Policy Panel
Total	$369,265	

Source: Federal Election Commission, *Committee Index of Candidates Supported/Opposed, 1983-1984*. Data cover the contributions of sixteen leading SDI contractors to these candidates.

Table 7-5. Leading PAC Beneficiaries, 1985–86.

	Contribution	Committees
Senate		
Dan Quayle (R-IN)	$50,333	Chairman, Armed Services Subcommittee on Defense Acquisition Policy, Labor and Human Resources Subcommittee on Employment and Productivity; member, Subcommittee on Strategic and Theater Nuclear Forces, Committee on the Budget
John Glenn (D-OH)	44,500	Member, Armed Services Subcommittee on Preparedness, Subcommittee on Defense Acquisition Policy, Governmental Affairs Subcommittee on Energy, Nuclear Proliferation, and Government Processes
Bob Packwood (R-OR)	42,100	Chairman, Commerce, Science, and Transportation Subcommittee on Surface Transport, Committee on Finance; vice-chairman, Committee on Taxation
Jeremiah Denton (R-AL)	39,000	Chairman, Judiciary Subcommittee on Security and Terrorism; member, Armed Services Subcommittee on Manpower and Personnel, Subcommittee on Preparedness, Subcommittee on Sea Power and Force Projection
Arlen Specter (R-PA)	38,850	Chairman, Appropriations Subcommittee on District of Columbia; member, Select Committee on Intelligence
Steve Symms (R-ID)	35,850	Member, Committee on Budget, Committee on Finance, Joint Economic Committee
Bob Dole (R-KS)	35,750	Member, Committee on Finance; ex officio member, Select Committee on Intelligence; Senate majority leader
Slade Gorton (R-WA)	35,733	Chairman, Commerce, Science, and Transportation Subcommittee on Science, Technology and Space; member, Committee on the Budget
James Abdnor (R-SD)	35,250	Vice-chairman, Joint Economic Committee; member, Appropriations Committee
Bob Kasten (R-WI)	34,199	Chairman, Appropriations Subcommittee on Foreign Operations; member, Subcommittee on Defense, Committee on the Budget

(R-UT)	33,332	Chairman, Committee on Banking, Housing and Urban Development, member, Appropriations Subcommittee on Defense
Ernest Hollings (D-SC)	28,950	Member, Appropriations Subcommittee on Defense, Committee on the Budget; Select Committee on Intelligence
Total	$453,847	

House

William O. Dickinson (R-AL)	$33,000	Ranking minority member, Armed Services Subcommittee on Research and Development and Defense Policy Panel
Bill Chappel Jr. (D-FL)[a]	31,500	Member, Appropriations Subcommittee on Defense
Robert H. Michel (R-IL)	31,500	Ex officio member, Permanent Select Committee on Intelligence; minority leader
Joseph M. McDade (R-PA)	26,000	Member, Appropriations Subcommittee on Defense
Joseph P. Addabbo (D-NY)[b]	24,830	Chairman, Appropriations Subcommittee on Defense
Les Aspin (D-WI)	23,600	Chairman, Committee on Armed Services, Defense Policy Panel
W. G. (Bill) Hefner (D-NC)	21,050	Member, Appropriations Subcommittee on Defense, Committee on the Budget
John Murtha (D-PA)	20,500	Member, Appropriations Subcommittee on Defense
Norman Dicks (D-WA)	18,975	Member, Appropriations Subcommittee on Defense
Dan Daniel (D-VA)	18,125	Chairman, Armed Services Subcommittee on Readiness
Beverly Byron (D-MD)	16,350	Member, Armed Services Subcommittee on Investigations, Subcommittee on Procurement and Military Nuclear Systems
Sam Stratton (D-NY)	14,500	Chairman, Armed Services Subcommittee on Procurement and Military Nuclear Systems
Total	$279,930	

a. Congressman Chappel replaced Congressman Addabbo as chairman of the Appropriations Subcommittee on May 7, 1986.

b. Congressman Addabbo died on April 11, 1986. He was replaced in office by Congressman Walden. His vacancy on the Appropriations Subcommittee on Defense was filled by Congressman Martin Sabo (MN-Democrat-Farmer-Labor Party) on May 1, 1986.

Source: Federal Election Commission, *Committee Index of Candidates Supported/Opposed, 1985–1986.* Data are through June 1986 and cover the contributions of sixteen leading SDI contractors to these candidates.

ship—received 35 percent of total SDI PAC contributions to House members, suggesting how accurately PAC monies are pinpointed. In the Senate, the pattern is similar but less marked: the thirty-six members of the corresponding Senate committees received 56 percent of SDI PAC contributions to Senate members, although they account for little more than a third of the Senate membership.

The pattern in the 1985–86 election cycle is even more striking. A disproportionate 30.3 percent of the $2.4 million in PAC contributions poured into the campaign coffers of just twenty-four congressional candidates (see Table 7–5). Not surprisingly, many of these members chair key military-related committees or subcommittees. Seventeen are members of either the Armed Services or Appropriations Subcommittee on Defense in both houses.

SDI PACs have not played party favorites. Republicans received 56–57 percent of the contributions by sixteen leading SDI contractors, and Democrats received 43–44 percent. Because funds flow most freely to chairs of key committees, each party has done substantially better in the house of Congress it controls. The Democrats received 54 percent of the total donations to the House in 1983–84, 58 percent in 1985–86; the Republicans garnered almost 73 and 79 percent in the Senate, respectively, for each election cycle.

EMPLOYMENT LINKED TO PAC INFLUENCE

Arguments to increase funding for SDI often assert that the program's related activities in laboratories and military bases will create additional jobs and income. About 49 percent of PAC contributions from the sixteen leading SDI contractors in 1985–86 went to senators and representatives in just ten states—all key SDI strongholds (see Table 7–6). Not surprisingly, California, which received the lion's share of all SDI contracts since FY 1983, was also the largest recipient of PAC money.

Silicon Valley, long considered the military-industrial capital of the world, is actively encouraging Congress to take note of the jobs issue. Rockwell International, headquartered in southern California and the recipient of over $197 million in SDI contracts to date, manufactures ideological ammunition to justify support for SDI. In a widely circulated booklet entitled *Space: America's Frontier for Growth, Leadership and Freedom,* Rockwell warns about the United States' declining economic growth, dependence on imported fossil

Table 7-6.   PAC Contributions to Major SDI States, 1985–86.

State	Total PAC Contributions
California	$188,730
Pennsylvania	142,245
New York	129,430
Washington	126,458
Texas	112,075
Alabama	111,350
Illinois	95,110
Georgia	91,583
Ohio	77,700
Virginia	62,125
Massachusetts	30,250
Colorado	22,350
Total	$1,189,406

Source: Federal Election Commission, *Indexes of Candidates Supported/Opposed*; data are for 1985 through July 1986.

fuels, loss of military superiority, and "decline in international morale." The space program, the company claims, is "at the very frontier of technology" and "spawns technological advancement that will ultimately help foster higher productivity, open new markets, and develop novel products."[3]

In areas like Huntsville, Alabama, home of the Army's Ballistic Missile Defense System Command, the jobs issue is likely to garner significant constituent support for SDI. Huntsville's population grew from 17,000 in the 1950s to more than 120,000 in mid-1960 on the strength of missile and space contracts from the Army and NASA. But in the 1970s, the town lost 11,000 jobs as a result of cutbacks in missile and space programs.[4] SDI's kinetic energy weapons program, which will be used for early deployment, promises a new military boom for Huntsville. From 1983 to 1986, Alabama senators have consistently voted against every amendment that cut into the SDI program, including the more recent 1986 amendments to reduce SDI spending or to bar tests of any nuclear weapon in connection with SDI.

Colorado is also well positioned to increase its share of Star Wars funding over the next decade. As home to the new U.S. Unified

Space Command, which will oversee space activities of all three services, Colorado Springs will become "the space capital of the free world," according to Colorado Representative Ken Kramer. He claims that "in ten to fifteen years, time, space, and the technology that goes along with it will be the number one factor in Colorado's economy."[5] Kramer, moreover, is not leaving his state's future benefits from SDI to chance. He is the principal sponsor of the pro-Star Wars "People Protection Act" (legislation that calls for creation of the Unified Space Command) and has founded a lobbying organization, the U.S. Space Foundation, to promote a wide range of military and civilian uses of space, including SDI.

SDI PACS INFLUENCE VOTES

SDI money is already talking on Capitol Hill. And many of our elected representatives seem to be listening. In three key House votes in June 1985, the twelve leading recipients of SDI PAC money voted more than 83 percent of the time against restraining SDI money. The closest vote was a 221–195 defeat of an amendment introduced by Norman Dicks (D-WA), which would have reduced the fiscal 1986 SDI authorization from $2.5 billion to $2.1 billion and limited the amount spent on programs with potential to violate the Anti-Ballistic Missile Treaty. PAC-supported representatives of the Armed Services Committee and Defense Appropriations Subcommittee in both houses voted more than two to one against the amendment. Rep. Dicks, whose district received SDI contracts, was confronted by the Star Wars chief. He recalled, "Abrahamson and the SDI top brass said to me, 'Why are you so critical? We're doing a lot of work in your area?'"[6]

SDI contractors influenced Senate votes as well. Leading PAC recipients in both election cycles voted against lowering the SDI budget 83 percent of the time in five key votes between 1984 and 1986. The closest vote was a 45–47 defeat of an amendment by Senator Kennedy to transfer $62 million from the SDI budget into the budget for certain nutrition programs. Since 1985 they cast 91 percent of their votes against three attempts to bar or delay antisatellite testing. In 1985 they unanimously voted for continuing the controversial SDI nuclear program, which involves activating an x-ray laser by an atomic explosion. Since SDI was initially touted as a nonnuclear defense system, this program has stirred considerable debate.

More recently, Congress has shown growing skepticism about the technical and strategic feasibility and the cost of a strategic defense system. In 1986, forty-eight senators signed a letter questioning the goals of the program and calling for a 43 percent cut in the president's 1987 $5.4 billion budget request for SDI. The defense establishment was considerably rattled by the fact that J. Bennett Johnston (D-LA) and Sam Nunn (D-GA)—generally considered reliable pro-arms senators—were among the skeptics. Senator Johnston is a particularly surprising exception to the PAC rule. Although he received $40,700 in PAC dollars from leading SDI companies between 1983 and 1984, he has rejected funding increases for the program.

As Congress becomes more skeptical about SDI's technical prospects, military boosters will have to fight an uphill battle to win support for the program. In the aftermath of the *Challenger* explosion and the bombing of the *U.S.S. Stark*, the risks inherent in SDI can only loom higher, as will its costs in light of ever-growing deficits. Even escalated contractor PAC contributions and more aggressive lobby campaign tactics that play up on the dependence of constituents on military jobs may be insufficient to win the day on Capitol Hill in November 1988.

In the interim, we may well see more aggressive tactics, like Rockwell International's successful campaign to restore the B-1 bomber program. In 1973, Rockwell initiated a letter-writing campaign among its employees, which generated over 80,000 messages to Congress in support of the bomber. A similar tactic was used by Martin Marietta in 1983. In a letter to his employees, the company's president pointed to their economic interest in the continued production of the MX missile and urged them to "let your Congressmen know how you feel."[7] Both Rockwell and Martin Marietta saw their programs restored.

If congressional opposition threatens to slow down the SDI program drastically, SDI contractors could be more likely to resort to aggressive tactics. One well-funded pro-SDI group, the High Frontier, has already devised a strategy aimed to ensure the survival of SDI.

LOBBYING AT THE HIGH FRONTIER

The High Frontier ballistic missile defense proposal, which helped encourage President Reagan to deliver his Star Wars speech in 1983, entails using existing off-the-shelf kinetic energy technology to destroy Soviet warheads before they reach U.S. soil. Retired Army General Daniel Graham, the creator and leading advocate of this revamped ballistic missile defense (BMD) concept, claims that a nonnuclear system could be deployed in as little as five years at a cost of about $15 billion.[8] To promote this version of a strategic defense system, Graham organized High Frontier Inc.

Operating out of Washington, D.C., High Frontier publishes a steady stream of reports, books, and newsletters promoting Graham's proposal. Because of Internal Revenue Service restrictions on tax-exempt organizations, however, High Frontier Inc. cannot engage in direct political activity. The American Space Frontiers Committee (ASFC), a PAC also headed by General Graham, has taken on an SDI congressional contribution campaign.

According to Federal Election Commission data, the ASFC overwhelmingly supports candidates from the ultraconservative side of the political spectrum. The committee spent $54,039 between 1983 and the spring of 1985 on PAC contributions.[9] Republicans were supported over Democrats by a ratio of 19 to 1. In the House, the largest share of PAC funds, almost $5,000, went to Robert Dornan (R-CA), a member of the Foreign Affairs Subcommittee on Arms Control and the International Security and Science Committee. In the Senate, Phil Gramm (R-TX), a member of the Armed Services Subcommittee on Defense Acquisition Policy, took the lead with over $4,000. Mack Mattingly (R-GA), Jesse Helms (R-NC), and Ed Bethune (R-AR) followed with $2,000 each. The committee also spent $18,863 on behalf of a losing campaign for U.S. Senate candidate Roger Jepsen (R-IA) between 1983 and 1984.

To bolster promotion of his High Frontier BMD concept, General Graham formed the Coalition for SDI in September 1985.[10] Composed of over seventy-five pro-SDI organizations, the Coalition's goals are (1) to prevent further erosion in the SDI budget during the authorization process, and (2) to show grassroots support for SDI so that it will not be negotiated away in the arms control process. The Coalition has committed its funds to an aggressive public relations campaign to counter rising media criticism of SDI.

Conservatives from the New Right dominate the Coalition's membership. Among the congressional cochairmen of the Coalition are Senator Malcolm Wallop (R-WY), an ardent advocate of early deployment of a strategic defense system, and Representative Jack Kemp (R-NY), a leading recipient of campaign contributions from the High Frontier PAC, who vowed to transform the 1988 presidential race into a "national referendum" on SDI. "The Strategic Defense Initiative is the greatest peace initiative of our time, and we can deploy it," Kemp stated as he announced his candidacy for president of the United States.[11] Graham boasts another sixty cosponsors on Capitol Hill. "Millions of Americans support the SDI program," he says, "and the Coalition for SDI will channel that support to ensure SDI is not derailed or slowed down."[12]

An insight into the Coalition's public relations strategy is provided by an ambitious 1983 memorandum on SDI submitted to High Frontier by John Bosma, then a consultant to the organization and now editor of *Military Space.* Bosma developed strategies for selling the concept of ballistic missile defense as "a new approach to arms control." The paper advocated creating sufficient programmatic momentum to keep "the BMD program alive in 1984 and to make it impossible to turn off by 1989," even by a Democratic administration. Among the proposed strategies for accomplishing this goal is "a drastic reorientation of the arms control debate in such a way as to make it politically risky for BMD opponents to invoke alleged 'arms control arguments' against an early BMD system. In fact, the project should unambiguously seek to recapture the term 'arms control' and all the idealistic images and language attached to it."[13]

To make this strategy effective, the memorandum suggests a radical approach "that seeks to disarm BMD opponents . . . by stealing their language and cause (arms control)."[14] While pro-BMD New Right conservatives such as representatives Ken Kramer, Gingrich, and Whitehurst, and senators Heflin, Wallop, McClure, Symms, and Armstrong are to be supported, the memorandum calls for involving as many liberal or moderate constituencies as possible, including Nuclear Freeze supporters and other peace groups. It identifies as its "declared enemies" the *Washington Post, New York Times, Christian Science Monitor*, "elite media" networks (CBS, NBC, ABC), and professional societies, including the Institute of Electrical and Electronics Engineers among others. On the other hand, it targets SDI supporters among the aerospace industry "for $ reasons," the science fiction community, *Reader's Digest*, the Rand Corporation, and others.

PUTTING A LID ON LOBBYING

Although our analysis reveals a politically and systematically moti-vated pattern of PAC contributions, such an approach is perfectly legal. SDI contractors are merely playing by the rules of campaign financing. Nonetheless, their astute use of PAC contributions and economic leverage for political ends raises serious questions about the potential for independent, objective congressional review of the SDI program.

Many lawmakers believe campaign money erodes the integrity of Congress, making it seem more responsive to the whims of the rich than the needs of the ordinary citizen, let alone the unemployed or handicapped. The Senate majority leader, Bob Dole, adds, "When these PACs give money, they expect something in return other than good government." [15]

In a recent effort to correct the unwarranted influence of PACs, Senator David Boren (D-OK) introduced a bill that would lower the ceiling on a PAC contribution from $5,000 to $3,000 per candi-date. [16] In addition there would be ceilings on total PAC receipts by candidates. Senate candidates could take between $175,000 and $750,000 depending on state population, and House candidates could receive no more than $100,000 from all PACs combined. How-ever, because many legislators are worried about voting against PACs and cutting off a major source of revenue, the chances for im-mediate change are slim.

This legislation would be a significant step in the right direction. But merely limiting corporate contributions, as proposed by the Boren bill, will only stem the momentum unleashed by PAC lobby-ing for SDI. To reform PAC spending, therefore, the entire contro-versy over public versus private campaign financing must be reopened. One viable alternative to free congressional military decisions from economic concerns is an economic conversion bill of the type cur-rently proposed by representatives Ted Weiss (D-NY) and Nicholas Mavroules (D-MA). [17] Conversion legislation would offer protection to workers and communities dependent on weapons production for jobs and income in the event that a defense project is cut back or canceled.

While federal funding of campaigns or stricter limits on PAC spending could diminish the influence of corporate lobbying on the political process, they would not sufficiently rein in the power behind sheltered military interests in the SDI program. Corporations would still maintain a mutually beneficial bond with the Pentagon that ensures them a significant degree of continued support for weapons programs.

To help control the momentum of the president's Star Wars crusade, Congress should consider measures that would free decisions on defense programs from the concentration of power and economic influence detailed above. Only then would we be assured that decisions on military programs are being based on our need for national security.

THE SDI TAX BURDEN: REGIONAL INEQUALITIES

The pattern of contracting for SDI is one that enriches only a few regions. This uneven distribution of SDI money also creates an imbalance in the SDI tax burden imposed on the nation's states. To study the distribution of SDI funds, the share of SDI taxes drawn from each state and from twenty-five major metropolitan areas was compared with the value of strategic defense contracts. Although SDI currently makes up only a fraction of the federal budget, it could create severe economic dislocations if this imbalance continues once the program begins to spend its multibillion dollar production contracts.

To calculate an "SDI tax"—the amount of taxes each state pays to cover SDI expenditures—the following method was used: first, the amount of personal federal income taxes paid by residents of each state for the last four years was identified; second, SDI outlays as a percentage of total federal outlays for each of those years was determined. By applying this percentage to each state's personal federal income tax payments, the SDI tax was derived. Finally, the actual amount of SDI contract money spent, or obligations, was compared to the SDI tax for each state and ranked according to a net loss or gain.

Since the analysis is based solely on personal federal income taxes and includes neither excise taxes, corporate taxes, gift and estate taxes, customs duties, and other miscellaneous receipts nor accounts in any way for the deficit, SDI contract obligations exceed the SDI share of taxes. Personal federal income taxes, on the average, make up 45 percent of all federal tax receipts. If additional taxes are taken into account, the share of SDI taxes paid by each state would be considerably higher and thus result in even greater net losses for many states.

Since 1983 the federal government has funneled SDI tax money out of a majority of states into those few that have large military bases or already have high proportions of SDI contracts.[18] Such regional imbalance means that while some areas prosper, others in need lose vital tax dollars, employment, and consumer spending.

Between FY 1983 and FY 1986, a total of 43 states comprising 80 percent of the nation's population suffered net losses from the uneven distribution of SDI money. Of these, ten states received no SDI money although they paid 6.5 percent of the taxes to finance the program. In contrast, only seven states and the District of Columbia, home to 20 percent of the U.S. population, received more from SDI contracts than they paid out in SDI taxes for the program (see Table 7-7).

For California, the heart of the military industrial complex, SDI has become a major source of revenue. Its position as leading beneficiary of SDI funding stems from its receiving over $3.2 billion in contracts to research various technologies, including nonnuclear kinetic energy weapons being tested for early production and deployment. These weapons range from Lockheed's Exoatmospheric Re-Entry Vehicle Interceptor Subsystem to EG&G's High Endoatmospheric Defense Interceptor to Rockwell International's Electromagnetic Railgun.

Georgia represents the other extreme of the spectrum. Having paid almost 7 percent of the taxes to finance SDI, the state received a mere 0.2 percent of all contracts to research such areas as optical computing and logic arrays for the Small Radar Homing Interceptor Technology, a kinetic energy weapon. Like midwestern states experiencing considerable decline in agricultural exports, Georgia would have benefited from alternative civilian uses of its share of SDI taxes. For example, the 300,000 farmers who have been forced off their land during the Reagan administration's years could be gainfully employed with the help of price and income supports, crop insurance and credit, and agricultural research. Instead, the Reagan administration continues to shrink the appropriations for such rural programs.

In the middle of these two extremes lies a host of midwestern states that both contribute little in taxes to finance the program and receive a negligible portion of the SDI pie. Idaho, Montana, North Dakota, Oregon, and Wyoming, for example, paid 1.6 percent of all SDI taxes in the last four years; except for Montana and Oregon, which split contracts amounting to $567,000 (.02 percent of the total), these states received no SDI money. According to the Census Bureau, these are the same five states that together lost 99,000 people between April 1980 and July 1986 due to a lack of jobs.[19]

The SDI budget distribution also affects metropolitan economies. Of the twenty-five most populous metropolitan areas in the United States, seventeen areas with almost 64 million people, or over 27 percent of the nation's population, are suffering a net drain of their economic resources. Only eight metropolitan areas with 14 percent of the U.S. population paid 19.2 percent of the taxes for SDI and received 62.8 percent of SDI contract obligations (see Table 7-8). Many of the regions sustaining net losses from the SDI program are already undergoing severe economic problems, such as the decline of the auto and steel industries in Detroit and Pittsburgh.

SDI is, consequently, an ongoing source of economic drain on manufacturing and agricultural regions already hampered by sluggish productivity growth, low exports, high interest rates, a bloated budget deficit, and rising demands for trade protection. If this distribution pattern persists, SDI funding will help sustain America's current bicoastal economy characterized by economic growth in coastal regions and economic decline in at least thirty-one midwestern states. While business is booming for advertising firms, Wall Street, retail trade, and others in major coastal metropolitan areas, the departure of bankrupt farmers and the decline in basic industries such as mining and textiles has weakened rural and interior industrial America.

Although the Reagan administration championed a laissez-faire economy that, it predicted, would achieve a 4 to 5 percent annual economic growth, actual growth in the past seven years has averaged only 2.3 percent. According to a 1986 Joint Economic Committee study, California and sixteen states on the East Coast experienced an annual 4 percent rate of economic growth between 1981 and 1985—about the level that the United States as a whole enjoyed during the 1960s. These areas, however, represent only 42 percent of the population. In contrast, economies in the rest of the country, representing 58 percent of the population, grew by a mere 1.4 percent annually.[20]

Any attempt to correct these regional imbalances, which may be aggravated by the largest military project yet, must first come to

Table 7-7. SDI Taxes and Prime Contracts, by State, FY 1983–86 (million dollars).

State	% Share of Total SDI Taxes[a]	% Share of Total SDI Obligations[b]	$ SDI Taxes	$ SDI Obligations	Net Losses/Gains
Losers					
Georgia	7.0	0.2	139.1	8.8	130.3
New York	8.4	1.9	166.4	66.9	99.5
Illinois	5.2	0.2	103.0	6.4	96.6
New Jersey	4.4	0.4	88.1	13.9	74.2
Michigan	3.6	0.03	71.4	1.0	70.4
Pennsylvania	4.2	0.6	84.2	21.5	62.7
Florida	4.9	1.2	97.8	43.2	54.6
Ohio	3.5	0.6	70.4	20.6	49.8
North Carolina	2.0	0.01	39.0	0.4	38.6
Indiana	2.0	0.01	39.2	2.1	37.1
All other states[c]	34.5	8.45	686.7	305.8	419.5
Totals	79.7%	13.6%	$1,585.3	$490.6	$1,133.3

Gainers

California	11.8	42.6	235.0	1,532.2	1,297.2
New Mexico	0.4	13.6	8.6	488.2	479.6
Alabama	1.1	9.9	22.3	355.7	333.4
Massachusetts	3.0	10.3	59.0	369.6	310.6
Washington	1.8	6.7	36.1	243.6	207.5
Colorado	1.4	2.0	27.7	70.9	43.2
Utah	0.4	0.7	8.6	26.8	18.2
District of Columbia	0.4	0.6	7.4	21.7	14.3
Totals	20.3%	86.4%	$404.7	$3,108.7	$2,704.0

a. To estimate "SDI Taxes," the percentage of SDI outlays of total federal outlays was applied to the total personal federal income tax payments of each state for each year (1983–1986). Since excise taxes, corporate taxes, estate and gift taxes, and customs duties are not included, the total SDI taxes are understated.

b. SDI Obligations refer to the amount of the total SDI contract value that was spent for that year.

c. These include all other states except the gainers.

Table 7-8. SDI Taxes and Prime Contracts, by Major Metropolitan Area, FY 1983–86 (million dollars).

Metropolitan Area	% Share SDI Taxes	% Share Total SDI Obligations	$ SDI Taxes	$ SDI Obligations	Net Losses/ Gains
Losers					
New York, North New Jersey, and Connecticut	10.3	1.7	205.7	61.9	143.8
Chicago, Gary, and Lake Country	3.5	0.2	69.2	5.6	63.6
Philadelphia, Wilmington, and Trenton	2.7	0.4	53.7	13.0	40.7
Detroit and Ann Arbor	2.0	0.03	39.9	1.0	38.9
Houston, Galveston, and Brazoria	1.9	0.0	37.6	0.0	37.6
Miami and Fort Lauderdale	1.4	0.0	28.1	0.0	28.1
Cleveland, Akron, and Lorain	1.2	0.2	23.0	8.5	14.5
St. Louis, East St. Louis, and Alton	1.1	0.2	21.5	7.9	13.6
Pittsburgh and Beaver Valley	0.9	0.2	18.6	6.4	12.2
Kansas City	0.6	0.0	12.2	0.0	12.2
Milwaukee and Racine	0.6	0.0	11.8	0.0	11.8
Atlanta	1.0	0.2	20.2	8.8	11.4
Other metro areas[a]	4.1	1.6	82.6	55.8	26.8
Totals	31.3%	4.7%	$624.1	$168.9	$455.2

Gainers

Los Angeles, Anaheim, and Riverside	7.3	21.9	114.4	788.6	674.2
San Francisco, Oakland, and San Jose	3.1	14.8	61.6	531.7	470.1
Boston, Lawrence, and Salem	2.0	10.2	40.7	366.7	326.0
Seattle and Tacoma	1.0	6.7	20.1	241.6	221.5
San Diego	0.9	2.6	17.6	92.0	74.4
Dallas and Fort Worth	1.9	3.0	37.2	107.3	70.1
Denver and Boulder	0.9	1.5	17.7	54.9	37.2
Washington, D.C.[b]	2.1	2.1	42.4	76.5	34.1
Totals	19.2%	62.8%	$351.7	$2,259.3	$1,907.6

a. Other metropolitan areas include Minneapolis, St. Paul, Cincinnati, Hamilton, Tampa, St. Petersburg, Phoenix, and Baltimore.

b. Although Washington, D.C.'s, share of SDI taxes and SDI obligations are equal, this metropolitan area is likely to be a winner in the long run given the great number of small consulting and high technology firms likely to receive SDI contracts.

terms with the considerable power the arms industry holds over the SDI purse strings. The politics of contracting and the economics of electoral politics have considerable influence over future funding for the program and allocation of SDI contracts. Through PACs and other political mechanisms, contractors finance the re-election of friendly legislators and influence votes in favor of SDI funding. A feedback loop is created whereby contractors finance legislators and promise to provide home district jobs, which persuades constituents to vote for legislators who sponsor SDI legislation, which enriches contractors who finance legislators. . . . Thus Detroit's taxes end up financing Silicon Valley's SDI contracts.

8

TECHNOLOGICAL RENAISSANCE
OR BRAIN DRAIN?

America continues to regard the rest of the world through the foggy lenses of cold-war diplomacy rather than through the clear glasses of commercial competition.

—Robert Reich
November 1, 1982

Beyond the dollars-and-cents issues of who pays for SDI and who will benefit from the effort to develop a strategic defense system lies a broader question: how will an expanding SDI program affect U.S. technological growth and the competitiveness of our nation's high technology industries?

As in earlier debates over space and defense programs, advocates of SDI contend that it will produce a cornucopia of valuable spinoffs that will improve productivity and enhance the competitiveness of the U.S. economy. Critics, on the other hand, argue that the extreme performance goals, relative inattention to cost, and secrecy that characterize this program and other military-sponsored R&D efforts will minimize spinoffs to civilian industry. Moreover, many economists and science policy experts maintain that in the highly competitive international environment of the late twentieth century, the United States cannot afford to devote substantial portions of its technical talent and resources to an SDI megaproject and strengthen crucial industries at the same time.[1]

While the future of SDI should depend primarily on its strategic and technical merits rather than on its implications for U.S. economic policy, its effects on civilian technological development cannot be ignored. This chapter will analyze three key questions that bear on SDI's potential impact on U.S. high technology. Will SDI divert a substantial proportion of U.S. scientific and engineering talent from potential civilian projects? What are the prospects for significant civilian spinoffs from SDI research? Will SDI evolve into the de facto U.S. industrial policy for high technology development, and if so, what will be the consequences for U.S. competitiveness?

SDI: A TRILLION DOLLAR BRAIN DRAIN?

Fears about the adequacy of the U.S. technical work force were raised in 1980 by the Reagan administration's decision to undertake the largest peacetime military build-up in U.S. history. At a time when many firms were reporting the need to raise salaries to attract sufficient engineering talent and deans of engineering schools were complaining that industry demand was drawing talent away from universities, how could the nation afford to devote additional resources to the military?

As rapid expansion in the military aerospace and electronics industries strained the existing supply of engineering talent in the early 1980s, industry leaders began to express concern about the quantity and quality of the U.S. technical work force. John R. Opel, chief executive officer of IBM, observed that "the United States is slipping in the race to strengthen not its capacity in buildings and machines, vital as they are, but the capabilities of its people: . . . the ultimate resource in any nation." As a result, he cautioned "we risk losing out against tougher, more pragmatic, more adventurous international contenders in the years ahead."[2]

But the president's call for intensive development of strategic defense technologies, combined with an expanding military budget and high economic growth, may revive labor market shortages in highly trained personnel. In the following section we examine the current market for engineering and scientific talent, review projections of future conditions, and estimate the demand created by the

Strategic Defense Initiative for certain types of technical personnel, placing that assessment in the context of labor market conditions.

Shortages Have Subsided after Recent Problems

Employers surveyed by the National Science Foundation (NSF) in the fall of 1981 reported shortages of qualified candidates for jobs in the computer and engineering fields.[3] Over 50 percent of surveyed firms reported shortages of qualified computer engineers and scientists. Employers could hire only 40 to 50 percent of their target number of new bachelor's and master's degree applicants in these fields. The demand for new electrical engineers also exceeded supply. More than half the firms reported shortages, and the hiring success rate was only about 40 percent. The survey indicated less severe shortages of electronic and petroleum engineers and systems analysts.

Data on starting salaries and unemployment rates indicate that the early 1980s was a period of moderate tightness in the engineering job market.[4] Average starting salary for engineers was 13 percent greater than the average starting salary in five other professional occupations in 1966, a year in which the engineering market was strained by the Apollo project and the Vietnam War.[5] By 1981, the relative advantage of engineering graduates had climbed to 21 percent. The unemployment rate for engineers was 1.5 percent in 1981, down from 2.6 percent in 1975, when engineers were in surplus, but somewhat higher than during the shortages of the mid-1960s. Overall, an analyst for the Bureau of Labor Statistics concluded in 1983 that "there probably have been shortages of some types of engineers in recent years, but the shortages have not been severe."[6]

Increased recruitment expenses and higher salaries were among the major costs of the tight engineering and scientific labor market, according to the NSF survey. Forty percent of the employers reporting shortages stated they expanded recruitment, 30 percent reported raising salary offers, and 15 percent said they improved benefits. In addition, over 10 percent of the firms experiencing shortages reported hiring and retraining persons with inappropriate training. Only 3 percent of the firms stated they had to reduce production or cancel research.[7]

The impact of tight job markets for technical personnel was felt beyond industry. Deans of engineering schools worried that the labor shortages would reduce the quality of engineering education by drawing away present and future faculty members. For example, between 1972 and 1982, the share of new scientific and engineering Ph.D.s with definite employment commitments in industry grew from 18 to 34 percent, while the proportion with academic employment commitments fell from 59 to 42 percent.[8]

Bachelor's and master's degree graduates were lured out of the universities by higher salaries in industry.[9] As industrial employment became more attractive than further education, the number of doctoral degrees awarded declined. In 1971, 3,498 new Ph.D.s were awarded; this figure dropped to 2,528 by 1981.[10] Moreover, an increasing percentage of the Ph.D.s awarded are earned by foreign students. In 1981, 51.5 percent of the doctoral degrees were awarded to foreign students, up from 29.8 percent in 1971.[11]

With fewer Ph.D.s awarded and industry positions becoming increasingly attractive, engineering colleges reported 10 percent of their faculty positions were vacant in the fall of 1980.[12] Meanwhile, full-time undergraduate enrollment increased 66 percent between 1969–70 and 1981–82 (from 233,500 to 387,600), while the number of faculty increased by just 11 percent (from 16,200 to 18,000). During this period, the student-teacher ratio for undergraduates rose from 14.4 to 21.5.[13]

Engineering education suffered as a result of these trends. Of the engineering school deans that reported difficulty recruiting or retaining faculty in 1980, 80 percent believed teaching loads had increased as a result of vacancies. Over half also indicated their schools were unable to offer courses in some areas. To compensate for the shortages, 66 percent of the deans reported greater reliance on graduate teaching assistants and part-time faculty. About 35 percent of the deans felt the vacancy problem forced their remaining faculty to curtail research activities.[14]

The deep recession that began in 1981 mitigated the problems somewhat. A 1983 NSF survey of the recruiting experience of 351 industrial firms found 60 percent of the companies felt it had become easier to hire scientists, engineers, and technicians than in the past year.[15] The proportion of employers reporting shortages of technical personnel in any category also fell substantially—from 60 percent in the 1981 survey to 28 percent in 1983. No single science or engineering occupation was reported to be in short supply by more than 10 percent of the employers in 1983; such shortages were reported by as many as 60 percent of the employers in 1981 and 30 percent in 1982.

Starting salaries and unemployment rates for engineers also indicate that shortages have subsided since the early 1980s. In 1983, the average starting engineering salary was 19.6 percent greater than the average starting salary of five other professional occupations. It had been 21.1 percent higher in 1981. The unemployment rate for engineers rose from 1.3 percent in 1980 to 3.0 percent in 1983. In 1986, the unemployment rate rose again to 2.6 percent after dropping to 1.9 in 1985.

A recent report by the National Academy of Engineering concluded that defense needs for engineers are not overwhelming the supply except for certain subspecialties. The study also found that salaries in defense and civilian industries are equivalent in most areas, making competition unnecessary.[16]

Future Shortages?

In the simplest terms, a shortage of engineers or scientists occurs when demand exceeds supply at a given price and point in time. Given the dynamic nature of the labor market, however, this static definition is inadequate. Employers can adjust to limited supply of engineers and scientists in a variety of ways, though each has its price. They may try to attract needed staff by raising salaries, intensifying recruiting, and broadening hiring standards, or they may substitute capital equipment for labor. The side effects of these adjustments can include higher costs, production delays, reduced quality, and lower productivity.[17] More sophisticated understanding of shortages must therefore include the costs imposed to reach market equilibrium.

New entrants to the skilled professional labor market consist of recent graduates, immigrants, and occupational transfers into the field. New demand may be created by economic growth, transfers out of the field, and attrition. An analyst for the Bureau of Labor Statistics (BLS) estimates that an average of 138,500 engineering job openings will occur every year between 1982 and 1995.[18] On average, 45,000 of these positions will be created by growth in demand. Another 93,500 will come open as a result of transfers out of the profession and attrition. Forty-six percent of those openings are projected to be filled by new graduates, the other 54 percent by occupation transfers and immigrants.

If demand for engineers at a particular price outstrips supply, industry might adjust by drawing more people from academia; by encouraging sales or managerial personnel with experience in engineering to return to the field; by training individuals with technical experience in allied fields such as mathematics and physics; and by attracting more students to the field.

Firms' efforts to correct engineering and scientific labor shortfalls exact a price, however. Increasing salaries and benefits to attract employees raises production costs and can undermine the competitiveness of a firm's goods in the international market. Mobility may also involve administrative sacrifices, including higher staff turnover and recruitment costs as professionals strive to better their situation in a favorable job market. Retraining personnel from allied fields adds further costs. Labor force quality may suffer as well from high mobility. Technicians may be required to do tasks usually performed by engineers. Finally, favorable salaries in industry can draw personnel out of the educational system—lowering the quality of the future engineering work force.

Bureau of Labor Statistics projections show a rough overall balance between engineering requirements and available labor over the next decade. But the BLS concludes that "imbalances over short periods of time among specialties are inevitable, given the nature of the engineering labor market."[19] If imbalances, or the accommodations they require, persist, they may hinder the growth and international competitiveness of U.S. industries.

The Manhattan project is frequently mentioned as a model for assessing the labor market impact of SDI, but NASA's Apollo program offers a better economic parallel. Whereas the effort to build the atomic bomb took place during wartime, when the economy was tightly controlled, the Apollo project occurred during a period of high military spending and strong economic growth, similar to the situation SDI could face if it moves to full-scale engineering and production. During the peak year of the Apollo program, 1966, it absorbed 13.5 percent of all research and development spending in the United States; NASA as a whole took 20.8 percent. Full-scale deployment of an SDI system would probably consume an equally large share of the nation's R&D resources.

Before the Apollo program, NASA was not a significant competitor with private industry for technical staff. Although the number of scientists and engineers employed by NASA and its contractors more than tripled (from 10,800 to 33,200) between 1960 and 1962, there was no significant drain of talent from civilian industry, for three reasons. First, 40 percent of NASA's in-house employees hired during this period came from other government agencies, particularly the Department of Defense.[20] These transfers were encouraged by special legislation allowing NASA to offer higher salaries than other federal agencies.[21] Second, almost half the new scientists and engineers hired by NASA contractors were lateral transfers from major aerospace firms. Since the aerospace market was slack because of the 1960–61 slowdown, these transfers did not strain the labor supply.[22] Third, and most important from a program management standpoint, NASA made a strong effort to avoid competition with the private sector by stimulating the expansion of the technical manpower pool. In 1962, the agency began to establish cooperative training and recruiting relationships with major U.S. universities. NASA sought to add 1,000 Ph.D.s annually to space-related fields by offering training, research, and facility grants to universities. In 1965, NASA gave training grants to 142 institutions, made twenty-seven facility grants, and supported over 3,000 students.[23] No such programs have been planned to ease the potential strain of SDI on labor markets for technical personnel.

Despite these efforts to accommodate the needs of civilian industry, members of Congress began to express concern that the space program might drain off technical manpower.[24] In 1963, as the Apollo program geared up, NASA almost doubled its technical staff, employing over 4 percent of the scientists and engineers in the United States. By 1966, strains in the science and engineering labor market were evident. NASA was employing almost 92,000 scientists and engineers, a full 5.5 percent of the national total. The unemployment rate for engineers dropped to 0.7 percent from 1.5 percent two years earlier, starting salaries for engineers increased substantially, and the demand for scientists and engineers outstripped supply by 5.2 percent, compared with a gap of only 3.9 percent in 1963.[25]

Competition with space and defense programs for professional engineers and scientists clearly hurt U.S. industry. As NASA requirements expanded from zero to almost 17 percent of the total industrial R&D labor pool between 1957 and 1964, the cost of employing

R&D scientists and engineers grew dramatically for civilian industry. Basic industries were forced to match high aerospace and electronic industry salaries in an attempt to retain skilled personnel.[26] R&D labor costs grew by 80 percent for the ferrous metals industry, 78 percent for chemicals, and 41 percent for fabricated metals, even though these industries' demand for scientists and engineers did not increase.[27]

Demand During SDI Research and Production

The number of scientists, engineers, and technicians required by SDI in the longer term will depend on executive and congressional decisions about whether to move toward deployment of a strategic defense system. Estimates of SDI's personnel requirements for the period through 1991 can be derived from data on budgetary outlays and DOD R&D employment requirements.

The first step is to determine actual SDI dollar outlays for each year (as opposed to budget authority, which simply represents congressional permission to obligate funds, which may be spent over a number of years). Under current budget projections SDI outlays are slated to more than triple from roughly $2.3 billion in FY 1986 to over $7.6 billion in FY 1991 (Table 8-1).

These outlay estimates then must be translated into SDI-related production by industry. We have assumed that SDI spending will have the same production requirements in each industry as the average DOD RDT&E program, because many of the technologies being explored for the initiative are very similar to those developed for other major Pentagon projects. Moreover, like other RDT&E projects, the current SDI program emphasizes full-scale development over technological exploration. Since total production includes many products and services produced by intermediate suppliers and incorporated into the final product or service purchased by DOD, the figure for total production shown in Table 8-1 is roughly twice the direct SDI outlay. In other words, this method measures both direct and indirect employment stimulated by R&D outlays.

Finally, we determined SDI employment requirements by industry and estimated the share of scientific, engineering, and technical personnel in that total. This analysis involved multiplying SDI production by the average number of jobs generated per million dollars

Table 8-1. SDI Budget Authority and Outlays, FY 1986-91 (*million 1985 dollars*).

Year	Budget Authority	Outlays 1986	1987	1988	1989	1990	1991
1982	$ 882	$ 9					
1983	1,036	31	$ 10				
1984	1,149	69	34	$ 11			
1985	1,621	567	97	49	$ 16		
1986	2,949	1,622	1,032	177	88	$ 29	
1987	3,285		1,807	1,150	197	99	$ 33
1988	5,731			3,152	2,006	344	172
1989	6,386				3,512	2,235	383
1990	7,335					4,034	2,567
1991	8,113						4,462
Total		$2,298	$2,980	$4,539	$5,819	$6,741	$7,617

Sources: Spendout rates to convert budget authority to outlays are from William Kaufmann, John F. Kennedy School of Government, Harvard University. *RDT&E Programs (R-1) Department of Defense Budget for Fiscal Year 1987* (Washington, D.C.: DOD, February 4, 1986); data for FY 1989-91 from *Selected Weapons Costs from the President's 1987 Program* (Washington, D.C.: Congressional Budget Office, Defense Cost Unit, April 9, 1986).

of RDT&E employment for each industry (Table 8-2). These figures on SDI employment by industry were then multiplied by the average percentage of skilled employees (by category) in each industry to arrive at a figure for total scientific, engineering, and technical personnel required by SDI (Table 8-3). In 1986, SDI used an estimated 9,000 engineers, scientists, and technicians. By 1991 that figure will triple, to roughly 28,500, if current budget projections hold true.

Barring a return to rapid economic growth and an acceleration of military spending in the next five years, this level of demand should not provoke shortages in qualified technical talent in industry or other government programs. However, some specific fields of research, such as optics, software, and fusion energy, could experience shortages even in the short term. SDI will, in addition, impose some opportunity costs—money that could be spent for other purposes—in specific technological areas.

Table 8-2. Estimated SDI Employment in FY 1986 and 1991 (millions 1985 dollars).

Industry	SDI Production		Employment (per 1 million 1985 dollars)	SDI Total Employment	
	1986	1991		1986	1991
Radio and TV communication equipment	472	1,417	10.8	5,098	15,304
Management, consulting, and labs	331	1,154	21.8	7,216	25,157
Complete guided missiles	267	758	10.6	2,830	8,035
Nonprofit organizations and miscellaneous profit services	217	794	35.0	7,595	27,790
Electronic measuring instruments	220	676	15.0	3,300	10,140
Electronic computing equipment	149	625	12.5	1,863	7,813
Wholesale trade	158	510	16.4	2,591	8,364
Aircraft	131	353	10.0	1,310	3,530
Real estate	103	343	5.1	525	1,749
Measuring and control instruments	91	270	15.1	1,374	4,077
Hotels and lodging places	81	262	44.2	3,580	11,580
Eating and drinking places	71	234	31.3	2,222	7,324
Electronic components, NEC	66	230	14.3	944	3,289
Electric utilities	64	214	4.4	282	942
Inorganic and organic chemicals	63	193	5.4	340	1,042
Computer and data processing	61	212	21.8	1,330	4,622
Other motor vehicles	57	171	6.5	371	1,112
Gas utilities	49	146	2.6	127	380
Aircraft engines and engine parts	48	122	10.0	480	1,220
Engineering and scientific instruments	45	141	15.1	680	2,129
Twenty industry total	2,744	8,825		44,058	145,599
All other industries	1,429	4,608	15.4	22,007	70,963
Total	4,173	13,433		66,065	216,562

Source: Defense Economic Impact Modeling System (Washington, D.C.: OUSD (PA&E) Economic Analysis Division, 1986).

More importantly, if SDI proceeds to actual development and deployment, it will far outstrip the size of the Apollo program. Harvey Brooks, a science policy expert and member of the Harvard faculty has observed:

> Given the many technical unknowns, not to mention likely Soviet countermeasures, the estimated costs of an ultimate deployed SDI system . . . have a much less firm technical basis than the cost estimates President Kennedy had available when he made a somewhat analogous public commitment to the Apollo program. . . . Not only is the likely ultimate cost of SDI less certain, but I would hazard a guess that the scope of the research, development, testing, and evaluation (RDT&E) involved in bringing the SDI to initial operating capability would be between ten and one hundred times greater than any major military or civilian project undertaken by the United States in the past.[28]

U.S. science and engineering resources have increased considerably since the Apollo era. Nevertheless, Brooks estimates that if SDI is to be made operational, "the ratio of the magnitude of the RDT&E effort to the capacity of the existing industrial and science/engineering infrastructure necessary to undergird it will prove far larger than for any previous technical megaproject."[29]

The Council on Economic Priorities has examined the impact a substantial strategic defense deployment might have on the demand for scientific and engineering resources. Our assessment indicates that full-scale deployment of an SDI system will require between 130,000 and 180,000 scientists and engineers each year over a ten-year period. This is about twice the number of specialists required each year during the most intense period of the NASA program. The hypothetical SDI deployment would require about 5.1 percent of the scientific and engineering talent pool between 2001 and 2010. In comparison, the NASA effort required 4.1 percent on average between 1961 and 1968 (Figure 8-1).

This analysis assumes that a preliminary "alpha" defense system costing $160 billion is deployed between 1995 and 2000, and the remaining components of a "gamma" system costing $600 billion are deployed between 2001 and 2010 (Figure 8-2). As noted earlier, this cost estimate by Blechman and Utgoff is probably optimistic. The hypothetical program is deployed over fifteen years in keeping with the SDIO position that a strategic defense system would be deployed in phases. By comparison, the NASA project spent roughly

Table 8-3. Estimated Engineering, Scientific, and Technical SDI Employment, 1986 and 1991.

	Scientists		
	Share of Total (percent)	Employment	
Industry		1986	1991
Radio and TV communication equipment	2.3	117	352
Management, consulting, and labs	5.3	382	1,333
Complete guided missiles	2.7	76	217
Nonprofit organizations and miscellaneous profit services	0.3	23	83
Electric measuring instruments	1.2	40	122
Electronic computing equipment	6.6	123	516
Wholesale trade	0.8	21	67
Aircraft	1.9	25	67
Real estate	0.0	0	0
Measuring and control instruments	1.2	16	49
Hotels and lodging places	0.0	0	0
Eating and drinking places	0.0	0	0
Electronic components, NEC	1.4	13	46
Electric utilities	1.3	4	13
Inorganic and organic chemistry	4.1	14	43
Computer and data processing	4.0	53	185
Other motor vehicles	1.2	4	13
Gas utilities	1.3	2	5
Aircraft engines and engine parts	1.9	9	23
Engineering and scientific instruments	1.2	8	26
Twenty industry totals[a]	2.1/2.2	930	3,160
All other industries[a]	2.1/2.2	462	1,561
Total[a]	2.1/2.2%	1,392	4,721

a. Percentages are for 1986 and 1991, respectively.
Source: CEP estimates and U.S. Department of Labor, Bureau of Labor Statistics, "Employment by Industry and Occupation, 1982 and Projected 1985 Alternatives," unpublished data.

Table 8-3. continued

	Engineers			Technicians			Total Set Employment	
Share of Total (percent)	Employment 1986	1991	Share of Total (percent)	Employment 1986	1991	Share of Total (percent)	Employment 1986	1991
15.0	765	2,296	8.6	438	1,316	25.9	1,320	3,964
3.4	245	855	4.6	332	1,157	13.3	959	3,345
25.9	733	2,081	9.6	272	771	38.2	1,081	3,069
0.1	8	28	0.4	30	111	0.8	61	222
7.7	254	781	7.6	251	771	16.5	545	1,674
11.9	222	930	9.4	175	734	27.9	520	2,180
0.8	21	67	2.0	52	167	3.6	94	301
10.9	143	385	5.4	71	191	18.2	239	643
0.0	0	0	0.0	0	0	0.0	0	0
7.7	106	314	7.6	104	310	16.5	226	673
0.0	0	0	0.0	0	0	0.0	0	0
0.0	0	0	0.0	0	0	0.0	0	0
7.2	68	237	7.7	73	253	16.3	154	536
4.8	14	45	5.6	16	53	11.7	34	111
5.6	19	58	5.9	20	61	15.6	53	162
12.2	162	564	16.4	218	758	32.6	433	1,507
7.7	29	86	7.6	28	85	16.5	61	184
4.8	6	18	5.6	7	21	11.7	15	44
10.9	52	133	5.1	24	62	17.9	85	218
7.7	52	164	7.6	52	162	16.5	112	352
6.2	2,899	9,042	4.9/4.8	2,163	6,983	13.6/13.2	5,992	19,185
6.2	1,452	4,400	4.9/4.8	1,078	3,406	13.6/13.2	2,992	9,367
6.2%	4,351	13,442	4.9/4.8%	3,241	10,389	13.6/13.2%	8,984	28,552

Figure 8-1. NASA and SDI Labor Requirements (*share of total U.S. scientists and engineers*).

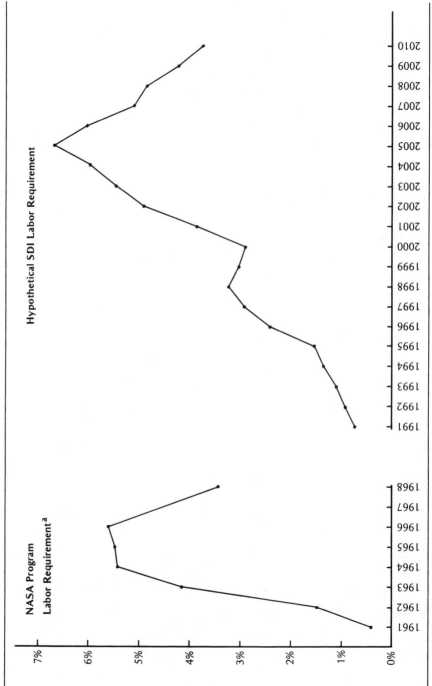

a. Based on figures from Arnold Levine, *Managing NASA in the Apollo Era* (Washington, D.C.: National Aeronautics and Space Administration

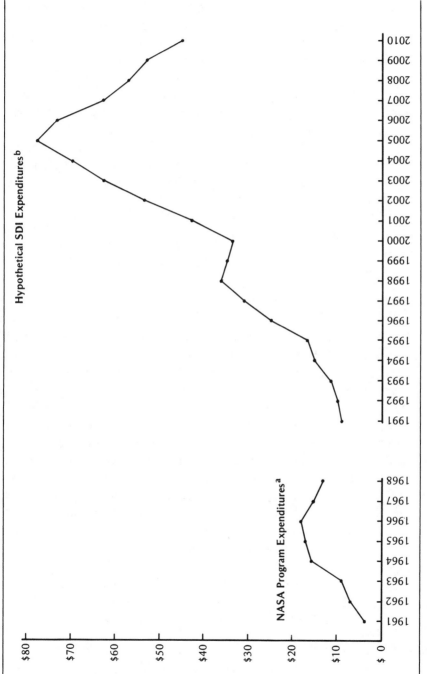

a. Based on figures from the *Federal Budget*, Fiscal Years 1963–1971 (Washington, D.C.: U.S. Government Printing Office, 1962–1970).

b. Based on estimates from Barry Blechman and Victor Utgoff, Johns Hopkins Foreign Policy Institute.

$91 billion (in constant 1987 dollars) between 1961 and 1968. Our forecast further assumes that the mix of scientists and engineers required for deployment does not dramatically differ from that of the R&D stage. This assumption may overstate the scientific talent requirement but it almost certainly understates the demand for engineering labor. Finally, our estimate of the total pool of scientists and engineers was extrapolated at a moderate growth rate from an estimate by the National Science Foundation of the pool in 1987.

In view of the likely labor demands of an SDI deployment, the economic implications of such a program should be carefully considered before proceeding. Would this program requirement come on top of the current military demand for technical talent? Can the commercial market compete successfully in world markets without such a large portion of our most talented scientists and engineers for such a sustained period? These are the types of questions that must be answered before undertaking this technological megaproject.

SDI AND COMMERCIAL SPINOFFS

Even if SDI proceeds to deployment, consuming hundreds of billions of dollars and employing a substantial proportion of the nation's scientific and engineering personnel, its drain on the economy could be mitigated or even neutralized if the program yields substantial commercial spinoffs that improve the competitiveness and productivity of U.S. civilian industries. The SDI Organization has opened an Education and Civil Applications Office to explore spinoff possibilities and educate the public about these potential benefits of strategic defense research. In the words of Capt. Chuck Houston of the new office, "the American taxpayer deserves some return that he or she can look at, and see that something other than defense can come out of SDI."[30]

Captain Houston acknowledges that "there aren't a whole lot of applications yet," citing contracts with ten universities to investigate the medical uses of free electron lasers (FELs) as the most promising area so far. Even here, the adaptation for civilian use may take some time. "The technology is still quite new, and has mostly physics applications," says Houston. "The FEL is quite large—not the size of a refrigerator, but the size of a room—and the mobility is very limited. There are only a few of them available in the United States. It's not yet available in stores—you can't just go and pick one up."[31]

Over time, however, former SDIO chief scientist Gerold Yonas argues that the program offers a broad range of potential commercial spinoffs:

> For the civilian economy, there are reasonable expectations that SDI research in lasers, particle beams, sensors, computer systems and software, and hardening will find applications in high strength, high temperature and wear-resistant materials, nondestructive testing, optics and holography, pattern recognition and artificial vision, faster and more sophisticated computers, improved commercial air traffic management, and automated methods for manufacturing high technology components at low cost.[32]

The difficulties of accurately predicting commercial spinoffs of a major R&D effort like SDI are daunting at this stage. Nonetheless, several features of this program and other related military R&D efforts indicate that the likely spinoffs will be relatively limited.

Does Government R&D Stimulate Productivity Growth?

Government research and development is justified primarily by the assumption that private industry is not likely to invest in activities, such as expanding basic knowledge and protecting the nation, that do not have direct commercial payoffs or are too expensive for one company to undertake alone. By funding basic research and making early use of innovations, government expands the nation's technological base and thus contributes to economic health. Numerous studies, employing a variety of methodologies, have attempted to substantiate this assumption empirically.

The space program has probably been the most carefully analyzed government R&D effort. Motivated in part by a desire to strengthen its position in the yearly budget battle, the National Aeronautics and Space Administration commissioned a variety of studies examining the economic benefits of space science. The results of these studies, and the responses they stimulated, clearly bear on our understanding of how SDI will affect the national economy.

In one of the most important of these studies, in 1965 Chase Econometrics examined the relationship between NASA R&D expenditures and productivity growth.[33] Through statistical testing, Chase concluded that NASA R&D was strongly associated with rising productivity between 1960 and 1974. For every $1 million spent by NASA in 1976, Chase predicted productivity improvements resulting from the expenditure would enhance economic output by \$23 million in 1984.[34] This is clearly quite a high rate of return on a R&D investment.

The General Accounting Office (GAO) took issue with the Chase study, noting that its conclusion "would indicate an enormous impact on the economy. The literal interpretation is that, if NASA had spent nothing in R&D, productivity would have declined in the United States between 1965 and 1974. That is, NASA R&D is given credit for all of the nation's productivity growth, and more besides."[35] In examining Chase's statistical analysis, the GAO found that the results were very sensitive to the assumptions made. For example, if the time period and variables used in the statistical testing were altered slightly, the relationship between NASA R&D and productivity became weaker and results were statistically insignificant.[36]

Academic studies by economists not associated with the space program cast even greater doubt on the Chase conclusion. A series of econometric studies have found that while industry-financed R&D is significantly related to productivity, government-supported efforts apparently are not.[37] Moreover, industries that are major recipients of federal R&D funds have the lowest productivity return on R&D from both sources.

There are at least three possible explanations for these findings. First, by lowering the marginal cost to the firm of performing R&D, government R&D may encourage the firm to undertake more R&D.[38] (In fact, most of the government's R&D dollars are spent in R&D-intensive industries.[39]) But when a single factor of production is increased, marginal returns on that factor will eventually decline, since the most profitable opportunities will already have been fully explored.

A second theory is that most of the government's R&D goes for developing products for its own use, such as aircraft and communications equipment, instead of improving the production process for commercial goods. The distinction between product and process improvements is important. Product innovations are normally useful only in the specific market for a given product. Process innovations diffuse throughout the economy.[40] This explanation suggests that government development work does not necessarily improve the productivity of commercial enterprises.

Finally, federal efforts may "crowd out" commercial research. A study by Frank Lichtenberg of Columbia University found that among industrial firms, increases in federal R&D were associated with *reductions* in company-financed research. His statistical analysis suggests that "a federally funded increase of 100 R&D scientists and engineers this year will result in a reduction of company-sponsored employment of 39 within a year, essentially no change next year, and an increase of 7 in two years."[41]

Clearly the statistical evidence is mixed on the proposition that federal R&D stimulates productivity growth. Without specific evidence that a particular government R&D effort will aid development in certain areas, there is no strong empirical basis for assuming that beneficial spinoffs will occur—at least not at a level adequate to justify a large investment. Indeed, the president's own Commission on Industrial Competitiveness recently concluded that "in the years following World War II, federally funded R&D projects were important catalysts to commercial industries such as aircraft and electronics. Today the roles have been reversed in many technologies. Industry is the principal initiator of technological advances—such as state-of-the-art VLSI (very large-scale integration) electronics—and Government is a net user."[42]

One cannot assume a specific government project will either help or hinder private sector technological growth. The burden of proof clearly resides with those who would justify government projects on the basis of their commercial impact. Unless the supporters of a specific project can demonstrate how it will help, we should assume that the effect is at best neutral.

SDI: Spinoff or Spin In?

How does SDI fit this general pattern of distribution of government R&D activities? A key factor affecting spinoffs from any government research program is the mix of basic and applied research involved in the project. Basic research allows more room for innovation, is conducted in an open environment conducive to the dissemination of research findings, and is generally considered to have more potential for commercial spinoffs. In contrast, applied research is mission oriented, frequently restricts disclosure of its findings, and usually results in fewer commercial spinoffs because of these restrictions.

SDI research funding has accelerated at a time when the Pentagon already controls a growing share of the nation's R&D funding. Under the Reagan administration, the Pentagon's share of government funding for research has risen from 50 percent in 1980 to 73 percent in 1986. DOD's role is particularly strong in certain key fields critical to high technology growth: more than half of all federal research in mathematics and computer sciences is Pentagon sponsored, as is over 80 percent of research in electrical engineering (see Table 8–4). At the same time federal support for civilian R&D programs declined by roughly 20 percent in real terms between 1981 and 1985.[43] If SDI continues on its current funding path, federal R&D funding will be tipped further toward military projects.

Current DOD-sponsored R&D is heavily weighted toward development efforts, which are least likely to yield civilian spinoffs. In FY 1985, 90 percent of DOD R&D was devoted to development of specific weapons systems, while less than 3 percent went for basic research. By contrast, basic research accounts for more than 37 percent of civilian R&D programs sponsored by the federal government, development for only 30 percent.[44] As the Congressional Budget Office has noted, "the predominance of development within the DOD R&D budget has been increasing. . . . The smallest increase has been in the category of 'technology base,' which has the greatest relevance for civilian industrial activities."[45] In effect, the growth of DOD R&D has shifted the entire federal R&D budget away from basic research toward development efforts, to the detriment of the future civilian technology base.

SDI is sure to accelerate this trend. Gerold Yonas has asserted that "about one third" of current SDI funds "will be spent to develop the technology base."[46] If so, SDI would be much more oriented toward basic research than is the average DOD R&D program, although still lagging the average federal civilian R&D program in this regard. However, SDI research may already be moving away from this basic research orientation. Independent estimates indicate that 49 percent of the FY 1987 SDI budget request was for experiments.[47] The three program elements that represent the bulk of SDI funding—surveillance, acquisition, tracking, and kill assessment; directed energy weapons; and kinetic energy weapons—have emphasized hardware demonstrations and prototype development in their budget plans for the next five years.[48]

Table 8-4. Pentagon Share of Federal Research Funding, by Major Field of Science, FY 1986.

Field	Funding (thousand dollars)		DOD Share of Total (percent)
	Total Federal	DOD	
Mathematics/ computer sciences	$ 635,279	$ 367,684	57.9
Mathematics	191,545	61,679	32.2
Computer sciences	293,113	168,808	57.6
Math and computer sciences not else- where classified	150,621	137,197	91.1
Engineering	3,537,580	1,609,573	45.5
Aeronautical	780,604	248,175	31.8
Astronautical	334,521	68,838	20.6
Chemical	136,750	39,259	28.7
Civil	215,669	64,334	29.8
Electrical	688,046	572,610	83.2
Mechanical	266,150	190,539	71.6
Metallurgy and materials	375,675	219,398	58.4
Other engineering	740,165	206,420	27.9
Environmental sciences	1,315,830	274,123	20.8
Atmospheric	473,033	95,925	20.3
Geological	377,141	61,188	16.2
Oceanography	381,153	83,479	21.9
Environmental sciences not elsewhere classified	84,503	33,531	39.7
Psychology	304,487	116,804	38.4
Physical sciences	3,040,143	637,248	20.9
Astronomy	437,321	19,221	4.4
Chemistry	622,665	159,829	25.7
Physics	1,822,802	339,548	18.6
Other physical sciences	157,355	118,650	75.4
Life sciences	6,039,916	272,510	4.5
Social sciences	417,260	7,445	1.8

Source: National Science Foundation, Division of Science Resources Studies, *Federal Obligations for Research by Agency and Detailed Field of Science, Fiscal Years 1967-1986* (Washington, D.C.: NSF, 1985).

A further factor likely to limit commercial spinoffs from SDI is the program's extreme performance requirements and "gold-plated" technologies. While military research in the post-World War II era helped usher in the age of computers and commercial airliners, the requirements for operations in space are so different from those on earth that there is little likelihood of similar breakthroughs spinning off from SDI research. In fact, civilian spinoffs from military spending have become harder to find as defense moves into space and as weapons become highly complex and expensive. Such overdesign, often the rule rather than the exception, produces little benefit for the cost-conscious civilian market.

Some of the work performed within SDI will have commercial value, for example, very high speed integrated circuits (VHSIC) are being developed for the near real-time data processing required by a strategic defense system. Yet it is hard to imagine private uses of such major SDI technologies as high-energy lasers, particle beams, large optics, or infrared sensors. Hans Peter Durr, director of Munich's Werner Heisenberg Institute for Physics, has raised this question with respect to SDI: "The ability to forge a sword may be useful for making plowshares—but do we need the ability to burn holes in metal at a range of 1,800 miles?"[49]

The third major obstacle to spinoffs from SDI is the aura of secrecy and security restrictions within which the research is likely to be carried out. Those SDI innovations that do have commercial potential—such as new software languages, next-generation computers, and new integrated circuit designs—may be classified for years to come. The Pentagon has already begun to control the dissemination of scientific findings in the name of national security. This trend will clearly reduce the possibility of spinoffs from SDI. Pentagon restrictions on disclosure of information about VHSIC chips, for example, are so tight that "close-up, head-on photographs of VHSIC chips cannot be published because of concerns that the Soviets might be able to determine the chip architecture and reverse engineer the device from such data."[50]

The Reagan administration has issued new guidelines to federal agencies restricting the release of a broad range of government data that are unclassified but considered sensitive.[51] Already, the DOD has restricted access to several civilian engineering meetings, including the March 1985 meeting of the Society of Photo-Optical Engineers, at which unclassified research on high-energy lasers was being presented. Restraining access to technological advances hinders their commercial development by industry. Manufacturers of VHSIC chips, for instance, may have to obtain security clearance for all employees, visitors, and even some suppliers. Moreover, chip designs used by the military may have to be reworked before they can be used in civilian products. One manufacturer asks, "How much must I change my VHSIC gate-array design to escape security restrictions?"[52] In contrast, programs like those of Japan's Ministry of International Trade and Industry (MITI) and France's European Research and Coordinating Agency (Eureka) program, developed for the purpose of advancing high technology, are unimpeded by security restrictions and benefit from easy diffusion to the commercial sector. While U.S. industry waits for access to this restricted information, France, Japan, and other competitors will be forging ahead with private and civilian programs to sharpen their competitive position in high technology markets.

Finally, there may be "negative spinoffs" from SDI research. That is, some areas of technology or equipment designs may be developed or maintained in civilian use despite flaws in safety, performance, or cost-effectiveness because military research subsidies have pushed development in a particular direction that would not have been pursued if the goal was commercial technological development. John P. Holdren and F. Bailey Green argue that "the pressurized water reactor (PWR), developed to power nuclear submarines and transferred to the civilian sector as the mainstay of the U.S. commercial nuclear power program" is one such negative spinoff.

> The PWR's high power density and very high-pressure coolant—results of criteria appropriate for the submarine application—make it inherently more vulnerable to accidents, earthquakes, and sabotage than are a number of other reactor designs that might have materialized from a strictly civilian reactor program. Tacked-on safety systems motivated by these vulnerabilities have greatly inflated the cost of PWRs and their close relatives, boiling water reactors, and it is possible to suppose that the commercial nuclear industry would be better off today if it had done without the spinoff of military reactor technology.[53]

While a strict balance sheet cannot be calculated at this early point in the SDI program, the details of its content and structure that are already known suggest it is extremely unlikely to spawn substantial civilian spinoffs, and it will certainly not generate enough commercial activity to "pay for itself." At best, the likely commercial effect of SDI will be comparable to the limited impact of military R&D on the electronics industry, in the view of the Office of Technology Assessment: "Although there have been many examples of secondary and indirect impacts, in no case can *recent* military spending in the United States, France, or the United Kingdom be shown to have stimulated commercial developments in a major way."[54]

SDI: A DE FACTO INDUSTRIAL POLICY?

Although some SDI supporters claim the program "will lay the foundation for an educational-vocational renaissance for the American labor force," there is serious concern among economic policy experts that the growth of strategic defense research could place the Pentagon in charge of the nation's de facto industrial policy, thereby distorting the entire direction of U.S. high technology development.[55]

Robert Reich, industrial policy expert and author of *The Next American Frontier*, estimates that the SDI Organization alone will control roughly 20 percent of U.S. high technology venture capital in the next four years, with potentially disastrous results for U.S. competitiveness. The military will be the principal sponsor of research in key areas such as very high speed integrated circuits, advanced computers, and optics. According to Reich, "The problem is that never before on this scale have we entrusted so much technological development to the Pentagon in so short a time. A handful of Pentagon officials are pre-empting scientific resources and picking winners and losers of the technology race, with large defense contractors advising them."[56]

In contrast to the United States, Japan funds civilian high technology research directly through MITI. This policy helps explain Japan's edge over the United States in the development of affordable, high-quality commercial electronics and computer products. Numerous studies also indicate a strong correlation between high levels of military spending and relatively low levels of economic performance. Since the Japanese government spends less than one-sixth of what the United States spends on military R&D, it can spend proportionately more for civilian research through MITI without straining its budget.[57]

The Japanese government is cooperating directly with civilian industry, through MITI, in developing its next-generation civilian products in the critical field of information technology. Japan's very large scale integration (VLSI) semiconductor project, initiated in 1976, is designed to develop state-of-the-art technology in logic and memory circuits for civilian application. The government is supplying 40 percent of the research funding for this venture, in which Toshiba, Hitachi, Mitsubishi, and other major Japanese electronics firms are participating.[58]

The latest example of Japanese government-business cooperation in high technology research and development is the "fifth-generation" artificial intelligence computer project, in which MITI and the eight leading Japanese computer companies have invested 100 billion yen. Robert S. Ozaki, an expert on technology development in Japan, argues that the United States' overreliance on military R&D puts it at a competitive disadvantage:

> In the U.S., where the government heavily subsidizes defense-related R&D, private firms are allowed to make commercial application of what was initially defense-oriented research; on the other hand, joint government-business financing of nondefense projects is generally considered illegitimate. Freed from this sort of ideological muddle, MITI has been participating in joint high-technology research with private producers in information electronics, an area that it envisions will be playing a strategic role in forthcoming years.[59]

Some economic analysts see no particular problem in this dichotomy between the U.S. and Japanese methods of developing new technologies. Wolfgang Demisch, an analyst at First Boston Corp., says "'Star Wars' is the American answer to MITI."[60] Furthermore, he argues, this is the only politically feasible approach: "The U.S. has no political consensus for industrial policy or technology development except for issues dealing with national security."[61]

The problem with relying on military R&D to lead the way in technology development is twofold, as Ann Markusen, professor of city and regional planning at the University of California at Berkeley, has argued. First, it condemns important industries like steel, automobiles, and metalworking to technological neglect. Markusen points out that the steel industry "has been denied $15 *million* by the Reagan Administration for its project of 'leapfrog technology;' U.S. high-tech industries, on the other hand, will enjoy the benefits of $30 *billion* in research outlays under SDI."[62]

Moreover, in those areas that do receive substantial military R&D funds, it is not at all clear that U.S. industry can compete by using spinoffs in areas where Japan and other industrial competitors are investing directly. For example, while U.S. artificial intelligence research is focused heavily on developing battle management systems (for strategic defense and other military purposes) at the expense of "intelligent libraries" and computer-assisted education, Japanese research in artificial intelligence is focused directly at improving business and consumer productivity and improving the delivery of social services.[63]

Perhaps the greatest danger is that the Star Wars vision will divert attention, leadership, and energy from other pressing national problems. Economist Lester Thurow has summed up this argument eloquently: "In many ways, a prosperous civilian economy is our best military defense. The real economic case against Star Wars is that the civilian economy—battered by trade deficits that have no parallel in human history—could well use some of the time, attention, and money now being lavished on Star Wars."[64]

SOVIET STRATEGIC DEFENSE PROGRAMS
A Decade Behind the United States

Our government has kept us in a perpetual state of fear—kept us in a continuous stampede of patriotic fervor—with the cry of grave national emergency. . . . Always there has been some terrible evil to gobble us up if we did not blindly rally behind it by furnishing the exorbitant sums demanded. Yet, in retrospect these disasters seem never to have happened, seem never to have been quite real.

> —*General Douglas MacArthur*
> *July 30, 1957*

The Reagan administration has justified its pursuit of a vigorous SDI program in part by claims that the Soviet Union will cooperate in establishing a defensive regime in space and in part by claims that the Soviets are already pursuing a similar program. Indeed, some officials point to a "defense gap" between the level of U.S. and Soviet SDI research and claim that the Soviets are ahead in certain key technology fields. They compound this with the alleged Soviet violations of the 1972 ABM Treaty. The administration concludes that SDI is an idea whose time has come. This fear of a Soviet Star Wars that could disarm America, however, is greatly exaggerated.

The USSR is pursuing its own version of a strategic defense program along radically different lines from that of the United States. In addition to the many research problems common to both countries, the Soviet Union must confront unique technical and logistic barriers to success. Its computer and sensing and tracking technologies put it perhaps a decade behind the United States. These problems, together with the different strategic motivations underlying its program, have led the USSR to emphasize off-the-shelf technologies over exotic new initiatives and to develop demonstration systems (however ineffectual) in tandem rather than as a successor to research efforts.

The Soviet Union appears to be directing its attention toward two distinct options in its strategic defense program. A great deal of effort is currently devoted to the development and small-scale deployment of conventional-technology ballistic missile defense (BMD) systems and antisatellite (ASAT) weapons, primarily in the form of surface-to-air missiles. The second approach explores new technologies such as lasers, particle beams, and kinetic energy weapons.

SOVIET CONVENTIONAL TECHNOLOGIES

Ballistic Missile Defense Systems

President Reagan's 1983 speech was by no means the beginning of strategic defense research. Rather he attempted to accelerate and tie together a variety of existing programs, some of which date back to about 1946. An independent Soviet ballistic missile defense organization was first established under the auspices of the air defense command in 1958, according to defense analyst David Rivkin.[1] In the same year the U.S. Defense Advanced Research Projects Agency (DARPA) initiated a particle beam program, code named SEE-SAW, intended to act as a ground-based ABM system. By 1961, the USSR was aggressively pursuing a BMD development program based on ground radar stations and surface-to-air interceptor missiles at the Sary Shagan missile testing site on Lake Balkash in Central Asia. This program culminated in the deployment of very primitive BMD systems around Moscow and Leningrad by the mid-1960s.[2]

The most conspicuous product of the early Soviet BMD systems experiments is the Galosh system surrounding Moscow, also known as the ABM-1B system. Based on a coordinated network of large radars located around the USSR's periphery, each known as a Hen House, it provides early warning and target tracking information to the main complex near Moscow.[3] A large radar at the central site, called the Dog House, then provides battle management data for the entire interceptor force. The Dog House was supplemented in the 1970s by the Cat House, a similar huge phased-array radar that also tracks a number of targets simultaneously.[4] The interceptor system itself consists of four batteries, each with two identical installations of three target tracking and acquisition radars and eight Galosh interceptor missiles. These missiles, larger than the U.S. Minuteman ICBMs, are exoatmospheric nuclear armed interceptors with a range estimated at 200 miles.[5]

The Galosh BMD system is vulnerable in several respects. Hen House radars constitute extremely large, soft targets that may be neutralized either by a direct nuclear hit or by the blinding effect of a nearby nuclear blast. While the Hen House system may be able to transmit some tracking data before its demise, loss of the Cat House and Dog House installations (both vulnerable to these same tactics) could critically degrade the entire system's ability to track and assign targets to the batteries for a coordinated response. Because the battery-level radars appear to have very limited tracking capabilities, they are vulnerable to saturation either by a large-scale attack or by decoys (dummy warheads) and chaff (thin metal strips that reflect radar waves).[6]

In the late 1970s, the USSR embarked on a program to modernize its conventional-technologies BMD systems. It appears to be replacing the aging Galosh system with a new generation of interceptors called the SH-08, often compared to the decade-old U.S. Sprint hypersonic missiles. In conjunction with a new phased-array radar, Soviet missiles appear to form part of a transportable and rapidly deployable ABM system called the ABM-X-3. Because of their high acceleration rates—they are reportedly capable of a 100g launch acceleration with speeds exceeding Mach 5 (five times the speed of sound)—these missiles allow the Soviets more time to discriminate targets from chaff and decoys before committing to a given target. The Soviet Union appears also to have added a new radar to the system at Pushkino (near Moscow) and may be preparing to replace the Galosh missiles themselves with a new, large interceptor missile designated SH-04. This will serve as an exoatmospheric complement to the shorter-range capabilities of the mobile system. Some experts contend the new ABM-X-3 system components "are equivalent to American ABM technology of the early to mid-1960s" and "share many of the technical limitations and vulnerabilities of the U.S. Nike-Zeus."[7]

An apt summary of the Soviet position in conventional BMD technologies is offered by former CIA deputy director of intelligence Sayre Stevens: "While the Soviet BMD program has momentum and has made significant technological progress over the past decade, it really has only reached the level of technology that was available to the U.S. ten years ago. The major difference is that the Soviet technology is much closer to application."[8]

Antisatellite Systems

U.S. interest in ASATs began with the Air Force Project SAINT, which ran from 1956 to 1962, probably predating Soviet efforts. After a lull, the Pentagon in 1975 redoubled its efforts to develop a sophisticated and versatile ASAT system of its own, which appears to be considerably more effective than the Soviet systems.

The Soviet Union has the only fully deployed ASAT system in existence, centered at Tyuratam, in Kazakhstan, 1,500 miles southeast of Moscow. It relies on the cumbersome technology of the 1960s. The Soviet ASAT program began in 1963 or 1964, but the first tests of interceptors against target satellites commenced in 1967. The ASAT rocket uses a booster identical to the booster in the obsolete liquid-fueled SS-9 ICBM, to loft a 4,400- to 6,000-pound warhead into near-earth orbit.[9]

The Soviet Union has conducted two series of ASAT tests since 1967. The first, running from October 1968 to December 1971, included seven interceptor launchings. The sequence of events in all tests was generally the same. First a target satellite was launched into orbit. Soon after, the interceptor was launched and, after one or two orbits, it attempted to intercept the target satellite. The interceptor then exploded, either near the target or, following the interception maneuver, some distance away. Five of these first seven tests were probable successes, according to U.S. officials.[10]

The Soviet Union began its second round of ASAT tests in February 1976. This series, which continued until June 1982, included thirteen interception attempts. There were no major departures from the sequence of events typifying the earlier tests. The two major technical changes were the incorporation of a more maneuverable low-thrust engine on the interceptor and the use of optical infrared sensor systems in six of the interceptors to supplement the standard radar detectors used earlier. Nine of these thirteen tests failed, including all six interception tests using the optical-infrared sensor systems.[11]

The Soviet ASAT program does not currently appear to present a very serious threat to U.S. satellites. For one thing, the Soviet system is extremely cumbersome and inflexible. It uses a large booster for launching, with only one set of facilities (at Tyuratam) equipped for launching. The low fuel capacity of the hunter-killer satellite and consequent limitations on its maneuvering capabilities restrict its interceptions to times when the target passes almost directly over the Tyuratam launch site.[12] Furthermore, as the twenty tests showed, the Soviet system is far from reliable. This low reliability in carefully planned trials cannot offer much promise for success under war-time conditions. Finally, all ASAT tests conducted by the Soviet Union occurred in orbits below an altitude of 1,100 miles and with inclinations between sixty-two and sixty-six degrees. The only U.S. satellites in low orbits with similar inclinations are ocean reconnaissance satellites and a few communications satellites. Because they follow highly elliptical orbits, the latter would be moving approximately 1,000 miles per hour faster than the Soviet ASAT at potential intercept altitudes and would therefore be difficult to intercept.[13]

The United States is far ahead of the USSR in ASAT capabilities. It conducted the world's first ASAT demonstration in 1959 and in 1963 began developing two ground-based ASAT systems, one using the Nike-Zeus ABM and the other using the Thor intermediate-range ballistic missile (IRBM). Only a few were deployed, but the nuclear-tipped Thor system remained operational until 1975.[14] Between 1964 and 1968 the U.S. Air Defense Command conducted sixteen ASAT tests, under the project name SQUANTO TERROR, at Johnston Island, southwest of Hawaii. Using a Thor missile carrying a simulated nuclear warhead, the system attacked debris and dead U.S. satellites at altitudes up to 700 nautical miles. Since 1976, the U.S. Air Force has been developing and testing an F-15 aircraft-launched miniature homing intercept vehicle for ASAT use. This small (30 X 30 centimeters) infrared-guided, direct ascent missile-mounted vehicle is capable of speeds exceeding 30,000 miles per hour. This means it is at least 7,000 miles per hour faster than any earth-orbiting satellite. The interception is made via collision to destroy the target satellite.[15]

The Soviet Union continues to emphasize the conventional strategic defense that began about twenty years ago. Its efforts appear to be focused on BMD systems, and there is no evidence that any ASAT vehicle modernization program is in the offing. Neither its BMD nor its ASAT systems represent a major threat to U.S. military programs. Both test results and systems characteristics suggest that the Soviet systems are rather unreliable and ineffective in the execution of their missions. Even with the Galosh system enhancements, it is difficult to imagine that Soviet BMD capabilities could repel a determined U.S. attack.

Thus far the Soviet Union's technology lags about eight to ten years behind U.S. capabilities in these missions. The new generation of Soviet BMD interceptors is considered by most experts, both within and outside the Pentagon, to resemble the Sprint ABM missiles, which the United States abandoned ten years ago as expensive and ineffective. The Soviet ASAT systems seem similar to, if more accurate than, the U.S. Nike-Zeus and Thor systems of the early to mid-1960s. Certainly the Soviets have no demonstrated technologies to rival the versatility and effectiveness of the new U.S. airborne miniature homing intercept ASAT vehicles.

Whereas U.S. weapons systems are characteristically not deployed until they have been perfected, the Soviet military seems more inclined to deploy a system relatively early and correct its shortcomings through field modifications later on. The Soviets are also more reluctant to retire aging and obsolete armaments. As a result, they now possess the only operational ASAT system and BMD network, albeit rudimentary ones. Although this deployment strategy may have won the Soviet Union a little of the international prestige for which it yearns, it comes at the cost of a sizable investment in an already obsolete technology. Moreover, reluctance to write off these sunk costs by abandoning the present systems may lock the USSR into a technology of dubious long-term value while inhibiting exploration of more promising although riskier avenues. The only advantage of the Soviet system may be that it serves as a foundation for an extensive and thorough testing program that may contribute some incremental improvements.

NEW TECHNOLOGIES APPEAR

Like the United States, the Soviet Union is aggressively exploring some relatively exotic technological options in its pursuit of strategic defense. Although information on Soviet programs in lasers, particle beams, and antisatellite weaponry is difficult to come by and often untrustworthy, some facts are emerging.

Soviet ground-based gas-dynamic lasers capable of damaging or destroying optical sensors of low-orbit U.S. reconnaissance satellites may already exist.[16] There are also reports of a short-wavelength, multishot excimer laser that, within a few years, may be able to strike satellites in orbits as high as 3,000 miles.[17] It is believed the Soviet Union may deploy several ground-based ASAT lasers over the next ten years.

Ground-based lasers, in both BMD and ASAT modes, have an advantage over space-based systems: size and weight are not critical constraints. They suffer, however, from problems of bending, dissipation, and energy attrition as they pass through the clouds and atmosphere. For this reason, airborne and space-based laser systems appear very attractive. President Reagan's special advisor on arms control, Paul Nitze, predicts the Soviet Union could have deployable ASAT space-based lasers by the mid-1990s and airborne systems before then.[18] Even if the USSR can solve the serious logistic and theoretical problems of designing an adequate power source compact enough for space use, other problems will remain. It will still be forced to confront its present inadequacies in precision tracking and aiming, rapid retargeting, and early warning technologies, which are required for any space-based BMD system. In ASAT applications, space-borne lasers may be vulnerable to comparatively simple countermeasures, such as protecting a satellite with small, primitive exploding ASAT missiles or fitting reflectors on U.S. satellites.

The Soviet Union has been active in particle beam technology since the 1950s and has been researching the feasibility of space-basing modes of this weapons since the 1970s.[19] Analysts Longstreth, Pike, and Rhinelander contend that most Soviet work in this area has been basic research, and no tangible weapons applications seem imminent.[20] According to Nitze, other areas of Soviet interest include radio frequency ASAT weaponry and kinetic energy weapons. But no testing of systems based on these principles is expected in the next fifteen years.

The Soviet new technologies program is probably no further ahead in any meaningful sense than its American counterpart. The Soviet Union has made some provocative and impressive strides in bringing the exotic technologies closer to prototype systems. Still, such a move has its own costs. Rapid development and deployment programs are often more expensive than selective and gradually accelerating research. Soviet emphasis on premature development or coproduction, therefore, runs the risk of fostering large investments in technology that further research might ultimately prove to be unsatisfactory. Moreover, given the inertia apparent in the Soviet acquisition and production processes, an inferior technological path could be locked in for a few years while the government tries to recoup early sunk costs.

The Soviet Union also appears to be emphasizing the more conspicuous, technologically prestigious components of a strategic defense system while devoting fewer resources to the essential underpinnings of an integrated overall system. In particular, the USSR is at a serious disadvantage relative to the United States in electrooptical sensing, surveillance and tracking, optics, high-speed signal processing, battle management and communications, microelectronics, computer hardware and software, and possibly even rocketmotor and fuel technologies. No amount of development in lasers and other weapons technology will be sufficient for the implementation of an effective integrated defense system until shortcomings in these areas are remedied.

Overall the Soviet Union appears able to design and even test systems at the level of basic scientific research or in one-step-removed applications. But its inadequacies are reflected in an inability to produce successful integrated systems or to mimic sophisticated U.S. applications of scientific innovations. Many small-scale subsystems and demonstration prototypes are developed, but there is no evidence of an integrated systems capability that combines early warning, sensing, battle management, engagement, and overall electronic data processing with real-time coordination functions into a single unit (i.e., one that could execute the tasks quickly enough to be useful in a real setting).

All in all, the USSR lags behind the United States by about ten years both in conventional strategic defense technologies and in the vital integrative technologies required to meld fragments of systems into a coordinated, functioning unit. The Soviets are about five to eight years behind in most of the more exotic technical areas, except particle beam technology, where Soviet theoretical and basic research may closely parallel the capabilities of the United States. However, the serious problems that still plague all attempts to move from theory to a practical weapons system may ultimately render moot the race for supremacy in this technology.

HOW IMPORTANT IS TECHNOLOGICAL CAPABILITY?

The Soviet Union's recent experience with SDI-like programs will no doubt play a major role in determining the characteristics of its future ASAT and BMD efforts. A second factor, however, is likely to be equally influential. The relative adequacy of the Soviet techno-logical base, with its particular strengths and weaknesses, will deter-mine not only how fast the USSR progresses in advanced technolo-gies strategic defenses but also which directions will be emphasized. For example, Soviet difficulties with heavy rocket booster develop-ment might limit the exploitation of space-based technologies. Infra-red sensor problems might result in a relative emphasis on radar-based detection. This bias, coupled with the USSR's chronic prob-lems with both signal processing and computer speeds, could pre-clude the development of a coordinated nationwide defense sys-tem and increase interest in autonomous pockets of terminal stage defenses.

The U.S. Department of Defense's annual *Program for Research, Development and Acquisition* compares U.S. and Soviet achievement in twenty of the most important areas of basic technology for mili-tary uses (Table 9-1). These DOD data indicate that the USSR does not lead in any of these technological areas. The two nations are rated as approximately equal in five areas, including conventional and nuclear warheads, and directed energy. The United States leads in fifteen technologies. Its lead is diminishing in six, stable in eight, and increasing in computer and software technology.[21]

U.S. superiority may be even stronger than this assessment implies. All of the six areas in which the U.S. advantage is said to be diminish-ing have been so described ever since 1980, yet none has had its status downgraded to that of U.S./Soviet equality.

Table 9-1. Relative U.S./USSR Standing in the Twenty Most Important Basic Technology Areas, 1985.

Technology	U.S. Superior			U.S./USSR Equal	USSR Superior
	Lead Increasing	Lead Stable	Lead Decreasing		
Aerodynamics/fluid dynamics				X	
Computers and software	X				
Conventional warheads				X	
Directed energy (laser)				X	
Electro-optical sensors		X			
Guidance and navigation			X		
Life sciences		X			
Materials			X		
Micro-electronic materials and integrated circuit manufacturing		X			
Nuclear warheads				X	
Optics			X		
Power sources				X	
Production/manufacturing		X			
Propulsion			X		
Radar sensor			X		
Robotics and machine intelligence		X			
Signal processing		X			
Signature reduction (stealth)		X			
Submarine detection			X		
Telecommunications		X			
	1	8	6	5	0

Source: Department of Defense, *The FY 1986 Department of Defense, Program for Research, Development and Acquisition* (Washington, D.C.: U.S. Government Printing Office, 1986), p. II-5.

At least three technologies are critical to the success of any SDI system: microelectronics, satellites, and computers. The USSR has lagged behind the United States in the development of each successive generation of military electronics. Miniature vacuum tubes, used in U.S. military equipment since about 1950, began to appear in Soviet equipment only some ten years later. By that time the United States was already switching to discrete semiconductors, a move the USSR did not emulate until the mid-1970s. In fact, the Soviet MiG-25 interceptor jet that Lt. Viktor Belenko flew to Japan when defecting from the USSR in 1976 contained only vacuum tubes and no solid state circuitry in its avionics, despite its relatively recent 1973 manufacture.[22] The U.S. development of integrated circuits (ICs) began in the early 1960s, and were incorporated into military hardware by the early 1970s, about a decade before their Soviet counterparts. Five years ago the United States moved from development to deployment of yet another generation of electronics, that of large-scale integrated functional circuits (LSIs); it is now rapidly moving toward the succeeding generation of very large-scale ICs. The Soviet Union is still in the process of LSI functional circuit development. In general, the USSR lags about ten years, or one generation, behind the United States in the evolution of advanced military electronics (see Figure 9-1).

Because of its similarity to SDI technologies, satellite technology provides a useful indicator for some aspects of the USSR's capacity to launch an SDI-like program. Soviet difficulties with advanced systems reliability and durability partly explain the striking contrast between the longevity of Soviet and American satellites. In every class of mission—communications, reconnaissance, early warning, and navigation—the lifespan of U.S. satellites now in service exceeds that of Soviet satellites by a factor of two to five.

Because of their shorter lifespans and more limited capabilities, the Soviet Union launches far more satellites each year than does the United States. For example, the USSR uses twenty-seven low-orbit satellites to provide its tactical and strategic communications capability, while U.S. military communications requirements are met by thirteen satellites.[23] By the end of 1980, the USSR had launched almost twice as many payloads into orbit as the United States.[24] Thus the Soviet Union has had significantly more launch experience than the United States.

Figure 9-1. U.S. and Soviet Introduction of Various Generations of Military Electronics.

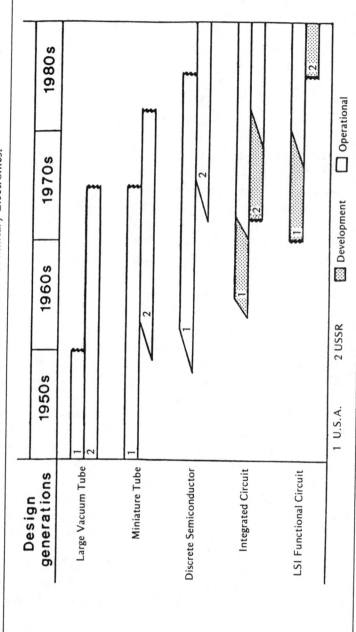

Source: Reprinted by permission from *International Defense Review*, June 1982, p. 712. Copyright 1982 Interavia S.A., Geneva, Switzerland.

To compete in a Star Wars race, or in modern weaponry in general, the USSR cannot afford to stand idly by while the United States solidifies its imposing superiority in computer technology. Nor does it appear that the Soviet Union intends to relinquish this high technology field quite so easily. In the fall of 1984, one year after DARPA announced its program, the Soviet Academy of Sciences launched a five-year, $100 million effort to develop its advanced computer technology, in an attempt to leapfrog a technological generation and establish itself at the forefront of international research in the field.[25] However, despite a concerted effort over the last fifteen years, the USSR still lags well behind U.S. computer capability. This gap, in addition to a number of systemic and institutional constraints, virtually assures a continuation of the five- to ten-year U.S. lead in new computer technologies that has prevailed since the mid-1960s.

Advances in computer technology are essential to high technology defense by the USSR. At the same time, Soviet state-of-the-art computer technology determines, at least in part, which modes of defense will be feasible. For example, the USSR may find it difficult to develop computers that can rapidly point and retarget beam weapons. In the short term, therefore, it may de-emphasize such systems in favor of missile-based defense systems. Or, if guidance computers present a problem, the Soviet Union might choose midrange and terminal defenses over long-range systems. If the entire constellation of computer systems and software development proves to be an onerous task, the USSR may direct its attention toward comparatively simple countermeasures, rather than relying on computerized defensive systems.

Table 9-2 illustrates the differences in Soviet and American diffusion of computers through the economy. Depending on the class of computer—mainframe, minicomputer, or microcomputer—the United States possesses from ten to a thousand times as many machines as the Soviet Union, and most of the U.S. machines have greater capabilities. For instance, many American supercomputers can process well over 100 million operations per second, and some can perform over 1 billion operations per second. Soviet supercomputers in serial production, by comparison, have yet to exceed 100 million instructions per second. Higher processing speeds are absolutely essential for a Star Wars effort.

Table 9-2. Comparison of U.S. and Soviet Diffusion of Computers.

1983 Production of 8-Bit Microcircuit Chips

USSR, total: 135,000   *U.S. microprocessors only: 15,000,000*

Soviet and U.S. Computer Stock: Mainframes and Minicomputers (units)

	1955	1960	1965	1970	1975	1977	1979	1984
Soviet		240	2,000	5–6,000	17,000	22,000	23,000	32,000
U.S.	240	5,400	24,700	74,060	200,000[a]	300,000		620,000
Lag (years)				10	12		14	18

Microcomputers—1985 (units)

U.S.	Annual Shipments	Total Installations	USSR
Business	3,330,000	9,000,000	Total Stock of
Households	3,200,000	15,000,000	Approx. 6–10,000
Total	6,500,000	24,000,000	microcomputers

Distribution of Computer Generations in USSR and U.S. Out of Total Computer Stock
(1st Generation: Vacuum Tubes, 2nd Generation: Transistors, 3rd Generation: Integrated Circuits)

	1960	1962	1964	1966	1968	1970	1972	1974	1975
USSR									
1st				65	43	23	4	—	—
2nd				35	57	77	95	91	83
3rd				—	—	—	1	9	17
U.S.									
1st	75	27.7	6.4	1.6	0.7	0.1	0	0	
2nd	25	72.3	93.6	74.1	30.0	12.3	7.4	4.4	
3rd	—	—	—	24.3	69.3	87.6	92.6	95.6	

a. Estimate extrapolated from 1973 and 1974 values of 133,250 and 165,040, respectively.

Sources: M. Cave, "Innovation Aspects of the Management Automation Programme in the Soviet Union," in R. Amann and J. Cooper, eds., *Industrial Innovation in the Soviet Union* (New Haven: Yale University Press, 1982); Martin Cave, "Computer Technology," in R. Amann, J. Cooper and R. W. Davies, eds., *The Technological Level of Soviet Industry* (New Haven: Yale University Press, 1977); D. Seligman, "The Great Soviet Computer Screw-Up," *Fortune*, July 8, 1985, pp. 32–36; D. R. Jones, ed., *Soviet Armed Forces Review Annual*, vol. 2 (Gulf Breeze, FL: Academic International Press, 1977; *Byte* Magazine research department, private conversation, July 1985; A. Beam, "Atari Bolsheviks," *The Atlantic*, March 1986, pp. 28–32; "Russia Gropes for a Way to Enter the High Tech Age," *Business Week*, November 11, 1985, p. 98; M. Phister, *Data Processing Technology and Economics*, 2d ed. (Bedford, MA: Digital Press and Santa Monica Publishing Co., 1979).

The USSR is well behind the United States in every aspect of computer technology, from circuit design and manufacturing to performance specifications, provision of infrastructure, software, support services, peripherals, and repairs. Moreover, much of current Soviet technology is based on American, and to a lesser extent European, computer systems and components. Although Soviet computers are "functional analogs," compatible with and based on American machines, they are not merely examples of reverse engineering of U.S. technology. A limited degree of indigenous integration and innovation finds its way into Soviet computer systems. However, it is highly unlikely that the Soviet Union has had enough experience with innovation to develop its own independent computer industry. This limitation casts doubt on its ability to make the advances in computer technology required to support SDI-like defenses, since advanced U.S. computer research for America's own defense programs is increasingly classified and more securely protected.

The shortage of computers and of well-trained, computer-literate specialists will prove to be a major impediment to advanced Soviet defense work. Problems will be particularly acute in software design. It has been estimated that the design, writing, and testing of computer codes for the U.S. SDI program could require tens of thousands of person-years of labor. Even with its 440,000 computer specialists, the United States will find it difficult to meet this demand. But it is utterly impossible to imagine the Soviet Union, with its vastly smaller stock of computer specialists, undertaking a similar project.[26]

Finally, because the USSR lags in computer speed, expertise, and miniaturization, it could probably not achieve the degree of subsystem integration and interlocking called for in U.S. defensive system plans. We should expect a Soviet defensive system to be designed in a more modular form, with each subsystem relatively independent of the others. While detection and sensing information may be shared, interconnections in battle management over wide expanses may be more loosely organized. This implies a design based on pockets of short-range terminal defenses to protect specific high-value locations, be they of military, industrial, or civilian significance. Such a strategy would minimize the disadvantages of the USSR's poor communications and coordination networks. Emphasis on shorter-range defenses may prove to be more rational in other respects as well. It would exploit the USSR's experience with Galosh, ASATs, and other rocket systems in which the gap between the two nations may not be as extreme.

The USSR's progress in high technology is also impeded by the inability of Soviet industry to accommodate the ever-increasing demand for precision and the exacting specifications required in the manufactured components that must support each successive generation of sophisticated armaments. Output quality problems and the maintenance of allowable engineering tolerances have been the nemesis of Soviet industry for decades. Such problems lead to less reliable components with higher maintenance requirements and shorter service lives. In 1980 Control Data Corporation specialists compared a Soviet microprocessor chip with the U.S. Intel 8080A, on which it was based. They estimated that these problems reduced Soviet manufacturing yields of acceptable chips by 50 percent and led to serious reliability problems with the chips produced. Soviet documentation revealed a failure rate twenty times higher than the U.S. failure rate.

Soviet chip manufacturing problems translate into further difficulties down the line. Technological progress in control systems, instrumentation, and of course computers is intimately linked to the progress and availability of semiconductor chips. The combination of low production yields, poor quality, and the military's priority claim on the best-quality products leaves civilian industries starved for components.

LABOR SUPPLY FOR SOVIET SCIENTIFIC AND ENGINEERING RESEARCH

The USSR's capacity for a large-scale strategic defense technology program also depends on the availability of skilled labor. While the Soviet Union employs one-quarter of the world's science specialists and one-half of its engineers, this statistic needs careful interpretation.[27]

So-called scientific workers make up the primary category of research personnel in the Soviet Union. These workers include all persons with advanced degrees or scientific titles, members of the USSR Academy of Sciences and its branches, other researchers and teachers, and the management of scientific research institutions. Excluded from the category are research technicians and assistants without higher education, individual inventors, graduate students, and research trainees.[29] Scientific workers totaled 1.43 million in 1982.[29] A breakdown by categories is presented in Table 9-3.

Although the scientific workers category is composed predominantly of research and development personnel, it would be an error to compare these raw statistics with those of the United States. Some categories of research workers, such as graduate students, that are generally included in U.S. statistics are excluded by the Soviet definition of scientific worker categories. Others included in Soviet statistics, such as nonresearch teachers, administrative personnel, and personnel in the humanities and social sciences, are normally excluded from U.S. statistics. Moreover, the Soviet statistics include all personnel involved in R&D work, while the U.S. figures prorate the content of work performed by personnel to the actual R&D activities involved. The Soviet statistical series can be adjusted to correspond to the U.S. conception of research and development personnel by excluding Soviet workers in the higher education system who are not actually doing research, prorating the research content of the work of graduate students, and excluding personnel employed in the social sciences and humanities.[30] Table 9-4 compares these adjusted figures with National Science Foundation estimates for U.S. R&D.

Following scientists and technicians, engineers are the third most important category of technical personnel in the USSR. Given the rigorous curricula and five-year training program, graduates of the full-time programs of Soviet universities and institutes are probably as competent as their American counterparts. Nonetheless, some adjustment of Soviet figures is necessary if they are to be compared with U.S. figures. According to education analyst David Bronson, the training received by part-time students of engineering in the Soviet Union is not up to U.S. standards. On-the-job training might eventually correct some of those shortcomings, however. Furthermore, about 20 percent of the personnel the USSR classifies as engineers perform functions not professionally recognized as engineering in the United States; this group includes crane operators, railroad engineers, and geodesic and meteorological workers.[31] An additional problem is that about a fifth of a Soviet engineer's time is spent on administration and tasks that do not correspond to those of U.S. engineers. When these and other factors are all taken into account, the Soviet supply of competent and fully employed engineers is substantially reduced from the 4.9 million reported in 1980.[32] Table 9-5 presents an adjusted estimate of Soviet engineering personnel, which repre-

Table 9–3. Soviet Scientific Workers, 1950–83 (*in thousands*).

	Total Scientific Workers	Advanced Degrees		Percent With Advanced Degrees	Professor Or Academy Member	Docent	Titles		Percent with Titles
		Doctor of Sciences	Candidate of Sciences				Senior SCI Worker	Junior SCI Worker	
1950	162.5	8.3	45.5	33.1	8.9	21.8	11.4	19.6	38.0
1955	223.9	9.5	78.0	39.1	9.0	28.6	14.6	17.1	31.0
1960	354.2	10.9	98.3	30.8	9.9	36.2	20.3	26.7	26.3
1965	664.6	14.8	134.4	22.4	12.5	48.6	28.7	48.9	21.0
1970	927.7	23.6	224.5	26.7	18.1	68.6	39.0	48.8	18.8
1975	1,223.4	32.3	326.8	29.4	22.9	87.9	53.3	45.0	17.1
1976	1,253.5	34.6	345.4	30.3	24.0	92.5	56.3	44.3	17.3
1977	1,279.6	36.0	358.4	30.8	25.3	96.6	59.3	43.2	17.5
1978	1,314.0	36.6	371.2	31.0	26.1	101.4	61.4	42.4	17.6
1979	1,340.6	37.1	383.6	31.4	26.9	105.8	63.8	42.3	17.8
1980	1,373.3	37.7	396.2	31.6	27.4	110.7	66.0	41.1	17.9
1981	1,411.2	38.7	409.7	31.8	28.1	115.7	68.6	40.2	17.9
1982	1,431.7	39.7	423.0	32.3	28.7	121.3	70.9	40.6	18.3
1983	1,444.0	41.0	435.4	33.0	29.4	125.4	73.5	42.0	18.7

Sources: L.E. Nolting and M. Feshback, "R&D Employment in the USSR—Definitions, Statistics, and Comparisons," in Joint Economic Committee, *Soviet Economy in a Time of Change* (1979) vol. 1, *Narodnoe khazaistvo SSSR*, vol. 1979, p. 107; vol. 1983, p. 94.

Table 9-4. Comparison of Soviet and U.S. Research Scientists
(*in thousands*).

Year	USSR			United States	
	Scientific Workers	Adjusted— Excludes Social Science and Humanities	Scientific Workers— Excludes Humanities Only	U.S. NSF Estimate of R&D Scientists[a]	BLS Estimate— Excludes Humanities and Social Scientists
1960	354.2	243.5	273.0	380.9	386.1
1965	664.6	423.3	474.5	494.5	513.2
1970	927.7	590.8	661.9	546.5	535.4
1975	1,223.4	779.3	873.5	534.8	—
1976	1,253.5	798.5	895.0	549.9	—
1977	1,279.6	815.1	913.6	568.2	—
1978	1,314.0	837.0	938.2	594.2	—
1979	1,340.6	853.8	957.0	622.0	—
1980	1,373.3	865.7	969.5	658.7	—
1981	1,411.2	889.6	996.2	691.4	—
1982	1,431.7	902.7	1,010.8	723.0	—
1983	1,444.0	910.5	1,019.6	750.0	—

a. NSF excludes humanities in all sectors and social sciences in industry.
Sources: L. Nolting and M. Feshback, *Statistics on Research and Development Employment in the USSR*, Series P-95, no. 76 (Washington, D.C.: U.S. Government Printing Office, Bureau of the Census, June 1981), p. 578; *Narodnoe khazaistvo SSSR*, vol. 1983, pp. 94, 97; author's calculations.

sents a first attempt to produce statistics comparable with U.S. data. These figures should be interpreted as rougher approximations than the estimates for R&D peronnel. In summary, the USSR appears to have a plentiful supply of well-trained and competent scientists and engineers, although perhaps not as plentiful as their raw statistics imply.

Training in engineering and the sciences appears to be fairly broad and rigorous. The USSR has greatly expanded its pool of engineering talent, as graduations in most subfields continue to rise (see Table 9-6). Although the number of U.S. natural science and engineering graduates has also been growing rapidly in recent years, it is still no more than half the Soviet figure. At the graduate level, the picture is reversed. The United States graduates about 295,000 M.A.s and

Table 9-5. Comparison of Soviet and U.S. Pools of Engineers (*in thousands*).

	USSR				United States	
	Number of Engineers	Per 10,000 of Population	(x.45) Adjusted Engineers	Per 10,000 of Population	Number of Engineers	Per 10,000 of Population
1950	400.2	22.2	180	10	408.0	26.8
1955	597.8	30.5	269	14	601.4	36.3
1960	1,135.0	53.0	511	24	801.1	44.3
1965	1,630.8	70.6	734	32	969.8	49.9
1970	2,486.5	102.4	1,119	46	1,098.2	53.5
1975	3,683.3	144.7	1,657	65	1,170.0	54.2
1976	–	–	–	–	1,214.0	55.7
1977	4,193.0	161.9	1,887	73	1,295.0	58.8
1978[a]	4,433.0[b]	169.7	1,995	76	1,297.0	58.3
1979	4,674.0[b]	177.4	2,103	80	1,421.0	63.1
1980	4,914.0	185.1	2,211	83	1,472.0	64.6
1981	5,246.0[b]	195.8	2,361	88	1,537.0	66.8

a. An estimate of the number of Soviet engineers is developed for 1981, one of three years for which no official estimate is published, by prorating the 1980 value according to the change in official Soviet figures for all technical personnel with higher education, adding 2.3 percent to account for the higher growth rate of the engineering population. 1978 and 1979 estimates derived by a linear extrapolation between 1977 and 1980.

b. Author's estimate.

Sources: L. Nolting and M. Feshback, *Statistics on Research and Development Employment in the USSR*, Series P-95, no. 76 (Washington, D.C.: U.S. Government Printing Office, Bureau of the Census, June 1981), p. 71; C. P. Ailes, F. M. Rushing, *The Science Race* (New York: Crane Russak, 1983), p. 101; John Scherer, ed., *USSR Facts and Figures Annual*, vol. 9, 1985 (Gulf Breeze, FL: Academic International Press, 1985), p. 40; Department of Labor, *Labor Force Statistics Derived from Current Population Survey: A Databook*, vol. 1, Bureau of Labor Statistics Bulletin #2096, September 1982, pp. 651–79; Bureau of the Census, *Statistical Abstract of the United States, 1985* (Washington, D.C.: U.S. Government Printing Office, 1984), p. 6; *Narodnoe khaziastvo SSSR*, vol. 1977, p. 393; vol. 1978, p. 377; vol. 1980, p. 368; vol. 1981, p. 407.

33,000 Ph.D.s annually. Of these, 44,000 are in engineering, math, and physical and biological sciences. In contrast, the USSR graduates a total of about 20,000 students in these disciplines annually.

U.S. government forecasts indicate that these Soviet trends will persist. Soviet higher education (diploma) graduations in the physical and life sciences and math are expected to continue at an annual level of 43,000 to 50,000. The number of engineering graduates is

Table 9-6. Comparison of Soviet and U.S. Graduations by Engineering/Science Specialties (*in thousands*).

USSR	1975	1980	1983	1983 (% distribution)	1975-83 Growth (% average)
Geology and Prospecting	5.9	6.2	6.2	1.5%	0.62%
Mining	8.3	8.7	8.8	2.1	0.73
Power source engineering	14.1	17.7	17.6	4.3	2.81
Metallurgy	7.8	8.7	9.2	2.2	2.08
Machine building and instruments	73.0	84.6	85.9	20.9	2.05
Electrotechnics, electro-instrument making and automation	49.6	52.9	55.5	13.5	1.41
Radiotechnics and communications	18.8	22.4	22.9	5.6	2.50
Chemical technology	15.4	14.7	14.6	3.6	-0.66
Timber engineering	4.7	5.7	5.8	1.4	2.66
Technology of food products	10.5	12.2	13.3	3.2	3.00
Technology of consumer products	7.6	8.9	9.8	2.4	3.23
Construction	44.8	61.3	63.9	15.6	4.54
Geodesy and cartography	1.3	2.0	2.0	0.5	5.53
Hydrology and meteorology	1.3	1.3	1.3	0.3	0.0
Agriculture and forestry	53.9	64.5	69.2	16.9	3.17
Transport	17.5	22.0	24.2	5.9	4.14

United States	1975	1980	1982	1982 (% distribution)	1975–82 Growth (% average)
Computer and information science	5.0	11.2	20.3	9.8	22.16
Engineering	46.9	68.9	80.0	38.8	7.93
Chemical	3.1	6.3	6.7	3.2	11.64
Petroleum	0.3	0.9	1.2	0.6	21.90
Civil	7.7	10.3	10.5	5.1	4.53
Electrical	10.2	13.8	16.5	8.0	7.11
Mechanical	6.9	11.8	13.9	6.7	10.52
Other	18.8	25.7	31.1	15.1	7.46
Mathematics	18.2	11.4	11.6	5.6	-6.23
Physics	3.6	3.3	3.5	1.7	-0.40
Chemistry	10.4	11.2	11.0	5.3	0.80

Source: *Narodnoe khazaistvo SSSR*, vol. 1983, p. 502; Bureau of the Census, *Statistical Abstract of the United States, 1985* (Washington, D.C.: U.S. Government Printing Office, 1984), p. 158.

predicted to remain between 350,000 and 440,000 per year until 1990. Because the rate of increase of the Soviet college-aged population is fairly low at present, the prospects are not good for a rapid near-term expansion in the pool of graduates unless standards are diluted. At the M.A. and Ph.D. level (the corresponding Soviet degree is the Candidate of Science), engineering, math, and science graduations are expected to decline slightly to about 18,400 a year until 1990.[33]

While U.S. graduation projections also show a gradual decline between the early 1980s and 1990, the order of magnitude is quite different. Math and science graduations at the B.A. level are expected to continue at a rate of 100,000 a year, about twice the Soviet rate. Engineering graduations are expected to fall slightly, to just under 80,000 a year, one-fifth the Soviet number. Earned M.A.s in physical and life sciences, math, and engineering will total just over 35,000, approximately double the Soviet rate for new Candidates in these disciplines. U.S. doctoral degrees are expected to dip to about 9,500 in engineering and science. At the graduate level, then, these projections suggest that the United States will annually award about 45,000 degrees in math, the sciences, and engineering, until the 1990s. In total, the United States is expected to have about 326,000 Ph.D.s in engineering, math, and the sciences by 1990.[34]

These projections have important implications for the way in which the USSR is expected to cope with the U.S. Star Wars program. Clearly the Soviet labor force in science and engineering exceeds that of the United States, even after some quality and equivalency adjustments for engineers and R&D personnel have been made. The Soviet total of these two personnel categories exceeds that of the United States by about 50 percent. Moreover, the Soviet educational quota system can be manipulated much more effectively to increase enrollments in designated specialties. The Soviet Union's real problem is the extreme scarcity of trained talent in the higher echelons of science. Its pool of both Candidates and Doctors of Science barely equals the U.S. pool of Ph.D.s alone in science and engineering. In addition, the United States has approximately 1 million M.A.s in engineering, math, and the sciences, providing an enormous supply of trained human capital for any major scientific effort. The Soviet Union, by contrast, has plenty of "foot soldiers of science" but few leaders. This problem is virtually intractable in the short term because there is a significant lag between initial graduate enrollment and the training and experience needed to qualify a project leader. Over a decade or two, the USSR may be able to expand its graduate program sufficiently to ameliorate this problem, but ultimately this may prove to be the Achilles' heel for any Soviet efforts to challenge the U.S. Star Wars program.

CONCLUSION

Both conventional and advanced Soviet strategic defenses are cumbersome, of dubious effectiveness, and highly vulnerable to attack. Except in particle beam technology, the USSR lags behind the United States in virtually every technological area relevant to strategic defense.

Soviet attempts to harness more advanced areas of defense systems research are hampered by their serious shortcomings in sensor technology, rocket booster propulsion, high-precision optics, and computer hardware development. As a result, they lag about ten years behind the United States in actual systems capabilities, despite their fragmentary progress in many other fields. Even the present level of U.S. computer technology is inadequate to meet the needs of an SDI program. Since Soviet computer technology and distribution throughout the economy lag from six to eighteen years behind the United States, the USSR is not even close to providing the capabilities necessary for viable advanced defenses.

Although unable to field large-scale working systems, the USSR has devoted considerable energy to the development and deployment of prototype testing and demonstration systems. This enthusiasm undoubtedly reflects the Soviet Union's long-standing ambition to be regarded as a worthy rival of the United States on the international stage. The early deployment of systems, however ineffectual, may be a bid for prestige among nations. By enhancing its image as a military superpower, the Soviet Union not only facilitates the task of intimidating lesser powers, but can cultivate additional clients in the increasing world competition for arms sales. The high visibility of its systems also enhances Soviet credibility during bargaining over treaty limitations on defensive systems, offering the potential to extract concessions far beyond any commanded by the inferior technological capabilities of the USSR.

This strategy is not without cost, however. Premature deployments may force the USSR into enormous expenditures on systems that may later be found wanting. The initial waste may then be compounded by efforts to improve the existing systems and amortize these costs, rather than abandon them in favor of a totally different approach. This in turn further delays the adoption of the next generation of technology. This phenomenon is typified by the Soviet experience with the aging Galosh ABM system. Saddled with an obsolete technological investment that they are reluctant to abandon, the Soviets continue to fall behind. It will be difficult for them to reverse this trend, both because continual marginal enhancements to existing systems offer safe and assured incremental improvements and because the incentive structure of the Soviet bureaucracy encourages risk aversion.

Whereas most facets of the U.S. SDI program have been pulled together under the auspices of SDIO, it does not appear that the USSR has taken similar steps to unify the supervision of its strategic defense efforts below the level of a service command (the National Air Defense Force). As a result, there is a greater danger that budget allocations may be based on the power and influence of the generals who control individual fiefdoms within the service command, rather than on a merit-based competition among rival schemes.

10

SOVIET SDI RESPONSE
A Nuclear Build-Up

The Strategic Defense Initiative will always be impossible from the point of view of military strategy, since any strong opponent with a sufficiently high level of technology can always overcome the technical achievements of the other side at all stages—and he (the opponent) won't even have to spend as much as the creator of SDI spends.

—Andrei Sakharov
December 28, 1986

Given the Soviet Union's present strategic defense capabilities, how is it likely to respond to SDI? How much would it cost to stock Soviet nuclear arsenals to a level that would overwhelm an SDI system in a massive attack? What other options are open to the USSR? One possible near-term response involves a build-up and diversification of its strategic nuclear arsenal in an effort to preserve the credibility of its deterrent in the face of potential erosion by SDI.

The overriding principle of a Soviet missile force expansion strategy is to overwhelm SDI defense by saturation beyond the defense system's response capacity. This increases the likelihood of Soviet warheads reaching their targets. There are two major methods by which the USSR could attempt to saturate U.S. defenses: (1) expansion of its missile and warhead force, and (2) construction of a bomber- and sea-based cruise missile fleet. A third possible Soviet strategy is, of course, to meet the U.S. strategic defense challenge head-on with direct competition through, for example, its military laser research program.

MISSILE FORCE EXPANSION

One way to expand the Soviet missile force would be to fractionate the missile payloads—that is, to install a larger number of smaller warheads within each existing missile or to replace older, single-warhead weapons with new MIRVed (multiple independently targetable re-entry vehicle) projectiles.

Fractionation cannot be extended indefinitely, however. As the desired force level increases, the Soviet Union would be compelled to expand its actual missile complement, either by deploying stockpiled missiles or by producing and deploying new re-entry vehicles. Either option could endanger the SALT II treaty.

Fractionation Costs

According to U.S. intelligence officials Richard Gates and Lawrence Gershwin, by 1990 the USSR could have more than 12,000 deliverable warheads in its intercontinental attack force while still observing the SALT II limits.[1] This figure includes both construction of new missiles and modifications of older systems, a process that often involves the fractionation of payloads. Our estimate will focus on the ground-based intercontinental arsenal, the largest and most readily available part of the Soviet nuclear stockpile likely to be fractionated.

The first step in estimating the cost of arsenal expansion through fractionation of payloads is to determine the maximum number of warheads that could be attained solely by this strategy. The Soviet land-based ICBM force currently consists of about 6,423 re-entry vehicles. The total yield of this force is 4,482 megatons, carried by 1,398 missiles (see Table 10-1). In addition, U.S. Department of Defense officials contend that deployment of the new SS-25 has begun, with twenty-seven or more already in place. By installing the maximum number of warheads on these existing missiles, the Soviets could expand their force to 7,460 warheads, with 3,760 megatons yield, a 16 percent increase. (Of course, if the present modifications underestimate the limit of feasible booster loading and the USSR

Table 10-1. Soviet Land-based ICBM Arsenal.

Missile Type	Modification	Year Deployed	Number (1985)	Range (km)	Warheads per Vehicle	Yield per Vehicle	Total Warheads	Total Delivery Capability (megatons)
SS-11	Mod 1	1966	220	10,500	1	0.950	220	209
	Mod 3	1973	300	8,800	3	0.350	900	315
SS-13		1968	60	10,000	1	0.600	60	36
SS-17	Mod 1	1975	130	10,000	4	0.750	520	390
	Mod 2	1977	20	11,000	1	3.6	20	72
	Mod 3	1979	?	–	4	0.750	–	–
SS-18	Mod 2	1976	115	11,000	8	0.900	920	828
	Mod 3	1976	23	16,000	1	20	23	460
	Mod 4	1982	170	11,000	10	0.500	1,700	850
SS-19	Mod 2	1978	20	10,000	1	10	20	200
	Mod 3	1979	340	10,000	6	0.550	2,040	1,122
			1,398				6,423	4,482

Source: There is some dispute regarding exact numbers of each modification type in the Soviet arsenal. The figures presented here are a compromise between several sources: T. Gervasi, *The Myth of Soviet Military Supremacy* (New York: Harper & Row, 1986), pp. 291, 336; J. Sands, "A Review of Soviet Military Power, 1985," Working Paper, National Resources Defense Council, Washington, D.C., June 1985, p. 69; Department of Defense, *Soviet Military Power, 1985* (Washington, D.C.: U.S. Government Printing Office, 1985), p. 80; International Institute of Strategic Studies, *The Military Balance* (London: IISS, various years, 1982–86); Robert Berman and John Baker, *Soviet Strategic Forces: Requirements and Responses* (Washington, D.C.: Brookings Institution, 1982), pp. 104–5.

could load more re-entry vehicles on the existing missile bus (the carrying structure within a missile payload that holds the warheads), the 16 percent growth would be an underestimate.)

The next step is to multiply the total number of warheads by the cost of a single warhead. Ideally one would like to have incremental cost estimates for the re-entry vehicles alone. Most of the many cost estimates for Soviet nuclear missiles that have appeared in the U.S. Congressional Record and in the House Armed Services Committee literature over the years pertain to average missile system cost per warhead. Estimates do exist, however, of average re-entry vehicle costs for U.S. systems. According to a 1979 article entered into the Congressional Record by Congressman L. Aspin, the cost of 2,000 warheads for the U.S. MX missile was expected to be $800 million, or $400,000 per warhead in 1978 dollars. The cost of warheads for each Minuteman III missile was estimated at $400,000.[2] A 1984 source estimates a cost of $840,000 (in fiscal 1982 dollars) for the MX missile W87 Mk21 warhead (about $600,000 in 1978 dollars).[3] Although Soviet costs would not be identical, we would expect a similar breakdown of total missile costs. The total cost of the twenty-one MX missiles, which hold ten warheads each, is $1.5 billion, or $7.2 million per warhead. Using the 1982 warhead cost estimate and adjusting for inflation, the warhead represents 12 percent of this cost. Assuming the same ratio of missile to warhead cost for the Soviet case allows us to estimate their average cost per missile and warhead.

S. Meyer and P. Amquist of the Massachusetts Institute of Technology have estimated costs (in 1978 dollars) for three Soviet missile types: the SS-17, $14 million; the SS-18, $28 million; and the SS-19, $19 million. These figures imply an average warhead cost of $500,000 for the SS-17 and $400,000 each for the SS-18 and SS-19. The cost of the SS-11 is estimated at $12-14 million (in 1971-72 dollars). The SS-11 warheads would cost between $500,000 and $725,000 each in 1971-72 dollars.[4]

Based on these estimates, the total cost of a 16 percent increase (from 6,400 to 7,460 warheads) in Soviet warhead deployment would be about $700-800 million (in 1978 dollars). If the USSR already maintains a stockpile of functioning warheads, this figure may be an overestimate. Moreover, these estimates represent an average cost. Since initial unit costs are likely to be extremely high, this average cost probably overstates the actual marginal cost per re-entry vehicle. Once quantity production levels are attained, true marginal costs may be considerably lower than the figure estimated here.

Expansion Costs

Because fractionation can be employed only to a certain point and because it implies reduced total megatonnage, a more practical way to expand the supply of deliverable warheads is to deploy more missiles. This could be accomplished either by deploying some of the extensive Soviet stockpile of stored ICBMs or by manufacturing new ones. Deploying those now in storage would be a less expensive option, but savings would come at the expense of accuracy and reliability.

Soviet land-based ICBM force expansion costs can be estimated on the basis of currently available information on missile production volumes and costs. The first step is to estimate Soviet missile shell costs and then to add the warhead and silo basing costs. To the extent that the USSR currently maintains a reserve supply of missile components and need not design and produce a new missile system from scratch, its costs will be lower. Thus a crucial step in the analysis is to estimate the level of the Soviet reserve stock of ICBMs.

For many years the Soviet Union has been producing considerably more missiles than it needs for deployment and testing. U.S. government estimates of annual Soviet ICBM production indicate a peak in the mid-1970s followed by a gradual decline in production volumes (Table 10-2). Throughout the period, however, Soviet ICBM production was maintained at substantial levels, totaling some 2,600 units in all.

Table 10-3, which presents annual missile deployment by type, shows that in 1972 the USSR had 1,527 ICBMs in place. By 1984, this number had dropped to 1,398, largely through retirement and replacement of older missile models. Given the production of 2,600 ICBMs and a net reduction of 129 in deployment, it would be possible for the Soviet Union to have a maximum of 2,729 missiles in storage, minus those used in testing and those destroyed after their retirement. If the total were actually this high, however, it would include many old SS-7, SS-8, and SS-9 missiles. Given their vintage and years spent in mothballs, the accuracy and reliability of these missiles would be dubious,

Table 10–2. Soviet ICBM Production Figure Estimates.

Source	1972	1973	1974	1976	1977	1978	1979	1980	1981	1982	1983	1984
Congressional Record[a]	150	150	200	250	300	225	225	250	200	175	150	
Joint Economic Committee 1982[b]					300	200	200	200	200			
Joint Economic Committee 1983[c]						225	225	250	200	175		
Department of Defense 1983 to 1985[d]						225	225	250	200	175	150	100
Department of Defense 1981[e]				300	300	200	200	200				

a. U.S., Congress, Senate, DIA data, 10 August 1984, *Congressional Record*, vol. 130, no. 107.

b. Joint Economic Committee, *Allocation of Resources in the Soviet Union and China—1982* (Washington, D.C.: U.S. Government Printing Office, 1982), pt. 8, p. 74.

c. Joint Economic Committee, *Allocation of Resources in the Soviet Union and China—1983* (Washington, D.C.: U.S. Government Printing Office, 1983), pt. 9, p. 13.

d. Department of Defense, *Soviet Military Power* (Washington, D.C.: U.S. Government Printing Office, 1983), p. 79; 1984, p. 98; 1985, p. 38.

e. Department of Defense, *Soviet Military Power* (Washington, D.C.: U.S. Government Printing Office, 1981), pp. 12–13.

A more reasonable assumption is that all retired SS-7, SS-8 and SS-9 missiles (a total of 497 since 1972) are militarily useless, given their age, and were disposed of. These 497 missiles were replaced with a net deployment of 360 new ICBMs out of the 2,600 manufactured by the Soviet Union. In addition, approximately 650, or 25 percent, of new Soviet production would have been consumed in testing, assuming Soviet testing practices are similar to those of the United States. This suggests a net stockpile of about 1,600 Soviet ICBMs.

The total number of warheads the Soviet Union could deploy on a land-based missile fleet depends on the composition of its missile reserve as well as its sheer size. The conservative assumption is that whenever Soviet missiles are withdrawn from the field, it is the least capable that are retired and placed in reserve storage while modern missiles are deployed in their stead. Under this assumption the reserve force will have much lower capabilities than if already deployed missiles were modified in the field and newly produced modern projectiles were put in storage.

Under these conditions, the Soviet reserve ICBM arsenal would include 750 SS-11 missiles and 495 more modern ones (SS-17s, SS-18s, and SS-19s), that had once been deployed and were later retired and replaced. Overall, the Soviet ICBM stockpile would be composed of 480 SS-11s mod 1, 500 SS-11 mod 3, 40 SS-17s, 260 SS-18s, and 260 SS-19 missiles.

Some experts believe that the current Soviet stockpile of ICBMs is smaller than the 1,600 missiles estimated here. Massachusetts Institute of Technology professor Stephen M. Meyer, a respected expert on Soviet military policy and technology and consultant to the Pentagon, puts the number at 1,000 missiles.[5] However, given Soviet production levels, a stockpile this low would imply that virtually all the stored missiles were pristine, never-deployed armaments and that the USSR has been scrapping most of its retired missiles. While possible, such behavior would run counter to all observations of the Soviet practice of warehousing or reselling retired arms from other branches of its armed forces.

Fielding this reserve of missiles would involve two major economic costs: the required missile silo infrastructure and warheads. Here we make the extreme assumption that all required silos and warheads for this force must be newly built. With its stockpile of missiles and its emphasis on preparation, however, the USSR surely already possesses

Table 10-3. Soviet Annual ICBM Deployment Totals.

Type	Modification	First Deployment	1972	1973	1974	1975	1976
SS-7		1962	190	190	190	190	130
SS-8		1963	19	19	19	19	19
SS-9		1966	288	288	288	288	248
SS-11	Mod 1	1966/73	970	970	970	970	890
SS-11	Mod 3	1973	–	20	40	60	60
SS-13		1969	60	60	60	60	60
SS-17	Mod 1	1975					
			–	–	–	–	–
SS-17	Mod 2	1977					
SS-18	Mod 1	1976					
SS-18	Mod 2	1977					
			–	–	–	–	60
SS-18	Mod 3	1979					
SS-18	Mod 4	1982					
SS-19	Mod 1, 2	1976/79	–	–	–	–	80
SS-19	Mod 3	1982					
Total			1,527	1,547	1,567	1,547	1,547
Annual new missile deployment (does not include modifications)				20	20	20	140

Sources: SIPRI, *SIPRI Yearbook* (London: Taylor and Francis Ltd., 1981, pp. 274–75; 1982, pp. 276–77; 1983, p. 49; 1984, p. 24); D. Jones, ed., *Soviet Armed Forces Review Annual 8* (Gulf Breeze, FL: Academic International Press, 1984), pp.102–103; J. Sands, *A Review of Soviet Military Power, 1985*, Working Paper, National Resources Defense Council, Washington, D.C., June 1985, p. 69; Department of Defense, *Soviet Military Power* (Washington, D.C.: U.S. Government Printing Office, 1985), p. 30.

Table 10-3. continued

1977	1978	1979	1980	1981	1982	1983	1984	1985
30	2	—	—	—	—	—	—	—
19	—	—	—	—	—	—	—	—
188	128	68	—	—	—	—	—	—
800	690	580	520	520	—	250	—	100
					520		520	
60	60	60	60	60		300		420
60	60	60	60	60	60	60	60	60
					120	130		
50	100	150	150	150			150	150
					30	20		
					—	—		
					175	115		
120	180	240	308	308			308	308
					58	23		
					75	170		
					60	20		
120	180	240	300	300			360	360
					300	310		
1,400	1,398	1,398	1,398	1,398	1,398	1,398	1,398	1,398
150	170	170	128	0	60	0	0	0

a large number of warheads and spare facilities components. As a result, this conservative assumption will lead to an overstatement of Soviet deployment costs.

To estimate the cost of building a silo, we turn to proposals for the MX missile. At the beginning of the Reagan presidency, U.S. government officials estimated that about $13 billion would be required for facility design and construction of 4,600 missile silos (twenty-three for each MX missile) and about half as much again for maintenance and operations.[6] Soviet costs per silo would presumably be higher, both because fewer are required (1,600 versus 4,600) and because of more difficult logistic and construction conditions and a hostile climate. The U.S. figures suggest that silo construction and operation might approximate 15 percent of missile procurement costs. Cost estimates for U.S. dense-pack basing schemes yield similar results. The Defense Department's 1984 annual report indicates that construction costs associated with the MX missile between 1984 and 1985 were expected to total 14.3 percent of the direct missile procurement costs, assuming a deployment of sixty-four MX missiles.[7]

Using this 15 percent ratio to approximate silo construction and missile maintenance costs, and the $500,000 per warhead figure derived above for warhead costs, we can estimate costs per missile and per warhead for deployment of Soviet reserve ICBM missiles. Table 10-4 presents these figures using U.S. price inflation figures to update the calculations to present-day dollars. Because Soviet inflation rates are generally lower, this procedure too will tend to overestimate Soviet costs.

Alternatively, the Soviet Union might expand its ICBM arsenal by building and deploying new models of missiles. While this option is the most expensive, it would assure the greatest accuracy and reliability. In 1981, Gen. K. Burke told the House Armed Services Committee that it would cost the USSR $5.95 million per re-entry vehicle to deploy new MIRVed ICBMs.[8] This is equal to about $6.75 million today.

The estimates above permit us to plot the cost of Soviet ICBM force expansion by the number of re-entry vehicles deployed. Figure 10-1 provides such a summary. It indicates that the USSR could expand its ICBM force by an additional 6,370 re-entry vehicles for $9.5 billion. This would double the total number of land-based re-entry vehicles in the Soviet arsenal, bringing the complement to

Table 10–4. Soviet Deployment Costs for Reserve Missile Force (*million 1978 dollars*).

Type	Modification	Silo Costs	Warhead Costs	Total Cost	Number of Warheads	Cost per Warhead	Total Reserves	Total Cost	Total Warheads
SS-11	Mod 1	4.5[a]	0.75	5.25	1	5.25	450	2,362	450
SS-11	Mod 3	4.5[a]	2.25	6.75	3	2.25	500	3,375	1,500
SS-17		3.1	3.0	6.1	4	1.53	40	246	160
SS-18		6.3	7.5	13.8	10	1.38	260	3,588	2,600
SS-19		4.4	4.5	8.9	6	1.48	260	2,301	1,560
								9,501	6,370

a. Missile cost of $12 million (1971–72 dollars) inflated by U.S. capital equipment price index to derive value of $30 million. Given lower Soviet inflation rates, this almost certainly overestimates their costs.

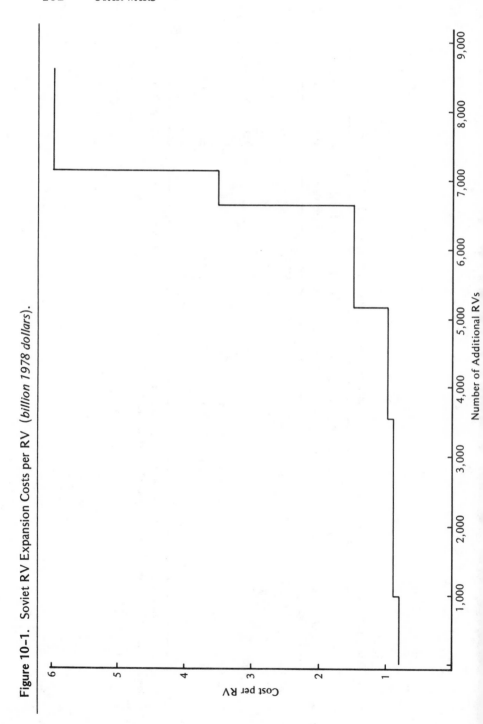

Figure 10–1. Soviet RV Expansion Costs per RV (*billion 1978 dollars*).

about 12,500. Expansion beyond this point, although limited by treaty restrictions, would cost approximately $6.75 million per additional re-entry vehicle. By merely replacing 520 of the 580 presently deployed SS-11 and SS-13 ICBMs with SS-18s and SS-19s, the USSR could add 4,200 re-entry vehicles to its deployed arsenal at a cost of about $5.9 billion. Such a move would expand the total Soviet land-based ICBM arsenal to about 11,000 warheads and a multitude of decoys.

Opponents of SDI often contend (and advocates sometimes acknowledge) that the program could not be effective without parallel cuts in the number of strategic warheads deployed by both sides. Otherwise the threat would remain that one side could attempt to overwhelm the other's defenses by saturating them with more targets than the defense system could handle in the limited time available. For example, a hypothetical system designed to destroy 75 percent of the incoming warheads in an attack of 2,000 missiles might be capable of destroying only 50 percent of the warheads in an attacking force of 4,000 projectiles in the same time period. In other words, by doubling the size of the attacking force, the attacker could more than double the number of successful strikes. An increase in the size of the attacking ICBM fleet could therefore pose extremely serious problems for SDI's capacity to ward off an attack, leaving the United States with a much weaker actual defense capability than originally promised.

CRUISE MISSILE FLEET

A longer-term response to a U.S. defensive build-up would involve the reconfiguration of the Soviet strategic nuclear arsenal away from the traditional ICBM and SLBM (submarine-launched ballistic missile) modes toward cruise missiles. Most nongovernment analysts agree that cruise missiles could circumvent strategic defenses, although a determined minority of SDI advocates insists otherwise. The short flight times of cruise missiles when launched from air and sea platforms near the United States, their ground-hugging flight paths, and their tiny radar cross-sections make them difficult targets to destroy. Given their accuracy, they are a formidable weapon indeed.[9] Moreover, the U.S. defenses against cruise missiles are modest. John L. Gardner, assistant director for systems in the SDIO, Department of Defense, contended late in 1985 that in a nuclear exchange most bombers and cruise missiles would arrive at their targets, even though many ballistic missiles might be shot down by the opponent's SDI-type defenses. His analysis suggested that 90 percent of the bombers and cruise missiles would penetrate SDI and antiaircraft defenses.[10] This position was also suggested in 1984 by the incumbent undersecretary of defense, Dr. Richard DeLauer, who reported that the USSR could only "get 10 percent" of any attacking U.S. cruise missiles.[11] Presumably the United States, which lacks the vast air defense network of the USSR, would fare much worse against a Soviet attack.

Intelligence officials Richard Gates and Lawrence Gershwin predict that by 1995 the USSR will "deploy 2,000 to 3,000 nuclear-armed [air-launched cruise missiles] ALCMs, sea-launched cruise missiles (SLCMs) and ground-launched cruise missiles (GLCMs)."[12] Yet today, only one type of Soviet long-range cruise missile is operational: the air-launched AS-15, currently mounted on newly manufactured propeller-driven Bear-H bombers. The U.S. Department of Defense contends that four other types of long-range cruise missiles are now under development in the USSR, including a large, ground-launched cruise missile and a sea-launched version that can be fired from standard torpedo tubes. A large SLCM, designated the SS-NX-24, is also reportedly being developed and may be intended for deployment on the converted Yankee-Class submarines.[13] The USSR could undoubtedly accelerate development of these systems rapidly if U.S. SDI plans move toward deployment. In addition to complicating the strategic nuclear equation, such a development would confront the United States with another threat against which no adequate defenses are available.

There are two distinct measures of cost for armaments like cruise missiles. The "flyaway cost" refers to the cost of a weapon itself as it leaves the assembly line. The "life-cycle cost," at the opposite extreme, includes not only the flyaway cost, but also costs of the basing mode and associated operating and maintenance expenses for the expected service life of the system. This analysis uses a life-cycle cost approach, a more inclusive measure of the true cost of a weapons system.

We can estimate the approximate life-cycle cost to the USSR in U.S. dollars for a Soviet fleet of cruise missiles by a comparison with the cost of U.S. Tomahawk class missiles. Of course, the application of U.S. cost estimates to Soviet data begs the question of potentially significant differences in input costs, output characteristics, and quality. It does, however, provide a clue to the magnitude of total expenses entailed by the Soviet cruise missile program.

The U.S. Department of Defense termed the Tomahawk missile "similar in design" to the Soviet AS-15.[14] The U.S. Tomahawk had an expected average flyaway cost of $790,000 (1981 dollars), while the SLCM counterpart averaged $1.40 million, with much of the difference attributable to a shorter production run.[15] Later flyaway cost estimates show a gradual rise. The 1983 Department of Defense budget estimates put the price at $1.51 million per missile for the ALCM and $4.33 million for the ground-launched cruise missile (GLCM).[16] The 1983 estimates for the Navy version of the Tomahawk were $2.44 million each.[17] The FY 1984 procurements budget for ALCMs averaged $1.76 million each.[18] FY 1985 costs for GLCMs and sea-based Tomahawks were estimated to be $4.76 million and $3.11 million, respectively.[19]

In addition to flyaway costs, expenses for the construction or reconfiguration of platforms for cruise missile basing should be considered in estimating the total life-cycle cost of a cruise missile fleet. One of the very few sources on which such estimates can be based is the U.S. experience with the conversion of B-52G aircraft to ALCM platforms. Those conversions cost $12 million (1981 dollars) per aircraft and permitted each plane to carry twenty missiles. The cost of an entirely new, modern ALCM-carrier aircraft is estimated to be $175-200 million in 1981 dollars.[20] Annual life-cycle costs, including operations and support, amount to about 10 percent of procurement costs for the ALCM and SLCM, and 2 percent for the GLCM.[21] Acquisition costs for a new ALCM platform are estimated to be between $2.5 million and $3.6 million per missile, with the total fifteen-year life-cycle cost ranging from $6.6 million to $8.0 million per missile (1981 dollars), assuming that the platform is either a B-52 type aircraft or a wide-bodied carrier. Conversion of Polaris submarines to carry SLCMs entails a fifteen-year life-cycle cost of $9.1-16.0 million per cruise missile.[22]

Assuming a fifteen-year life cycle for Soviet ALCMs as well, these missiles would cost approximately $4.4 million each, and SLCMs and GLCMs would cost about $7.8 million and $6.2 million, respectively. Assuming that refurbished aircraft are used (such as the BEAR-H bomber, which carries four AS-15s on external pylons), $4.5 million per warhead should be added to the cost of the ALCM for a total of about $9.9 million. If the ALCMs are to be deployed on new aircraft and the SLCMs on refurbished submarines, fifteen-year life-cycle costs on the order of $11.5 million and $20 million, respectively, could be expected. A force comparable in distribution to that of the United States, would cost roughly $40 billion over fifteen years, if it consisted of three-quarters ALCMs and one-eighth each SLCMs and GLCMs for a total of 2,500 missiles. (This is approximately the size predicted by U.S. defense analysts for the Soviet cruise missile fleet five years hence.)

According to a 1983 briefing given by Mr. Norbert Michaud and Major General Schuyler Bissell of the Defense Intelligence Agency (DIA) to the Joint Economic Committee of the U.S. Congress, the Soviet 1981 defense budget totaled $220 billion in U.S. dollars. This figure implies an average annual real growth rate since 1970 of 3 percent, which the DIA expects to prevail for the foreseeable future.[23] On this basis the $40 billion expenditure on cruise missiles represents only 2.28 percent of the Soviet defense budget over the next five years. Furthermore, it is only 0.65 percent of the expected total Soviet defense expenditure over the fifteen-year life cycle of the cruise missiles, and would provide a fully deployed countermeasures system, not merely a research program and feasibility study. In fact, this expenditure would give the USSR an accurate and fairly reliable force of missiles, capable of attacking U.S. strategic targets from a stand-off launch position. In the absence of vastly improved U.S. air defenses, it could enable the Soviet Union to land 2,200 additional warheads on U.S. targets.

It is often asserted that it will be cheaper for the United States to install or incrementally improve SDI defenses than it is for the USSR to saturate or overwhelm them with more or better weapons. Advocates of SDI use this notion of "cost effectiveness at the margin" to argue that SDI will not lead to a renewed arms race. Knowing that the United States could counter an arms build-up at a fraction of the cost, they argue, the Soviet Union will recognize that a new arms race would lead only to its own bankruptcy.

Of course, this argument rests squarely on the assertion that SDI is cheaper than armed responses available to the Soviet Union. Present estimates of SDI's costs range from $400 billion to over $5 trillion. Moreover, there is no guarantee that the resulting defenses would adequately protect the U.S. populace from a massive attack by a determined adversary using not only ICBMs, but also submarine-launched missiles fired from just off the U.S. coast, cruise missiles, and possibly even small nuclear devices smuggled into American cities by terrorists. While enormous in the absolute sense, the potential cost of doubling the Soviet ICBM arsenal or deploying a fleet of 2,500 cruise missiles pales by comparison with SDI's cost estimates. Faced with expenditures of $10–40 billion to counter American strategic defenses costing from 10 to 200 times as much, it is difficult to imagine that the USSR would be the side most concerned about being bankrupted by the arms race.

SOVIET MILITARY LASER PROGRAM

In recent years the U.S. government has repeatedly drawn attention to the apparently large and well-funded Soviet military laser program. As long ago as 1979, the Department of Defense began issuing ominous warnings that the Soviet program was three to five times larger than the U.S. program. By 1982, more specific reports asserted that the Soviet Union was spending approximately $1 billion per year on the military applications of laser technology, while total U.S. expenditures since the early 1970s amounted to only $2 billion.[24] More recently, it has been reported that the Soviet program involves more than half a dozen research and development facilities and test ranges, and about 10,000 full-time scientists and engineers.[25] In 1985 a joint publication of the defense and state departments asserted that "a laser program of the magnitude of the Soviet effort would cost roughly $1 billion per year in the U.S."[26]

While these figures may be intended to provide a comprehensible basis for comparison between U.S. and Soviet laser efforts, they should not be accepted uncritically as a barometer of lagging U.S. efforts. Although SDI advocates have argued that a "beam gap" exists, it is wrong to interpret these statistics as showing that the United States has fallen behind the USSR, either in terms of the resources devoted to military lasers or in the results obtained. It is also wrong to infer that the United States must also spend at least $1 billion a year to keep up with the Soviet program.

Methods of Costing Soviet Military Programs

The Central Intelligence Agency (CIA) and the DIA use the so-called building-block method to make dollar-cost estimates for Soviet military programs such as their laser effort. This approach begins by listing the input components to the Soviet program, in the categories of procurement, construction, personnel, operations, maintenance, and research, development, testing, and engineering activities. These components are then priced in terms of what it would cost the U.S. Department of Defense to produce and staff a force of identical size and with the same equipment and operated in the same way that the Soviet Union operates its forces. These U.S. prices are then multiplied by the Soviet input quantities and summed to estimate the total cost of the Soviet effort in U.S. dollars. The estimates of quantities and item costs come either from within the U.S. government intelligence community or from U.S. government contract prices for manufacturers of similar equipment. The DIA maintains that "because this measure is in terms of U.S. costs, the magnitude of Soviet military forces and programs can be directly compared with U.S. military forces and programs."[27]

Three interrelated characteristics of this method exert a problematic effect on the estimation process and subsequent biases of the comparison. First, the building-block method of costing depends only on the *inputs* to Soviet forces. It does not and cannot guarantee that the products of these inputs, presumably our real concern, would be identical in the United States and the USSR. In other words, the method does not measure what the USSR produced with their effort, only what went into the process. The same inputs may produce different products in the two nations for a variety of reasons, including efficiency differences, unmeasured complementarities (the synergy between components), and qualitative differences in attributes that the U.S. intelligence community could not measure and therefore could not take into consideration.

Second, qualitative differences can be extremely important. If, for example, Soviet pilots are not as well trained, or Soviet scientists are not as productive with the same equipment as their U.S. counterparts, then it is not sensible to give the same economic value to their work in calculating the input costs of Soviet efforts.

Third, a subtle upward bias is introduced by different economic structures in using Soviet quantities with U.S. prices. Nations tend to use more of inputs that are relatively abundant and cheap to produce their output. If labor is cheap in the USSR while capital is cheap in the United States, then assigning high U.S. wages to Soviet use of labor will inflate the apparent dollar cost of the Soviet effort to a level well above the U.S. cost of achieving the same results using a more rational (for the United States) mix of more capital and less labor. For this reason, it is difficult to accept the DIA's insistence that Soviet dollar costs can "be directly compared" with U.S. costs. A CIA pamphlet makes this same observation:

> Dollar cost calculations tend to overstate Soviet defense activities relative to those of the United States. Given different resource endowments and technologies, countries tend to use more of the resources that are relatively cheap and less of those that are relatively expensive for a given purpose. A comparison drawn in terms of the prices of one country thus tends to overstate the relative value of the activities of the other.[28]

The wage difference between Soviet and U.S. scientists inflates the laser program dollar cost enormously relative to its actual cost in the Soviet Union. The U.S. government has reported that 10,000 scientists and engineers are working on the Soviet program. The U.S. Department of Labor's Bureau of Labor Statistics average annual salary rate for U.S. scientists and engineers can be used as a proxy for the value applied by the DIA to the Soviet scientists in calculating the dollar cost estimate for the Soviet efforts. The average 1984 civilian salary for professional engineers, chemists, and computer program analysts was $35,325. The average annual salary of engineering technicians, computer operators, key entry operators, and secretaries was $18,774. The BLS survey indicates an average ratio of 0.61 support staff to each professional in the services category.[29] Applying the $35,325 salary rate to the 10,000 Soviet scientists and engineers reportedly working on the program and assuming the same ratio of professional to support staff as reported by the BLS, the total wages for the Soviet military laser project amount to $468 million. This is about half of the entire dollar budget estimated by the U.S. government for the Soviet program.

When the Soviet salaries are calculated in rubles, however, a striking contrast appears. Soviet engineer-technicians earned 220.2 rubles per month in 1982, while clerks and support staff averaged 152.2 rubles per month.[30] These figures suggest that workers involved in Soviet military laser projects actually earned total wages of 31.3 million rubles, which at prevailing exchange rates was equal to about $40 million. The DIA dollar-cost estimate overstates the wages actually paid by the USSR by roughly a factor of twelve.

In similar contexts it has been argued that scientists are approximately equally productive whether employed in the USSR or in the United States. Valuing the Soviet worker at U.S. wage rates simply recognizes the fact that the U.S. government would have to pay more to get the same job done. Viewed in this light, the $1 billion figure is an estimate of what it would cost the United States to perform substantially the same research as the USSR. There are two flaws in this reasoning, however. First, it ignores the structural differences between the two economies, which determine the production mix of capital and labor that would be employed. In other words, the United States would not need to employ 10,000 scientists to do the same work. Second, this argument assumes that Soviet labor and capital are as productive as their U.S. counterparts. The evidence, however, points to the relative inefficiency of resources in Soviet hands.

Costs of the Military Laser Program

The correct way to measure the value of Soviet military laser efforts depends on the use to be made of the estimate. If our intention is to compare Soviet and U.S. progress, then the most sensible approach is to assess the concrete results of the rival research programs. Chapter 9 indicates that, on this basis, the United States holds the high ground. Alternatively, if we are interested in comparing dollar commitments as a measure of economic burden or the seriousness with which each government is pursuing its laser projects, then a quality-adjusted measure of the inputs is appropriate. For this purpose, U.S. average wage rates must be applied not to the total number of Soviet scientists and engineers, but rather to the number of U.S.-equivalent Soviet technical specialists. Similarly, capital must be measured in its U.S.-equivalent value. These adjustments correct the value of input units, but do not address the problem of the underlying structural differences in the two economies. While this method assigns a dollar-cost estimate to the Soviet program, it still overestimates the amount the United States would have to spend to keep up with the USSR.

Soviet quantities may be adjusted for productivity differences by using either deductive or sector-specific methods. Deductive techniques apply exogenously derived estimates of the relative efficiency of Soviet inputs in the economy as a whole to the quantities used in the laser program and then evaluate those adjusted quantities at U.S.

Table 10-5. Output Ratio Comparisons for United States and USSR, 1982.

	Output (billion dollars)	Capital (billion dollars)	Labor Force (million)
United States	$3,041.4	$5,296.2	110.2
USSR	1,787.0	not available	127.9
	(550.4 billion rubles)	(1,968 billion rubles)	
Ratios:			
Soviet (output/input)/U.S. (output/input)		0.487	0.506

Sources: U.S. GDP: Bureau of Census, *Statistical Abstract of the United States, 1985* (Washington, D.C.: U.S. Government Printing Office, 1984), p. 847; capital stock: ibid., p. 525; labor supply: *Economic Report of the President, 1985*, p. 266. USSR GNP (dollars): J. L. Scherer, ed., *USSR: Facts and Figures Annual*, vol. 9, 1985 (Gulf Breeze, FL: Academic International Press, 1985), p. 147; capital: ibid., p. 144; labor: ibid., p. 176; GNP (rubles): 1980 figure from Joint Economic Committee, *USSR: Measures of Economic Growth and Development, 1950–80* (Washington, D.C.: U.S. Government Printing Office, 1982), p. 54; growth rates to derive 1982 estimate from Scherer, *Facts and Figures*, p. 141.

prices. Sector-specific techniques begin by evaluating the relative level of Soviet laser program accomplishments and then work backward to derive the corresponding efficiency estimates. These are then used with U.S. prices to estimate program costs.

The simplest deductive comparison of U.S. and Soviet productivity assesses output per unit input for both capital and labor in the two economies. Although this measure has some flaws, it provides a useful initial approximation to the productivity differences. The comparison in Table 10-5 is based on 1982 data. The output measures are real gross domestic product for the United States and gross national product (GNP) for the USSR, evaluated in dollars. U.S. capital stock is defined as fixed nonresidential private capital. U.S. labor input is measured by the 1982 employed civilian labor force.

In both capital and labor, Soviet productivity is only about 50 percent of U.S. productivity. Therefore, the correct scaling of inputs to units of equivalent quality for the USSR and the United States produces an estimate of about $500 million for the Soviet laser program. This is considerably less than the $803.4 million budgeted by the Reagan administration for ground- and space-based high-energy research in FY 1986 and the $1,103.7 million projected for FY 1988.[31]

Abram Bergson, a Harvard University authority on the Soviet economy, using a more refined theoretical methodology, prepared an assessment of U.S. and Soviet factor productivity that confirms the computations above. With data from 1960, coupled with a few assumptions about the way capital and labor combine to produce output, Professor Bergson determined that Soviet productivity lies between 26.8 and 49.7 percent of U.S. productivity. His average estimate was 37 percent of U.S. levels.[32]

Using this ratio, Soviet laser expenditures would equal about $370 million worth of actual productive effort if performed in the United States. This represents less than two-fifths of the U.S. government estimate of dollar costs for the Soviet program.

These deductive techniques evaluate productivity for the Soviet economy as a whole, relative to the U.S. economy, and then apply the derived values to Soviet laser research efforts to estimate its U.S. equivalent. It can be argued that the organization and execution of Soviet military research and development are so different from the overall Soviet economic performance that numbers derived from a comparison of the two economies as a whole are of only limited applicability. It is difficult to determine whether Soviet military research is more or less productive than U.S. military research. Although the Soviet military reputedly has access to the best labor and capital inputs, it is not renowned for vigor or path-breaking innovation. By using the available data on Soviet and U.S. laser programs, one can develop an approximation of relative productivity on a sector-specific basis.

We first need to compare the output of U.S. and Soviet programs. Chapter 9 suggests that the United States and the Soviet Union have made roughly equal progress in SDI so far. (However, this assessment is probably overly generous to the Soviet Union.) Second, we assume that the output of the two research programs is produced in accordance with a Cobb-Douglas production function, $Q = K^a L^b$, where output (Q) equals labor (L) times capital input (K) raised to the powers of a and b. On the assumption that the ratio of capital investment in the two programs is identical to the ratio of the sizes of the programs as evaluated in dollars by the U.S. government, then Soviet capital investment has been three to five times that of the United States. If the programs began at roughly the same time, this implies that the Soviet capital stock devoted to this program must by now amount to about four times that involved in the U.S. laser program. If the U.S. program involves one-third of the staff that the USSR has devoted to laser research (again, based on the U.S. government comparison of overall program sizes), then the Soviet program productivity is about one-fifth that of the United States. In productivity-adjusted terms, it is worth about $200 million per year in U.S.-equivalent output or effort. This is roughly what the United States had been spending before the program was expanded under the auspices of the SDI effort.

Two important caveats should be considered before the U.S. government assessment of the Soviet military laser research program is accepted. First, because labor is considerably cheaper in the Soviet Union than in the United States, the U.S. government's dollar-cost estimate exaggerates the actual difference in Soviet and U.S. project expenditures. Fully half of the $1 billion estimate can be attributed to the conversion of Soviet wage rates to U.S. wage rates. Actual Soviet wage expenditures amount to only about 30 million rubles, or $40 million. Second, if the intent is to compare Soviet and U.S. efforts, rather than just the expenditures devoted to military applications of lasers, then some productivity adjustment is required to convert Soviet data into U.S.-equivalent productivity units, before costing at U.S. rates. If the productivity adjustment is inferred from a comparison of overall U.S. and Soviet economic performance, then the implied U.S. dollar value of the Soviet efforts is in the $370 to $500 million range. If the adjustment is based instead on the available information about Soviet laser progress and inputs, the U.S. dollar value lies between $200 million and $250 million per year. These amounts are close to the dollar resources the United States has been devoting to its counterpart laser program until recently, and considerably lower than the amounts the United States intends to spend during the next five years on SDI laser research.

IMPLICATIONS OF THE SOVIET RESPONSE

Inferior technological capabilities, military strategy, and competing demands for resources will undoubtedly deter the USSR from mounting a full-scale strategic defense effort of its own. Instead it will choose the more affordable and feasible option of building up its nuclear weapons (at one-tenth the cost of deploying SDI), probably in conjunction with continued SDI-like research. This response has serious strategic and economic implications for both the United States and the Soviet Union.

Several of the findings of this report have important implications for the design of American nuclear policy. Because a much larger fraction of the Soviet strategic arsenal is land based, and these ICBMs are slow to ready and launch, the USSR has more to gain from the development and deployment of local site-protecting missile defenses than does the United States. The USSR has conducted research in strategic defense and even deployed some rudimentary systems over the last twenty-five years, following similar American projects with a lag of four to eight years. Nonetheless, the Soviet Union is approximately a decade behind the United States in its ballistic missile defense capabilities, and there is no evidence whatever that this gap is closing. Moreover, it appears that no Soviet advanced technologies defense programs have yet progressed to the design and engineering phase.[33] In this context, the U.S. government's occasional references to SDI as a response to efforts initiated in the USSR appear to be an exaggeration.

Given current Soviet economic concerns, the technical difficulties and the enormous expense implied by an SDI-like effort both in the near term and in later years, it does not appear likely that the USSR will compete seriously with the United States in developing and deploying advanced technologies defenses. Its near-term response is more likely to involve a build-up and diversification of its strategic nuclear arsenal in an effort to preserve the credibility of its deterrent in the face of potential erosion by SDI. The costs of attempting to saturate SDI by doubling the Soviet land-based warhead contingent, or of escaping SDI altogether by relying on cruise missiles that can penetrate these defenses, are similar to the cost of the present U.S. SDI feasibility study itself. Our findings indicate that it is cheaper for the USSR to counter the U.S. SDI system by using offensive weapons than it is for the United States to deploy a strategic defense system.

A particularly disturbing aspect of this offense-defense arms spiral is that Soviet planners, responding prudently to their worst-case suspicions regarding the purpose and capabilities of SDI, may initiate a build-up that vastly overcompensates for any actual degradation SDI could impose. Moreover, they may take advantage of the long lead time involved in planning and deploying SDI systems to start producing missiles in anticipation of future needs. Then even if SDI never goes beyond the research stage, the offensive arms race could be rekindled if the United States felt compelled to respond to the Soviet build-up with one of its own.

The economic implications of the Soviet response to SDI are just as severe. Countermeasures, though perhaps only one-tenth as costly as a full-blown SDI defense, would tax the discretionary budget of any nation. This problem is especially pertinent to the leaders of the Soviet Union, whose economic performance is flagging.

General Secretary Gorbachev has designated economic "revitalization" (it is never called "reform" in the USSR) the top priority on the national agenda. He has repeatedly asserted that "our most important, top priority task" is to bring about "radical improvement" in the performance of the Soviet economy, and not simply through the setting of "new records in producing metals, oil, cement, machine tools or other products." Rather, he said, "the main thing is to make life better for people."[34] Recently announced targets for the 12th Five-Year Plan, running from 1986 to 1990, call for a boost of 13 to 15 percent in per capita national income and provision of a separate apartment or house for every family by 1990. Oil production is scheduled to rise 7.6 percent, and natural gas 31 percent. The fifteen-year projection, setting approximate goals for the economy to the year 2000, calls for a doubling of national income. Nonfood consumer goods production is scheduled to increase 80 to 90 percent from its present level of $100 billion per year. Real per capita income is to rise by 60 to 80 percent, and labor productivity by 130 to 150 percent, by the turn of the century.[35]

Public statements by Soviet leaders indicate that they are taking seriously the ascendancy of economic revitalization in the nation's priorities. Even members of the Soviet military establishment appear to have accepted that the economy's needs will be placed before the military's, for the short term at any rate (or have accepted temporary sacrifices with the notion that the military will do best when the economy is healthy). In a joint press conference with Chief of General Staff Marshal Sergei F. Akhromeyev, Kremlin spokesman Leonid M. Zamyatin insisted that "no matter how difficult it is to solve the military problems, we will not depart from our economic program."[36]

The Soviet economy today shows marked signs of stagnation or deterioration in virtually every major sector. Growth in gross national product suffered an unprecedented slowdown between 1979 and 1982. Over these four years, total growth in the economy was a mere 6 percent, or about 1.46 percent per year on average. Although the economy picked up somewhat in 1983, posting 3.2 percent growth, it seems to have expanded at a rate of only 1.5 to 2.5 percent since 1984. Between 1978 and 1984, per capita GNP rose only 6.7 percent, or about 0.9 percent per year. In recent congressional testimony, CIA analysts said they expected the Soviet economy's growth rate to remain near 2.0 percent per year at least until 1990. They also predicted that growth could be even slower unless steps are taken to correct problems in the agricultural and energy sectors.[37]

The Soviet economy, despite its obvious weaknesses and present troubles, is still the second largest in the world, with a GNP about three-fifths as large as that of the United States. It is robust and diversified and can rely on a staggering wealth of raw materials to fuel its recovery and growth. On the other hand, the Soviets are undoubtedly in for a difficult period economically. Between the Food Program, plant modernization, energy industry investment, transportation refurbishing, and the encouragement of increased effort by workers, the cost is likely to be many hundreds of billions of rubles over the next decade. It is easy to understand the Politburo's reluctance to involve the USSR in another all-out arms race with the United States. The Kremlin appears to have accepted the notion that economic revitalization will necessitate cutbacks in the share of national income going to defense expenditures, at least temporarily. It has translated this perception into action through its discouragement of U.S. SDI plans and its overtures toward re-establishing détente.

The United States thus confronts a difficult dilemma. Should it push the Soviet Union to the wall, using the SDI program as an economic cudgel, or should détente be encouraged, allowing a de-escalation of pressure both militarily and economically on both sides?

Bludgeoning the USSR into submission or reform does not appear to be a realistic possibility. Faced with economic and military pressure from the United States, the Soviet Union is more likely to batten down, marshal its resources, and respond in a similar manner— letting consumption falter in the meantime. Traditionally, the USSR has not liberalized in times of stress, but has gravitated toward increasing totalitarianism. U.S. pressure would also give the Kremlin a convenient excuse to demand further sacrifices from its people, exhorting them to meet the threat of American "aggression." By blaming the United States and insisting on its own willingness to negotiate on arms reductions and SDI, Soviet leaders could deflect any internal criticisms of the regime, dealing harshly with dissidents in a time of crisis. Such a strategy would prove entirely counterproductive to the long-term U.S. interest in encouraging freedom and democracy in the Soviet Union.

The alternative approach—to permit a de-escalation of the economic and military pressure—has much to recommend it. First, the United States, too could benefit from reduced military expenditures and tensions, which might more easily permit a reduction of the huge federal debt. Second, the ideal time to negotiate arms reductions is now, while the United States has the upper hand militarily and before the health of the Soviet economy has been restored. A stronger Soviet economy will inevitably reduce U.S. bargaining power, regardless of any continued military build-up here, because the Soviet incentive to negotiate will no longer appear so pressing. Third, while Gorbachev's avowed goal of modernization could be achieved either through increased centralization or through decentralization (probably a more effective path), easing of international tensions may encourage the latter approach. Economic decentralization may in turn lead to a greater degree of political decentralization over time, as the Soviet leaders recognize that the complexities of a modern, technological, flexible economy are incompatible with the stranglehold of control they now exercise. Moreover, while he may not be a closet capitalist, Gorbachev's flexibility and pragmatism are easier for the United States to deal with than the hard-line approach that may succeed him should his American policy and economic revitalization fail. If the United States wishes to encourage decentralization and freedom behind the Iron Curtain, this goal might be promoted most effectively by permitting the USSR to experiment with different approaches to innovation in a less tense international atmosphere.

11

THE FUTURE OF STAR WARS

In the past thirty years, had the total dollars we spent on military R&D been expended instead on those areas of science and technology promising the most economic progress, we probably would be today where we are going to find ourselves arriving technologically in the year 2000.

—*Simon Ramo*
America's Technological Slip, 1980

W hat role should the Strategic Defense Initiative play in American nuclear policy? The question is an immensely complicated one. Even at this early stage, the administration's program harbors intractable technical difficulties and serious threats to the economy that should be carefully considered before a decision about production and deployment is made. American strategic policy, however, does not operate in a vacuum. Soviet actions and reactions must also be taken into account, along with their effect on the USSR's politico-economic structure and on American policymaking.

Taken together, the SDI's liabilities make for a powerful economic undertow in which the losers would far outnumber the winners. Yet there is a clear danger that as remarkably generous funding for a few carefully selected contractors increases, lobbying for SDI will take on an irreversible institutional and economic momentum. As Hans A. Bethe stated, "When a trillion dollars is waved at the U.S. aerospace industry, the project will rapidly acquire a life of its own—

independent of its public justification; it will become an unstoppable juggernaut."[1]

Today we are at a critical juncture with regard to the future of SDI. Momentum is building both for negotiating weapons reductions with the Soviet Union and for early deployment of a partial defense system to protect missile silos. But as the negotiations in Geneva demonstrate, the two goals are on a collision course. If the Reagan administration forgoes the opportunity and the Soviet Union continues to regard SDI as an insuperable obstacle to significant arms accords, a historic opportunity for sizable mutual reductions of strategic nuclear weapons may be lost. It is therefore urgent that policymakers consider all the costs of the SDI program and evaluate the wisdom of proceeding with early deployment, before the program is irreversibly under way. To assist in the development of a U.S. strategic policy that effectively promotes American interests in light of probable Soviet reactions, the Council on Economic Priorities makes the following six recommendations.

1. ELIMINATE PROTOTYPE EXPERIMENTS

The Defense Department should reduce SDI's emphasis on developing prototype systems at least until the technological uncertainties of deploying an effective overall defense and its implications for the Anti-Ballistic Missile Treaty have been clarified. There are currently fourteen scheduled experiments, costing a total of $13 billion between FY 1987 and FY 1991, that are in potential violation of the ABM Treaty—which President Reagan's own Commission on Strategic Forces has described as "one of the most successful arms control agreements."[2] As one member of the Electronics Industries Association's SDI Subcommittee put it, "Any time one considers testing a weapon of these types in space, the potential to completely stop the show is there. It's entirely possible that development could continue on the ground for a long period of time, but as soon as one wants to do something, it could grind to a halt."[3]

Gerard Smith, ABM Treaty negotiator under the Nixon administration, has argued that even the SDI R&D program as currently outlined will undermine the treaty:

> By its very existence the Star Wars effort is a threat to the future of the ABM Treaty, and some parts of the announced five-year program raise questions of Treaty compliance. The current program envisions a series of hardware dem-

onstrations, and one of them is described as "an advanced boost phase detection and tracking system." But the ABM Treaty specifically forbids the testing of any "space-based" components of an anti-ballistic missile system. We find it hard to believe how a boost-phase detection system could be anything but space based, and we are not impressed by the Administration's claim that such a system is not sufficiently significant to be called a "component."[4]

Defense corporations and communities depending on these firms for jobs and income are unlikely to remain neutral as the debate over the maintenance of the ABM Treaty continues. Instead, the prospect of development and production programs may galvanize support for strategic defense as the research program sets the industry pork barrels rolling. It is therefore crucial to rein in the prototype experiments now, before they develop an unstoppable economic and institutional life of their own.

2. LIMIT FUNDING LEVELS

The Congress should significantly slow the growth of SDI funding until a more complete analysis indicates that the program's goal is technologically and economically feasible. In arguing for accelerated strategic defense funding, the administration has maintained that it is improper to criticize the proposal before we have explored the technologies sufficiently to ascertain whether such an important accomplishment is feasible. But this reverses the proper decision-making order. Until the prospects for success are established, the case for accelerating a massive funding effort has not been made. In light of the technical risks, one can justify only a significantly smaller and more appropriately targeted research effort.

The administration's budget request for FY 1988 is $5.8 billion—almost two times that of FY 1987 and an alarming 104.5 percent of all new funds for national research.[5] The Council on Economic Priorities recommends that Congress reduce the FY 1988 SDI budget to no more than $1.5 billion. This amount, based on the unaccelerated growth rate that was slated for ballistic missile defense research before the president announced his SDI program, is already a hefty increase and will support a level of research more than sufficient for the United States to maintain a strong negotiating posture in Geneva. It will also enable us to continue research at a level sufficient to hedge against a potential Soviet breakout of the ABM Treaty or breakthrough in BMD technology.

3. ESTABLISH AN INDEPENDENT REVIEW BOARD

Since the SDI Institute is not structured so as to provide an objective technical and strategic assessment of the SDI program, the Council recommends that Congress empower an independent board to review the overall program on an annual basis and ask the Congressional Budget Office to assess the budget for SDI. The board could be established through an amendment to the FY 1988 Defense Appropriations Bill and would replace the SDI Institute. To assure that its work receives top congressional and public attention, the board should be a blue-ribbon panel composed of independent experts in military science, technology, and strategy. These experts should have no significant private financial stake in strategic defense programs. Members of the board must be cleared for access to all classified materials pertinent to the assessment of the progress on SDI research. The board should submit an annual report, in both classified and unclassified versions, to Congress.

4. HOLD COMMITTEE HEARINGS ON SDI

The Council on Economic Priorities recommends that the House Armed Services Committee request a report from the Department of Defense explicitly outlining the precise mission intended for SDI and justifying the research in that context. A series of hearings would then be held to discuss the findings of the report and aid in the decision-making process regarding the future of SDI. If the goal is to protect missiles, one can legitimately ask, first, whether this is necessary or even desirable and, if so, whether conventional means already exist for this mission. If population defenses are the objective, one should explore the feasibility of this goal, given the existence of alternative enemy delivery systems and the dangers of fallout, nuclear winter, electromagnetic impulse, and so forth. In either case, cost-effectiveness at the margin must be clearly demonstrated.

The report should also consider the adaptability of the U.S. nuclear posture to Soviet responses to SDI. In particular, if the USSR expands and diversifies its nuclear arsenal, how would the United States respond? Since this Soviet response seems a strong possibility, is the United States willing to imperil prospects for arms control by continuing the SDI program in its present form?

Finally, the report should resolve the apparent contradictions among segments of the U.S. nuclear policy. For example, it is often argued that even a partly effective defensive shield is desirable because it would increase uncertainty about the Soviet Union's capability to launch a successful first strike against the United States.[6] This logic seems to suggest that greater uncertainty regarding nuclear strike capability would have a positive and stabilizing effect on the nuclear balance. However, the government took the opposite position in arguing against the Comprehensive Test Ban Treaty proposal. Opposition to this measure has been justified by Assistant Secretary of Defense Richard Perle precisely because a moratorium on testing increases the uncertainty in the Soviet Union's capacity to launch a nuclear strike. To establish a coherent U.S. strategic policy, contradictions such as this one should be explored and resolved.

5. PURSUE ARMS CONTROL AND VERIFICATION

The administration should vigorously pursue its goals of ensuring strategic stability and eliminating nuclear weapons through verifiable arms control agreements. Verification measures that would increase confidence in a ban on SDI production should be developed.

Restricting the SDI program and the size of the U.S. nuclear arsenal will release a considerable fund of federal resources. The Council on Economic Priorities recommends that a substantial fraction of these funds be rechanneled into the exploration of technologies related to the ability of the U.S. deterrent force to survive attack and to the strengthening of verification technologies for arms control proposals.[7] Further research directed at ensuring the survival of the U.S. military communications infrastructure and a retaliatory force— be it land, sea, or air based—will strengthen America's deterrent posture while increasing confidence in smaller U.S. and Soviet arsenals. A well-conceived program to support improved methods of verification could enhance negotiations of new arms control agreements to promote our mutual security and move our two nations back from the nuclear precipice.

6. NEGOTIATE A CONTINGENT TREATY

The hypothetical and distant promise of effective strategic defense of the entire population should not distract the nation from the more immediate prospects for meaningful arms control. The political momentum that will develop as a result of an accelerated program should not be allowed to drive the United States to develop defensive systems. Officials involved with the SDI effort, including scientists working on the defense research and military officers attached to SDIO, have publicly acknowledged that the effectiveness of SDI defenses depends on limitations on the size of the Soviet strategic nuclear arsenal. However, the USSR is most likely to respond to America's SDI program by expanding and diversifying its strategic arsenal. SDI promises, in effect, to launch a new offense-defense arms spiral. A fundamental irony of the SDI strategy is that the defenses cannot be effective unless arms limitations are negotiated, but an arms limitation agreement is made less probable by the U.S. refusal to negotiate on SDI. Even many program supporters have retreated from the early claim that SDI would be superior to the arms control process because the United States could pursue SDI unilaterally, without depending on Soviet adherence to treaties.

The Council on Economic Priorities therefore recommends negotiations intended to lead to the signing of a dual contingent treaty, covering both strategic defense and arms reductions. The first of these agreements would limit the development of advanced strategic defense systems to activities that can be performed within the confines of a laboratory or other enclosed structure as allowed under the ABM Treaty. This would permit a level of research adequate to hedge against a Soviet technological breakthrough while still maintaining the ABM Treaty. The second agreement would reduce the size of both nations' strategic nuclear arsenals as an initial confidence-building measure.

The treaties should explicitly define the proscribed activities, including types of development and testing work. They should limit especially weapons whose short flight times and minimal radar profiles impose the greatest burden on the speed and reliability of the adversary's means of detection. The treaties would be contingent in the sense that abrogation of the very specific and detailed provisions of one treaty by a signatory would render the other one null and void at the option of the other signatory. Although this type of package is likely to encounter definitional disputes, the problems should be avoided by a combination of rigorous attention to detail during negotiations and the institution of standard mechanisms to resolve disputes.

*   *   *

The Council on Economic Priorities suggests these measures in an effort to decrease the risk of nuclear war and to promote arms control. Decisions regarding the future of SDI must be based on sound objective analysis of the program on national security grounds and not on the vested economic interests of powerful arms lobbies.

Our analysis of SDI's program structure clearly shows that the original promise of population protection has been abandoned in favor of the only realistic goal—early deployment of a partial defense system intended to defend missile silos. Any hope for the feasibility of President Reagan's 1983 view of SDI has been dashed by the American Physical Society's April 1987 report, which concludes in unequivocal terms:

> In view of the large gap between current technology and the advanced levels required for an effective missile defense, the SDI program should not be a controlling factor in U.S. security planning and the process of arms control. It is the judgment of the Council of the American Physical Society that there should be no early commitment to the deployment of SDI components.[8]

Deploying an SDI system would not only fail to deliver a "nuclear-free world" but could also spawn a dual arms race that would destabilize the strategic balance, impair both U.S. and Soviet policy-making processes, and bring arms control negotiations to a stalemate. To be effective, a less than foolproof SDI system requires bilateral cutback of nuclear weapons. But in response to SDI the Soviet Union is more likely to produce and deploy cheaper and technologically proven nuclear missiles than to reduce its nuclear arsenal. This quagmire leads to the fundamental irony of the SDI program: SDI cannot succeed without arms control, but its very existence makes arms control highly improbable. Arms control agreements, on the other hand, can promote security without any reliance on SDI. And ultimately, SDI is unnecessary with them.

The American public chooses arms control over SDI. Seventy-four percent of the Americans polled by the Washington Post/ABC News in October 1985 thought it more important for the United States and the Soviet Union to agree to a substantial bilateral reduction of nuclear arms than for the United States to develop SDI.[9] Representative Duncan Hunter's (R-CA) May 1987 amendment to the 1988 Defense Authorization Bill to delete a provision that would require continued adherence to the traditional interpretation of the ABM Treaty was defeated by a margin of almost two to one (262 to 159).

Despite this diminishing support, the SDI Organization and the defense industry continue to pressure Congress to appropriate increasingly larger funds. The diversion to SDI of government resources on the scale planned by the Reagan administration will seriously weaken the nation's ability to meet the challenges of unemployment, export market loss, dwindling technological leadership, and antiquated industrial plants. If we fail to arrest the economic momentum of the SDI juggernaut, we will find ourselves paying for Star Wars well into the next century. We must seriously explore alternative peaceful solutions to the threat of nuclear war—now.

NOTES

CHAPTER 1: THE REAGAN SDI VISION

1. President Reagan, remarks to National Space Club, Washington, D.C., March 29, 1983.
2. Scowcroft Commission, *Report of the President's Commission on Strategic Forces* (Washington, D.C.: U.S. Government Printing Office, April 1983), p. 12.
3. Interview, "Developments in a Ballistic Missile Defense: We're Already There . . . in a Decade or So," *Government Executive*, July–August 1983, p. 21.
4. Kent Stansberry, acting director, strategic defense and arms control policy, Office of the Undersecretary of Defense for Policy, statement at a Capitol Hill seminar sponsored by the American Academy of Sciences, March 19, 1986 (author's notes).
5. National Academy of Sciences, "The Strategic Defense Initiative: A Survey of the National Academy of Sciences," conducted by Cornell University, the Floyd R. Newmann Laboratory of Nuclear Studies, Ithaca, New York, November 7, 1986.
6. American Institute of Physics, News Release, "APS Directed Energy Weapons Study Released," April 24, 1987, p. 1.
7. Lt. Gen. Abrahamson, director, SDIO, address to National Security Issues Symposium, Washington, D.C., October 25, 1984.
8. Douglas C. Waller and James T. Bruce, staff report submitted to senators William Proxmire and J. Bennett Johnston, "SDI: Progress and Challenges, Part Two," March 19, 1987, p. ii.

9. Charles Gellner, "The Strategic Budgetary Issues," Congressional Research Service, June 25, 1986.

10. D. Jones, ed., *Soviet Armed Forces Review Annual 8* (Gulf Breeze, FL: Academic International Press, 1984), p. 25.

11. David C. Morrison, "Shooting Down Star Wars," *National Journal*, October 25, 1986, p. 2548.

12. "Recent Public Opinion Findings on Nuclear Arms Control Issues," Council for a Livable World, Washington, D.C., April 7, 1987, p. 3.

CHAPTER 2: SPACE-BASED MISSILE DEFENSES

1. U.S. Congress, Office of Technology Assessment, Ballistic Missile Defense Technologies, OTA-ISC-254 (Washington, D.C.: U.S. Government Printing Office, September 1985), pp. 45–49.

2. Strategic Defense Initiative Organization, *Report to Congress*, June 1986, p. IV-12.

3. Douglas Waller, James Bruce, and Douglas Cook, "SDI: Progress and Challenges," staff report submitted to senators William Proxmire, J. Bennett Johnston, and Lawton Chiles, March 17, 1986.

4. Harold Brown, "Is SDI Technically Feasible?" *Foreign Affairs*, Spring 1986, pp. 435–54.

5. See *Washington Post*, May 4, 1986, which gives an account of a briefing by Lt. Col. Simon P. Worden of the SDIO.

6. See Herbert Lin, "The Development of Software for Ballistic Missile Defense," *Scientific American* 253, no. 6 (December 1985).

7. Eastport Study Group, Summer Study 1985, "A Report to the Director, Strategic Defense Initiative Organization," December 1985, pp. v, 9.

8. See James Fletcher, statement before the U.S. Congress, House Armed Services Committee, Subcommittee on Research and Development, mimeo, March 1, 1984, p. 8.

9. Waller et al., "SDI: Progress and Challenges," p. 2.

10. Ibid.

11. See David Lynch, "SDI: 58 Years of Shuttle Flights?" *Defense Week*, February 24, 1986, p. 7; Lynch, "U.S. Maps Out Plans for War in Space," *Defense Week*, April 28, 1986, p. 7; Fred Hiatt, "Space Launch Needs of SDI Are Estimated," *Washington Post*, June 27, 1986, p. A24; Charles Mohr, "Cost Cuts Sought in Missile Defense," *New York Times*, May 8, 1986, p. A24.

12. Lin, "Development of Software."

13. See, for example, Keith Payne, *Strategic Defense: Star Wars in Perspective* (Lanham, MD: Hamilton Press, 1986).

14. SDI Organization, *The President's Strategic Defense Initiative* (Washington, D.C.: U.S. Government Printing Office, January 1985), p. 5.

15. For just such an analysis, see Michael McGwire, *Military Objectives in Soviet Foreign Policy* (Washington, D.C.: Brookings Institution, 1987).

CHAPTER 3: WHAT PRICE STRATEGIC DEFENSE?

1. U.S. Senate, Committee on Foreign Relations, *Strategic Defense and Anti-satellite Weapons* (Washington, D.C.: U.S. Government Printing Office, April 25, 1984).
2. Testimony before the U.S. Congress, Senate Defense Appropriations Subcommittee, April 10, 1986.
3. According to data compiled by the Federation of American Scientists, the research and production costs (in 1986 dollars) of these nuclear weapons are as follows: B-1 bomber—$5 billion R&D, $24 billion procurement; Trident II—$10 billion R&D, $19 billion procurement; MX missile—$11 billion R&D, $17 billion procurement.
4. The Boston Study Group, *The Price of Defense* (New York: New York Times Book Company, Inc., 1979), pp. 232–41.
5. This Council on Economic Priorities estimate is based on the assumption that the $48 billion currently programmed for technological exploration would be about one-third of the total development cost, and development cost might be between one-quarter and one-eighth of total procurement cost.
6. Barry Blechman and Victor Utgoff, *Fiscal and Economic Implications of Strategic Defenses* (Washington, D.C.: Johns Hopkins Foreign Policy Institute, July 1986).
7. Ibid., p. 95. There are 86,789,000 households in the United States. U.S. Department of Commerce, Bureau of the Census, *Statistical Abstract of the United States 1986*, December 1985, p. 39.
8. Congressional Budget Office, *Analysis of the Costs of the Administration's Strategic Defense Initiative, 1985–1989* (Washington, D.C.: CBO, May 1984), p. 15.
9. Ibid., p. 18.
10. James Abrahamson, "Statement on the President's Strategic Defense Initiative," testimony before the U.S. Congress, Senate Appropriations Committee, May 15, 1984, p. 1.
11. John Pike, *Strategic Defense Budget* (Washington, D.C.: Federation of American Scientists, 1984).
12. Congressional Budget Office, "Analysis of Costs," p. 17.
13. Douglas Waller, James Bruce, and Douglas Cook, "Strategic Defense Initiative: Progress and Challenges," staff report submitted to senators William Proxmire, J. Bennett Johnston, and Lawton Chiles, March 17, 1986, pp. 10–11. Also see Congressional Budget Office, "Analysis of Costs," p. 5.

14. John Pike, *The Strategic Defense Initiative Budget and Program* (Washington, D.C.: Federation of American Scientists, February 10, 1985), pp. 32–41.
15. Franklin C. Spinney, "Defense Facts of Life," testimony before the U.S. Congress, Senate Subcommittee on Manpower and Personnel, Armed Services Committee, December 5, 1980; Franklin C. Spinney, "Plan/Reality Mismatch," December 1982 (unpublished).
16. George Leopold, "Subpanel Endorses Spending Plan Backing Reagan's SDI Request," *Defense News*, September 15, 1986, p. 5.

CHAPTER 4: STAR WARS: THE RACE FOR CONTRACTS

1. Brad Knickerbocker, "The Debate Over Strategic Defense," *Christian Science Monitor*, September 17, 1984, p. 1.
2. William D. Hartung and Rosy Nimroody, "Cutting Up the Star Wars Pie," *The Nation*, September 14, 1985, p. 200.
3. "The Star Wars General Gets a Taste of Hostile Fire," *Business Week*, May 14, 1984, pp. 180–85.
4. Ibid.
5. "The Federal Triangle: Step Taken to 'Star Wars' Defense," *Washington Post*, September 19, 1984, p. 25.
6. "SDI Architecture Proposals Due Oct. 18," *Aerospace Daily*, September 19, 1984.
7. David E. Sanger, "Pentagon and Critics Dispute Roles of Space Arms Designers," *New York Times*, November 5, 1985.
8. Walter Pincus, "'Star Wars' Plan Lost in Space," *Washington Post*, October 22, 1984, p. A8.
9. Walter Andrews, "Missile Interception Called Capable of 85% Protection," *Washington Times*, October 24, 1984.
10. Max Kampelman, Zbigniew Brzezinski, and Robert Jastrow, "Defense in Space Is Not 'Star Wars'," *New York Times Magazine*, January 27, 1985, pp. 28–51.
11. Defensive Technologies Study Team, *The Strategic Defense Initiative* (Washington, D.C.: U.S. Government Printing Office, April 1984).
12. Eastport Study Group, Summer Study 1985, "A Report to the Director, Strategic Defense Initiative Organization," December 1985.
13. Merton J. Peck and Frederic M. Scherer, *The Weapons Acquisition Process: An Economic Analysis* (Boston: Harvard Graduate School of Business Administration, Division of Research, 1962).
14. Ibid., p. 177.
15. Edmund Beard, *The Development of the ICBM* (New York: Columbia University Press, 1976).
16. The bill, known as the Alternative Strategic Defense Initiative Budget for FY 1986, was introduced on April 3, 1985, by senators William Proxmire, Dale Bumpers, Charles McC. Mathias Jr., and John H. Chafee.

17. Charlotte Grimes, "Star Wars Think Tank Draws Fire," *St. Louis Post Dispatch,* June 5, 1986, p. B7.
18. Fred Hiatt, "Senator Levin Attacks Rules for Forming Proposed 'Star Wars' Think Tank," *Washington Post,* May 11, 1986, p. 3.
19. Cosmo DiMaggio and Michael E. Davey, *The Strategic Defense Initiative Institute: An Assessment of DoD's Current Proposal* (Washington, D.C.: Congressional Research Service, August 11, 1986).
20. Grimes, "Star Wars Think Tank."
21. These figures are based on contracts compiled from Government Data Publications' *R&D Contracts Monthly,* March 1983 to December 1986, as well as responses to our Freedom of Information requests to various DOD agencies involved in the Strategic Defense Initiative.
22. Department of Defense, *100 Companies Receiving the Largest Dollar Volume of Prime Contracts, Department of Defense Awards, Fiscal Year 1985* (Washington, D.C.: U.S. Government Printing Office, 1985).
23. "Prime Contract Awards Alphabetically by Contractor, by State or Country, and Place," Directorate for Information Operations and Reports, Department of Defense, 1983–85.
24. Earl Lane, "New Horizon for Defense," *Newsday,* May 19, 1985, p. 5.
25. Department of Defense, *500 Contractors Receiving the Largest Dollar Volume of Prime Contract Awards for RDT&E, Fiscal Year 1985* (Washington, D.C.: Government Printing Office, 1985).

CHAPTER 5: PROFILES OF THE TOP TEN SDI CONTRACTORS

1. Figures on company dependency on Pentagon contracts are for FY 1984, from Linda S. Shaw, Jeffrey W. Knopf, and Kenneth A. Bertsch, *Stocking the Arsenal: A Guide to the Nation's Top Military Contractors* (Washington, D.C.: Investor Responsibility Research Center, 1985).
2. National Science Foundation, *National Patterns of Science and Technology Resources* (Washington, D.C.: National Science Foundation, 1984). Projections for 1985 through 1989 are extrapolated from the 5.87 percent real growth rate experienced in 1984.
3. SDI contract values indicated in the Lockheed profile include contracts for Sanders Associates, Inc., acquired by Lockheed on July 9, 1986. Before the merger, Sanders was awarded a total of $1.6 million in SDI contracts for the ballistic missile command, control, and communication (BMC3) program. All figures are for 1985. Obligations: Lockheed, $54.3 million; Sanders, $0.1 million. DOD RDT&E: Lockheed, $1,653.3 million; Sanders, $56.3 million. DOD prime contract awards: Lockheed, $5,082.5 million; Sanders, $467.9 million. Company sales: Lockheed, $9,535.0 million; Sanders, $885.8 million.

4. SDI contract values indicated in the General Motors profile include contracts for Hughes Aircraft Co. Before the merger, GM's Delco Electronics division received a total of $26.5 million in SDI contract awards for the kinetic energy weapons program. All figures are for 1985. Obligations: GM, $8.1 million; Hughes, $76.2 million. DOD RDT&E: GM, $31.9 million; Hughes, $474.9 million. DOD prime contract awards: GM, $1,614.2 million; Hughes, $3,462.0 million. Company sales: GM, $96,371.7 million; Hughes, $6,000.0 million.

5. Telephone interview, December 5, 1984.

6. Ibid.

7. TRW, 1985 annual report.

8. McDonnell Douglas representatives have spoken at conferences sponsored by the American Society of Mechanical Engineers (November 16, 1984) and the American Institute of Aeronautics and Astronautics (August 19, 1984).

9. SDI contract values indicated in the General Electric profile include contracts for RCA, acquired by GE in February 1986. Before the merger, RCA received a total of $9.3 million in SDI contract awards for the surveillance, acquisition, tracking, and kill assessment program. It also won a phase two systems architecture contract. All figures are for 1985. Obligations: GE, $9.6 million; RCA, $0.4 million. DOD RDT&E: GE, $885 million; RCA, $282 million. DOD prime contract awards: GE, $5,891 million; RCA, $1,315 million. Company sales: GE, $28,285 million; RCA, $8,972 million.

10. Rockwell International, *Space: America's Frontier for Growth, Leadership and Freedom* (October 1, 1981), pp. 8, 28.

CHAPTER 6: TARGETING ACADEMIA

1. "Senators and Scientists Object to SDI Costs and Uncertainties," *Physics Today*, July 1985, pp. 55–56.

2. Ibid., p. 55.

3. Office of Management and Budget, *Special Analyses Budget of the United States Government, Fiscal Year 1987* (Washington, D.C.: U.S. Government Printing Office), Tables K-9 and K-10, pp. K-20 and K-29.

4. Philip J. Klass, "SDI Office Pushes Innovative Science, Technology Research," *Aviation Week and Space Technology*, April 29, 1985, p. 225.

5. Kim McDonald, "Opposition to Reagan's Star Wars Grows Among Research Scientists; Many Spurn Funds from Pentagon," *Chronicle of Higher Education*, July 24, 1985, p. 2.

6. Ingrid Kock, "Star Wars on Campus," *Michigan Daily*, April 19, 1985; Jeffrey Smith, "Star Wars Grants Attract Universities," *Science* 228, p. 304.

7. James Ionson, *Strategic Defense Initiative Organization, Innovative Science and Technology Office* (Washington, D.C.: SDIO, March 1985).

8. David Parnas, Letter of resignation from SDI's panel on "Computing in Support of Battle Management," June 28, 1985.

9. "Senators and Scientists Object," p. 56.

10. Smith, "Grants Attract Universities," p. 304.

11. Ionson, *Strategic Defense Initiative Organization*, p. 26.

12. *New York Times*, September 13, 1985.

13. Ionson, *Strategic Defense Initiative Organization*, p. 5.

14. "Senators and Scientists Object," p. 57.

15. Ibid., p. 58.

16. Colin Norman, "Memo Sets Policy for 'Star Wars' Publications," *Science*, August 30, 1985, p. 843.

17. David J. Lynch, "Stop Exaggerating Our Star Wars Role, Schools Tell DoD," *Defense Week*, May 28, 1985, p. 16.

18. Ben Stanger, "Institute Graduates 1700, Gray and Iacocca Discuss MIT, National Policies," *The Tech*, July 9, 1985; Michael Weisskoph, "Universities Say Pentagon Misstated Role in SDI," *Washington Post*, June 7, 1985; Steve Curwood, "'Star Wars' Move Hit in MIT Talks," *Boston Globe*, June 4, 1985; "Senators and Scientists Object," p. 58; Scott Saleska, "Scientists Mount Campaign Against Star Wars," *The Tech*, September 17, 1985, p. 7.

19. Francis E. Low, "Concerns Over MIT's Involvement in SDI," letter to the editor, *The Tech*, June 3, 1985.

20. Lynch, "Stop Exaggerating," p. 16; Weisskoph, "Universities Say."

21. David E. Sanger, "Campuses' Role in Arms Debated as 'Star Wars' Funds Are Sought," *New York Times*, July 22, 1985.

22. Boyce Rensberger, "Physicists Launch Missive at Strategic Defense Initiative," *Washington Post*, July 12, 1985, p. 3; "Text of Scientists' 2 Petitions Opposing 'Star Wars' Studies," *Chronicle of Higher Education*, July 24, 1985.

23. Michael Weissman, telephone interview with Council on Economic Priorities, November 21, 1985.

24. David Wright, telephone interview with Council on Economic Priorities, November 21, 1985.

25. Lisbeth Gronlund, John Kogut, Michael Weissman, and David Wright, "A Status Report on the Boycott of Star Wars Research by Academic Scientists and Engineers," May 13, 1986; Colin Campbell, "Latest Cause on Campus: Saying No to 'Star Wars'," *New York Times*, September 15, 1985.

26. *Educational and NonProfit Institutions Receiving Prime Contract Awards for RDT&E, Fiscal Year 1985* (Washington, D.C.: U.S. Government Printing Office, 1985).

27. Sanger, "Campuses' Role," p. A12.

CHAPTER 7: THE PORKBARREL: WHO PAYS?

1. Examples can be found in voting records on the F-18 fighters, B-1 bombers, and A-10 attack planes.

2. Tim Carrington, "Scramble in Space: Star Wars Plan Spurs Defense Firms to Vie for Billions in Orders," *Wall Street Journal*, May 21, 1985.

3. Rockwell International, *Space: America's Frontier for Growth, Leadership, and Freedom*, October 2, 1981.

4. "Huntsville Planners Diversify to Non-Government Work," *Aviation Week and Space Technology*, March 21, 1983, pp. 90–91.

5. James Coates, "Star Wars Means the Sky's the Limit for City," *Chicago Tribune*, December 26, 1984. Norm Udevitz and Patrick Yack, "State Gets 'Pentagon of Space,'" *Denver Post*, April 27, 1985. Matthew Rothschild and Keenen Peck, "Star Wars: The Final Solution," *The Progressive*, July 1985.

6. Keith Ervin, "Boeing Launches a First-Strike in the Star Wars," *The Weekly*, November 20–26, 1985, p. 28.

7. Letter from Thomas G. Pownall to Martin Marietta employees, September 12, 1983. Quoted in Gordon Adams, *The B1: Bomber for All Seasons?* (New York: Council on Economic Priorities, February, 1982).

8. Lt. Gen. Daniel O. Graham, *We Must Defend America: A New Strategy for National Survival* (Chicago, IL: Regnery Gateway, Inc., 1983).

9. Federal Election Commission Committee, Index of Candidates Supported/Opposed by American Space Frontiers Committee, 1983–1986 (computer printout).

10. "Coalition for SDI Formed," *High Frontier Newsletter* 3, no. 10 (October 1985): 1–3.

11. David Shribman, "Kemp Joins GOP Race for Presidency, Vows to Make It Star Wars Referendum," *Wall Street Journal*, April 7, 1987.

12. Ibid., p. 1.

13. "A Proposed Plan for Project on BMD and Arms Control," study commissioned by the High Frontier, written by John Bosma in 1984 and obtained by the Council on Economic Priorities in 1985.

14. *Ibid.*

15. "Special Interest Snipers," *New York Times*, November 21, 1985.

16. Steven V. Roberts, "Some in Congress Say Money Talks Too Much," *New York Times,* November 19, 1985.

17. William B. Hartung, *The Economic Consequences of a Nuclear Freeze* (New York: Council on Economic Priorities, 1984).

18. Sources used for the tax analysis include: Supplementary Report of Metropolitan Statistical Areas, *1980 Census of Population,* U.S. Department of Commerce, Bureau of the Census, December 1984. *Survey of Current Business,* U.S. Department of Commerce, Bureau of Economic Analysis,

April 1986; *Statistical Abstract of the United States, 1986*, U.S. Department of Commerce, Bureau of the Census, December 1985, *Statistics of Income Bulletin*, Internal Revenue Service, Statistics of Income Division, Spring 1986; *Local Area Personal Income 1979–1984*, vol. 1, Summary, U.S. Department of Commerce, Bureau of the Census, September 1986; *Survey of Current Business*, U.S. Department of Commerce, Bureau of Economic Analysis, July 1986.

19. Robert Lindsey, "Economic Boom Out West Is Mostly Inside City Limits," *New York Times*, May 10, 1987, p. E4.

20. *The Bi-Coastal Economy*, staff study by the Democratic Staff of the Joint Economic Committee, Congress of the United States, July 9, 1986.

CHAPTER 8: TECHNOLOGICAL RENAISSANCE OR BRAIN DRAIN?

1. On this point see Ann Markusen, "The Militarized Economy," *World Policy Journal* 3, no. 3 (Summer 1986); Robert Reich, "High Tech, a Subsidiary of Pentagon Inc.," *New York Times*, May 29, 1985; and Lester Thurow, "The Economic Case Against Star Wars," *Technology Review* (April 1986).

2. Congressional Research Service, *U.S. Science and Engineering Education and Manpower* (Washington, D.C.: U.S. Government Printing Office, April 1983), p. 77.

3. National Science Foundation, "Labor Markets for New Science and Engineering Graduates in Private Industry," *Highlights*, June 9, 1982.

4. Douglas Braddock, "The Job Market for Engineers, Recent Conditions and Future Prospects," *Occupational Outlook Quarterly* (Summer 1983).

5. The five professional occupations are accountant, auditor, attorney, buyer and chemist. Ibid., p. 4.

6. Ibid., p. 6.

7. National Science Foundation, "Labor Markets," p. 5.

8. National Science Foundation, "1982 Doctorate Production Stable in Science and Engineering Fields, but Down in Science and Mathematics Education," *Highlights*, April 20, 1983, p. 3.

9. National Science Foundation, "1982 Job Market for New Science and Engineering Graduates About the Same as That of Previous Years," *Highlights*, April 30, 1984, p. 4.

10. National Science Board, *Science Indicators 1982* (Washington, D.C.: National Science Foundation, 1983), appendix Table 3-29, p. 272.

11. Ibid., appendix Table 1-39, p. 228.

12. National Science Foundation, "Engineering Colleges Report 10% of Faculty Positions Vacant in Fall 1980," *Highlights*, November 2, 1981.

13. John Geils, "The Faculty Shortage: A Review of the 1981 AAES/ASEE Survey," *Engineering Education* (November 1982), p. 148.

14. National Science Foundation, "Engineering Colleges," p. 3.

15. National Science Foundation, "Industry Reports Shortages of Scientists and Engineers Down Substantially from 1982 to 1983," *Highlights*, February 17, 1984.

16. National Research Council, "The Impact of Defense Spending on Non-Defense Engineering Labor Markets," a report to the National Academy of Engineering (Washington, D.C.: National Academy Press, 1986).

17. Telephone interview with Ray Stata, president of Analog Devices, Inc., Norwood, MA, July 1984.

18. Ronald E. Kutscher, "Future Labor-Market Conditions for Engineers," in National Research Council, *Labor-Market Conditions for Engineers; Is There a Shortage?* (Washington, D.C.: National Academy Press, 1984), pp. 27–28.

19. Ibid., pp. 32–35.

20. Arnold S. Levine, *Managing NASA in the Apollo Era* (Washington, D.C.: NASA, 1982), pp. 116, 118.

21. Robert L. Rosholt, *An Administrative History of NASA, 1958-1963* (Washington, D.C.: NASA, 1966), p. 4.

22. *Economic Report of the President* (Washington, D.C.: U.S. Government Printing Office, February 1984), p. 223.

23. U.S. Congress, Senate Committee on Labor and Public Welfare, *Impact of Federal Research and Development Policies on Scientific and Technical Manpower* (Washington, D.C.: U.S. Government Printing Office, June and July 1965), p. 865.

24. U.S. Congress, Senate Committee on Labor and Public Welfare, *Nation's Manpower Revolution* (Washington, D.C.: U.S. Government Printing Office, November and December 1963), pt. 8, pp. 2690–99.

25. Levine, *Managing NASA*, p. 116; Hugh Folk, *The Shortage of Scientists and Engineers* (Lexington, MA: D.C. Heath, 1970), pp. 160–62.

26. National Industrial Conference Board, *The Technical Manpower Shortage: How Acute?* (New York: NICB, 1970), pp. 48–55.

27. Folk, *Shortage of Scientists*, pp. 74–75.

28. Harvey Brooks, "The Strategic Defense Initiative as Science Policy," *International Security* 11, no. 2 (Fall 1986): 180.

29. Ibid., p. 180.

30. "SDI Opens Spin-Office," *Military Space*, July 7, 1986, p. 8.

31. Ibid.

32. Gerold Yonas, "Research and the Strategic Defense Initiative," *International Security* 11, no. 2 (Fall 1986): 188.

33. Michael A. Evans, *The Economic Impact of NASA R&D Spending* (Bala Cynwyd, PA: Chase Econometrics, April 1976).

34. A similar study using somewhat different assumptions, performed by the MidWest Research Institute (MRI), found the discounted rate of return to

be 33 percent. This and other studies are cited in David Bruce Hack, "Studies of the Economic Effects of NASA R&D," in U.S. Congress, House Committee on Science and Technology, *United States Civilian Space Program, 1958-1978* (Washington, D.C.: U.S. Government Printing Office, January 1981), pp. 975-99.

35. U.S. General Accounting Office, *NASA Report May Overstate the Economic Benefits of Research and Development Spending* (Washington, D.C.: GAO, October 18, 1977), p. 6.

36. In particular, GAO argued that Chase's regression analysis used too short a time period, which did not contain sufficient variation in NASA R&D levels. Also, Chase's NASA R&D variable was correlated with overall R&D, making it difficult to distinguish between the separate effects of the two variables. After making adjustments in Chase's assumptions, GAO's NASA R&D regression coefficient falls to 0.136 (a 14 percent rate of return) from Chase's 0.426. The t-statistic for GAO's coefficient also falls below 2 (1.73), which suggests statistical insignificance.

37. Three studies that did not find a statistical relationship between government R&D and productivity growth are cited by Eleanor Thomas, "Recent Research on R&D and Productivity Growth: A Changing Relationship between Input and Impact Indicators?" prepared for presentation at the Third Conference on Science and Technology Indicators, OECD Headquarters, September 15-19, 1980. Two, by Zvi Griliches (1973) and Nestor Terleckyj (1974), are not fully cited by Thomas. The third is William Leonard, "Research and Development in Industrial Growth," *Journal of Political Economy* 79, no. 2 (March/April 1971): 232-56. More recently, Zvi Griliches and Frank Lichtenberg obtained the same results in "R&D Productivity Growth at the Industry Level: Is There Still a Relationship?" in Zvi Griliches, ed., *R&D Patents and Productivity* (Chicago: University of Chicago Press, 1984), pp. 465-501.

38. Support for the view that government R&D stimulates private efforts can be found in Jeffrey Carmichael, "The Effects of Mission-Oriented Public R&D Spending on Private Industry," *Journal of Finance* (June 1981), pp. 617-27; Richard Levin, "Toward an Empirical Model of Schumpeterian Competition," unpublished paper, Yale University, May 1980; David Levy and Nestor Terleckyj, "Effects of Government R&D on Private R&D Investment and Productivity: A Macroeconomic Analysis," paper presented at the Southern Economic Association, November 1982.

39. Congressional Budget Office, *Federal Support for R&D and Innovation* (Washington, D.C.: CBO, April 1984), pp. 32-37.

40. Thomas, "Recent Research," p. 12. She cites Paul Kochanowshi and Henry Hertzfeld, "Often Overlooked Factors in Measuring the Rate of Return to Government R&D Expenditures," *Policy Analysis* 7, no. 2 (1981): 153-67.

41. Frank Lichtenberg, "The Relationship Between Federal Contract R&D and Company R&D," *American Economics Association Papers and Proceedings* (May 1984), p. 77.

42. *Global Competition: The New Reality,* report of the President's Commission on Industrial Competitiveness (Washington, D.C.: U.S. Government Printing Office, January 1985), p. 19.

43. Yonas, "Research and the Initiative," p. 188.

44. John P. Holdren and F. Bailey Green, "Military Spending, the SDI, and Government Support of Research and Development: Effects on the Economy and the Health of American Science," *FAS Public Interest Report* (September 1986), p. 16.

45. Congressional Budget Office, Natural Resources and Commerce Division, *Trends in the Consolidated R&D Budget,* May 11, 1983.

46. Yonas, "Research and the Initiative," p. 186.

47. See John Pike, *Strategic Defense Initiative Budget and Program* (Washington, D.C.: Federation of American Scientists: February 10, 1985).

48. Lt. Gen. James A. Abrahamson, "Statement on the President's Strategic Defense Initiative," before the U.S. Congress, Senate Appropriations Committee, May 15, 1984, pp. 4–6.

49. Hans-Peter Durr, "Could Star Wars Work?" *World Press Review,* September 1985, p. 29.

50. "Protecting Circuit Technology Raises Numerous Uncertainties," *Aviation Week and Space Technology,* July 30, 1984, p. 50.

51. Richard L. Berke, "U.S. Issues Guidelines to Restrict Release of 'Sensitive' Information," *New York Times,* November 13, 1986.

52. "Protecting Circuit Technology," p. 51.

53. Holdren and Green, "Military Spending," pp. 16–17.

54. Office of Technology Assessment, Industry, Technology and Employment Section, *Research and Development in the U.S. and the Other OECD Countries,* November 1983.

55. Rep. Ken Kramer, cited in Matthew Rothschild and Keenen Peck, "Star Wars: The Final Solution," *Progressive,* July 1985.

56. Reich, "High Tech."

57. For more on this point, see Chalmers Johnson, *The Industrial Policy Debate* (San Francisco, CA: Institute for Contemporary Studies, 1984).

58. Robert S. Ozaki, "How Japanese Industrial Policy Works," in Johnson, Ibid., p. 62–63.

59. Ibid., p. 62.

60. Earl Lane, "New Horizon for Defense," *Newsday,* May 19, 1985.

61. Fred V. Guterl, "Star Wars Is Bad for Business," *Dunn's Business Month,* September 1986.

62. Markusen, "The Militarized Economy," p. 504.

63. Ibid., p. 506; and Office of Technology Assessment, *Information Technology R&D: Critical Trends and Issues* (Washington, D.C.: U.S. Congress, OTA, February 1985), p. 96.
64. Thurow, "The Economic Case."

CHAPTER 9: SOVIET STRATEGIC DEFENSE PROGRAMS: A DECADE BEHIND THE UNITED STATES

1. David Rivkin, Jr., "What Does Moscow Think? *Foreign Policy* (Summer 1985), pp. 85–105; Sayre Stevens, "The Soviet BMD Program," pp. 182–300 in A.B. Carter and D.N. Schwartz, eds., *Ballistic Missile Defense* (Washington, D.C.: Brookings Institution, 1984).
2. Ibid.
3. D. Jones, ed., *Soviet Armed Forces Review Annual 6* (Gulf Breeze, FL: Academic International Press, 1984), p. 165.
4. Stevens, "Soviet BMD Program," p. 197.
5. C. Chant and I. Hogg, *Nuclear War in the 1980's?* (New York: Harper & Row, 1983), p. 104.
6. K. Tsipis, *Arsenal: Understanding Weapons in the Nuclear Age* (New York: Simon & Schuster, 1983), pp. 176–77.
7. T. K. Longstreth, J. E. Pike, and J. B. Rhinelander, *The Impact of U.S. and Soviet Ballistic Missile Defense Programs on the ABM Treaty* (Washington, D.C.: National Campaign to Save the ABM Treaty, 1985), p. 19.
8. Stevens, "Soviet BMD Program," p. 217.
9. *Soviet Armed Forces Review Annual 5* (Gulf Breeze, FL: Academic International Press, 1983), p. 103; J. Tirman, ed., *The Fallacy of Star Wars* (New York: Vintage Books, 1984), p. 198; *Soviet Armed Forces Review Annual 2* (Gulf Breeze, FL: Academic International Press, 1980), p. 104.
10. T. Karas, *The New High Ground* (New York: Simon & Schuster, 1983), p. 150; Tirman, *Fallacy of Star Wars*, p. 209.
11. Tirman, *Fallacy of Star Wars*, pp. 208–9, 211; *Soviet Armed Forces Review Annual 2*, p. 104.
12. *Soviet Armed Forces Review Annual 5*, p. 103.
13. Karas, *New High Ground*, p. 150; Tirman, *Fallacy of Star Wars*, p. 199.
14. P. Stares, "U.S. and Soviet Military Space Programs: A Comparative Assessment," *Daedalus* (Spring 1984), pp. 132–33.
15. Karas, *New High Ground*, p. 151.
16. "Soviets Build Directed-Energy Weapon," *Aviation Week and Space Technology*, July 28, 1980, pp. 47–50.
17. *Soviet Armed Forces Review Annual 5*, p. 106.
18. Paul Nitze, "SDI: The Soviet Program," *Current Policy*, no. 717 (1985): 2.

19. C. Robinson, Jr., "Beam Weapons Technology Expanding," *Aviation Week and Space Technology*, May 25, 1981, pp. 40–47; Department of Defense, *Soviet Military Power*, 1st ed. (Washington, D.C.: U.S. Government Printing Office, 1981), pp. 75–76.

20. Longstreth, Pike, and Rhinelander, *Impact of Programs*, p. 20.

21. Department of Defense, *The FY 1981 Department of Defense Program for Research, Development, and Acquisition* (Washington, D.C.: U.S. Government Printing Office, 1980), p. 82; Department of Defense, *The FY 1983 Department of Defense Program for Research, Development, and Acquisition* (Washington, D.C.: U.S. Government Printing Office, 1982), pp. 11–21.

22; Cecil Brownlow, "MiG-25 Based on Technology Spinoffs," *Aviation Week and Space Technology*, October 11, 1976, pp. 18–19.

23. Stares, "U.S. and Soviet Military Space Programs," p. 137.

24. U.S. Congress, Committee on Commerce, Science and Technology, *Soviet Space Programs: 1976–80* (Washington, D.C.: U.S. Government Printing Office, 1982), pp. 32, 39.

25. J. Jacky, "The 'Star Wars' Defense Won't Compute," *Atlantic Monthly*, June 1985, p. 20.

26. From unpublished information provided by the National Science Foundation.

27, H.D. Balzer, "Soviet Science in the Gorbachev Era," *Issues in Science and Technology* 1, no. 4 (Summer 1985): 30.

28. L.E. Nolting and M. Feshbach, *Statistics on Research and Development Employment in the USSR* (Washington, D.C.: U.S. Government Printing Office (for U.S. Bureau of the Census), June 1981), Series P-95, no. 76, pp. 7–18.

29. J.L. Scherer, ed., *USSR Facts and Figures Annual 9, 1985*, (Gulf Breeze, FL: Academic International Press, 1985), p. 339.

30. U.M. Kruse-Vaucienne and J.M. Longsdon, *Science and Technology in the Soviet Union* (Washington, D.C.: National Science Foundation, 1979), p. 69.

31. Nolting and Feshbach, *Statistics on Research*, pp. 39–41.

32. *Narodnoe Khaziastvo SSSR* v. 1981 p. 407; C.P. Ailes and F.W. Rushing, *The Science Race* (New York: Crane Russak, 1982), p. 99.

33. Ailes and Rushing, *Science Race*, pp. 188–92.

34. Ibid., pp. 194–204.

CHAPTER 10: SOVIET SDI RESPONSE: A NUCLEAR BUILDUP

1. R.M. Gates and L.K. Gershwin, "Soviet Strategic Force Developments," testimony before Subcommittee on Strategic and Theater Nuclear Forces

of the Senate Armed Services Committee and the Defense Subcommittee of the Senate Commission on Appropriations, June 26, 1985, p. 4.

2. L. Aspin, "Are We Standing Still?—U.S. Strategic Nuclear Forces in the 1970s and Early 1980s," *Congressional Record,* July 9, 1979, pp. E3448-53.

3. T. Cochran, W. Arkin, and M. Hoenig, *U.S. Nuclear Forces and Capabilities,* vol. 1 of the *Nuclear Weapons Databook* (Cambridge, MA: Ballinger Publishing Co., 1984), pp. 126-27; *Economic Report of the President, 1985* (Washington, D.C.: U.S. Government Printing Office, 1985), p. 297.

4. S. Meyer and P. Amquist, "Insights from Mathematical Modeling in Soviet Mission Analysis, Part II" (Massachusetts Institute of Technology, mimeo, April 1985), pp. 40-41. The $12-14 million range in 1971-72 dollars is given because imprecision in the source material prevented the analysts from accurately narrowing the value beyond the $2 million spread or determining the correct base year.

5. Charles Mohr, "'Star Wars' in Strategy: The Russian Response," *New York Times,* December 17, 1985, pp. 1, A16.

6. H. Scoville, Jr., *MX Prescription for Disaster* (Cambridge, MA: M.I.T. Press, 1982), pp. 161-64; Harold Brown, *Department of Defense Annual Report FY 1982* (Washington, D.C.: U.S. Government Printing Office, 1981), pp. 109-12.

7. Caspar Weinberger, *Department of Defense Annual Report to the Congress, FY 1984* (Washington, D.C.: U.S. Government Printing Office, 1983), pp. 220-21.

8. U.S. House Armed Services Committee, *Department of Defense Authorization for Appropriations for FY 1981* (Washington, D.C.: U.S. Government Printing Office, 1980), pp. 1869, 1872-73.

9. C. A. Robinson, Jr., "Soviets Test New Cruise Missiles," *Aviation Week and Space Technology,* January 2, 1984, pp. 14-16.

10. F. Kaplan, "Official Says Missile-Defense Plan Would Tilt Nuclear Balance to U.S.," *Boston Globe,* December 12, 1985, p. 29.

11. Quoted in Center for Defense Information, "U.S.-Soviet Nuclear Arms: 1985," *Defense Monitor* 14, no. 6 (1985): 6.

12. Gates and Gershwin, "Soviet Strategic Force Developments," p. 4.

13. Department of Defense, *Soviet Military Power, 1985* (Washington, D.C.: U.S. Government Printing Office, 1985), pp. 7, 25-35.

14. Ibid., p. 35.

15. John C. Baker, "Program Costs and Comparisons," in R. K. Betts, ed., *Cruise Missiles: Technology, Strategy, Politics* (Washington, D.C.: Brookings Institution, 1981), p. 106.

16. C. Robinson, Jr., "Defense Plans Spur Purchases, Research," *Aviation Week and Space Technology,* February 15, 1982, pp. 16-21.

17.   C. Robinson, Jr., "Defense Research Request Rises 14%," *Aviation Week and Space Technology,* February 22, 1982, pp. 53–56.

18.   C. Weinberger, *Department of Defense Annual Report to Congress FY 1985* (Washington, D.C.: U.S. Government Printing Office, 1984), p. 191.

19.   C. Robinson, Jr., "Defense Department Stresses Research, Readiness, Upgrades," *Aviation Week and Space Technology,* February 6, 1984, pp. 14–19.

20.   John C. Baker, "Program Costs and Comparisons, Appendix B: Additional Data on Costs," in Betts, *Cruise Missiles,* pp. 574–75, 587.

21.   Ibid., p. 586.

22.   Ibid., p. 591–92.

23.   Joint Economic Committee, *Allocation of Resources in the Soviet Union and China—1983, Part 9* (Washington, D.C.: U.S. Government Printing Office, 1983), pp. 19–24.

24.   J. K. Davis et al., *The Soviet Union and Ballistic Missile Defense* (Cambridge, MA: Institute for Foreign Policy Analysis, Inc., 1980), p. 59; C. A. Robinson, Jr., "GAO Pushing Accelerated Laser Program," *Aviation Week and Space Technology,* April 12, 1982, pp. 16–19; J. Rather, "The U.S. High Energy Program," in R. daCosta, ed., *Defense Thought 2001* (CA: daCosta Yglesias Publishing Company, 1983), p. 60.

25.   R. R. Ropelewski, "Soviet High Energy Laser Program Moves into Prototype Weapons Stage," *Aviation Week and Space Technology,* April 15, 1985, pp. 42–46.

26.   Department of Defense, Department of State, *Soviet Strategic Defense Programs* (Washington, D.C.: U.S. Government Printing Office, 1985), p. 13.

27.   Joint Economic Committee, *Allocation of Resources,* pp. 207–8.

28.   Quoted in F. Holzman, "Administration Misrepresentations of Soviet Military Spending," in R. V. Dellums, ed., *Defense Sense* (Cambridge, MA: Ballinger Publishing Company, 1983), p. 98.

29.   Bureau of Labor Statistics, U.S. Department of Labor, *National Survey of Professional, Administrative, Technical and Clerical Pay,* March 1984 BLS Bulletin #2208 (Washington, D.C.: U.S. Government Printing Office, 1984), pp. 11–13, 35.

30.   Central Statistical Agency, USSR, *Narodnoe Khaziastvo, SSSR, 1982* (Moscow: Central Statistical Agency, 1983), p. 370.

31.   John Pike, *The Strategic Defense Initiative: Areas of Concern* (Washington, D.C.: Federation of American Scientists, June 10, 1985).

32.   A. Bergson, *Productivity and the Social System: The USSR and the West* (Cambridge, MA: Harvard University Press, 1978), pp. 68–90.

33.   Comments by Dr. S. Meyer in "What the Soviets Are Doing," *Time,* June 23, 1986, p. 25.

34. George J. Church, "Moscow's Vigorous Leader," *Time*, September 9, 1985, p. 17.

35. "Soviets Seek Better Output and Quality for Consumers," *Boston Globe*, October 10, 1985, p. 4; "Soviets Set Schedule for Raising Incomes," *Boston Globe*, November 9, 1985, p. 20: Phillip Taubman, "Big News in Soviet: 5 Year Plan, Not the Summit," *New York Times*, November 17, 1985, p. 13; Serge Schmemann, "Labor Productivity Rise Stressed in Soviet Plans," *New York Times*, October 18, 1985, p. D1.

36. Phillip Taubman, "Moscow Vows to Match Space Arms," *New York Times*, October 21, 1985, p. A3.

37. Joint Economic Committee, *Allocation of Resources in the Soviet Union and China, Pt. 10, 1984* (Washington, D.C.: U.S. Government Printing Office, 1985), p. 76.

38. "Communism 'Doesn't Fit a Modern Industrial Society,'" *U.S. News and World Report*, February 4, 1985, p. 43.

CHAPTER 11: THE FUTURE OF STAR WARS

1. "'Star Wars' Seen as Unworkable and Dangerous," *Wall Street Journal*, January 2, 1985, p. 19.

2. Excerpted from prepared statement of Dr. Sidney D. Drell before the Committee on Foreign Relations, U.S. Senate, April 25, 1984. For more detail on the experiments, see Betty Lall, *Security Without Star Wars* (New York, NY: Council on Economic Priorities, January 1986).

3. Proceedings of conference on "The Military Electronics Market: Exploring the Opportunities," Electronics Industries Association, October 9–11, 1984, p. 202.

4. McGeorge Bundy, George F. Kennan, Robert S. McNamara, and Gerard Smith, "The President's Choice: Star Wars or Arms Control," *Foreign Affairs*, Winter 1984/85, p. 274.

5. Since the growth of the SDI budget between FY 1987 and 1988 ($2,002 million) is greater than the growth of the national research budget ($1,769 million), SDI funding growth represents more than 100 percent of all new funds for national research.

6. Comments by Dr. S. Meyer in "What the Soviets are Doing," *Time*, June 23, 1986, p. 25.

7. For more information on verification technology, see Lall, *Security Without Star Wars*.

8. American Institute of Physics, News Release, "APS Directed Energy Weapons Study Released," April 24, 1987, p. 4.

9. Jeffrey D. Alderman, ABC News/Washington Post Poll, Survey Pt. 203, 206, 209, July, October, and November 1985.